INTO AFRICA WITH MARGARET LAURENCE

INTO AFRICA WITH MARGARET LAURENCE

Fiona Sparrow

ECW PRESS

CHAMPLAIN COLLEGE

CANADIAN CATALOGUING IN PUBLICATION DATA

Sparrow, Fiona
Into Africa with Margaret Laurence

Includes bibliographical references.
ISBN 1-55011-169-8

1. Laurence, Margaret, 1926–1987 — Criticism
and interpretation. 1. Title

PS8523.A77Z8 1992   C818'.54   C92-095257-7
PR9199.3.L3Z8 1992

This book has been published with the financial assistance
of the Ontario Arts Council, The Canada Council,
and the Government of Canada Department of
External Affairs and International Trade.

Design & imaging by ECW *Type & Art*, Oakville, Ontario.
Printed and bound by Imprimerie Gagné, Louiseville, Quebec.
Cover photo courtesy of James Martin.

Distributed by General Publishing Co. Limited,
30 Lesmill Road, Don Mills, Ontario M3B 2T6

Published by ECW PRESS, 1980 Queen Street East, Toronto, Ontario M4L 1J2

To Bryan
"who shares my memories"

ACKNOWLEDGEMENTS

This book began life as a thesis, written at the University of Toronto. I was fortunate in its early stages to be advised by B.W. Andrzejewski of the London School of African and Oriental Studies. In Toronto many people gave me warm support and good advice and I would like to thank them all, in particular, Ted Chamberlin, Jim Howard, and Clara Thomas. I am also grateful to Jocelyn and David Laurence for their generous permission to use unpublished material. Others have helped the thesis become a book. I would like to thank Ellen Quiqley, who edited my manuscript, and Holly Potter and Robert Lecker of ECW PRESS, whose wholehearted support made its publication possible. I am also indebted to James Martin, who provided the photograph for the cover of the book. I am also grateful to the Archives and Special Collections of York University Library and the William Ready Division of Archives and Research Collections of McMaster University Library for allowing me access to the Laurence Papers they hold.

A very special thank-you goes to Bill Keith who encouraged and helped me every step of the way.

There has been considerable uncertainty about the spelling of African names and terms. This was particularly so in Somaliland in the years before an official orthography was adopted. The spellings favoured by Margaret Laurence, and these themselves varied from work to work, are used here except in direct quotations from other writers. Likewise, pre-independence names such as Somaliland and The Gold Coast are used where appropriate. The only exception to this general rule is the use here of today's spelling "Igbo" instead of "Ibo." The latter was the usual one when Margaret Laurence was writing.

CONTENTS

Into Africa

During the last year of her father's life Margaret Laurence, or Margaret Wemyss as she was then, lived in the red-brick house in Neepawa built by her paternal grandfather. Some of her memories of that year were inevitably unhappy but she recalls with pleasure the hours she spent in her father's study, remembering one detail in particular. On a shelf by themselves stood a long row of *National Geographic* magazines (see Laurence, *Dance* 55; Laurence, *Bird* 53). The eight-year-old child used to look through them, longing to see for herself the unfamiliar flowers and animals pictured in remote and fascinating lands. During the years she later spent in Africa such pictures came to life but familiarity did not in her case breed contempt, and the curiosity that had excited her childhood dreams of travel remained with her throughout her adult journey. Her keen and serious interest in her subject matter is everywhere evident in the writing that resulted from the time she spent in Africa.

Laurence has said in an interview with Rosemary Sullivan that "... it was just a stroke of good luck" that took her to Africa (63), but there were other factors at work, not least the curiosity that had been roused in her father's study. Margaret Wemyss married Jack Laurence in 1947, and in 1949, after he had gained a degree in engineering, they left for England. In 1950 Jack Laurence applied for a post with the Government of the British Protectorate of Somaliland, and as the year ended they set out together to travel east of Suez to the Horn of Africa. However, Laurence only accompanied her husband on this journey because of her own determination to do so and chance at this point needed a helping hand.

In 1950 the Government of the British Protectorate of Somaliland, headquartered in the inland city of Hargeisa, was expanding its development program, but housing could not be built fast enough to cope with the increase in staff. The Financial Secretary's draft estimates for 1949 to 1950 lament the housing shortage which meant warning the Colonial Office, who would be responsible for recruiting Jack Laurence, "that the accommodation is short and it will be necessary to withhold permission for new officers to bring their wives" (Great Britain, British Protectorate of Somaliland 11). The Laurences were duly advised by the Colonial Office that ". . . no accommodation for married couples seemed to be available in Somaliland at the moment, but perhaps Mr. Laurence's wife would be able to join him in six or eight months" (Laurence, *Prophet's* 3). The Colonial Office was persuaded to relent on the understanding that Margaret Laurence was quite prepared to rough it, in a tent if necessary, and so her African journey began.

She made the obligatory preparations for the journey, but she arrived ill-prepared in many ways for the experiences that awaited her. She had, however, read as much about the area as was possible. Research was a task she always took seriously and she had "ferreted out from libraries" as much of the history as she could (*Prophet's* 4). Of the works she read, the one that fascinated her most was *First Footsteps in East Africa*, written by the Victorian explorer Sir Richard Burton. It tells of a remarkable journey he made in 1854 across northern Somaliland to the city of Harar. His is the earliest work in English to give a detailed description of this region, and it was read by most of the visitors who followed in his footsteps. Some of these visitors also wrote about their experiences and their accounts cover many important historical events. Their record of Somaliland — much of which Laurence ferreted out of London's libraries — is of great interest and on the whole reflects an admiration and respect for the people of the region whose way of life is reported with integrity and sympathy, thus establishing a tradition that Laurence in no way betrayed.

Sir Richard Burton was, as Laurence observes in *The Prophet's Camel Bell*, a "compulsive traveller" (16), driven by curiosity and not by the hope of profit. Those who landed later at Berbera or Zeilah on the coast of Somaliland had other motives. Some came to hunt wild animals, and they traversed the region in pursuit of their quarry, but many more came for political reasons as British interest in the area grew. Officials concerned with safeguarding the route to India came to secure a foothold on the coast for the British imperial power. They left few traces of their incursions on the mainland and neither their language nor their religion took root there. The Bedouin in the inland desert areas of northern Somaliland resisted colonization and, indeed, for the first two decades of the twentieth century the British presence was vigorously challenged by the religious leader Mahammed 'Abdille Hasan,[1] who was known to his followers as the Sayyid and to the English as the Mad Mullah of Somaliland. The events of these twenty years form the core of the extensive documentation on Somaliland made by the British, and Laurence was to add a Canadian viewpoint when she wrote "The Poem and the Spear," her account of the Sayyid's life.

Laurence lived in the Protectorate in more peaceful times than those of the Sayyid. She arrived there in January of 1951 and left just over a year later as the spring rains began to fall (see Appendix). At this time the British were preparing the region for independence, which was granted when the Protectorate joined with Italian Somaliland to form the Republic of Somalia in 1960. Laurence's memoir *The Prophet's Camel Bell*, published in 1963, is based on the diaries she kept in Somaliland, and it gives a clear and accurate picture of the work of the administration during her stay, dwelling in particular on her husband's struggle to improve the water supplies for the desert Bedouin and their flocks. Much of her time was indeed spent roughing it, through wet and dry seasons, living in the desert, while she shared in her husband's work. Though it was written some time after she had left Africa, *The Prophet's Camel Bell* recreates with immediacy their life together in a foreign land.

While Laurence lived in Somaliland her own literary ambitions were not neglected. The urge to write was strong, and it found relief in her diaries. But she also turned her attention to what was to become her first published book, *A Tree for Poverty: Somali Poetry and Prose*. This highly esteemed anthology of Somali poems and stories, which she collected and translated into English, was published in Nairobi in 1954. Though she was at the same time trying her hand at fiction, she was never satisfied with the results, and only one short story, "Uncertain Flowering," published in 1953, survives from this period.

In 1953 the Laurences, now with a baby daughter who had been born during leave in England, started a new life in the Gold Coast, which was to become the independent nation state of Ghana on 6 March 1957. (Laurence left the Gold Coast to return to Canada a few weeks before the declaration of independence.) The Gold Coast opened up new perspectives for Laurence. She had come west across the continent to a humid tropical region, to an area that had for long been under British rule. There Jack Laurence, under contract for a second time to the Colonial Office, was "second-in-command of building the new port of Tema" (Laurence, *Dance* 142). Once again Laurence read avidly about the culture and history of the people she was living amongst, and her reading included works written by Ghanaians about their own traditions as well as books by European administrators and anthropologists. She used the knowledge she acquired from reading as well as her own immediate experiences when she embarked on her West African fiction. One of her most important sources was the work of Robert Sutherland Rattray, who wrote in great detail about the Ashanti people. She used his work extensively.

Laurence wrote much of her first novel, *This Side Jordan*, in the Gold Coast, though she finished it while living in Vancouver, and it was published in 1960. The West African stories that were collected in *The Tomorrow-Tamer* in 1963 were also largely written back in Canada. Her novel and stories portray the Gold Coast and the people who lived there with an immediacy that indicates a lively response to all about her but also with a depth that reveals the detailed knowledge she had gained from her wide reading. When Mary Renault reviewed *This Side Jordan*, she referred to its author as "[a] scholar and translator of African folklore and poetry . . ." (104). Today this would not seem the natural way to describe one of Canada's greatest writers of fiction but the scholar is more active in her work, above all her African work, than is generally recognized. Undoubtedly she will be remembered as a fiction writer, but most of her fiction benefits from her uncompromising standards of truthful reporting and careful research, which are the hallmarks of her non-fictional writing. Laurence's fictional portrayal of the Gold Coast and its people is convincing because it has a spontaneity and liveliness that might be expected from an interested and accurate observer, but also because it achieves a close identification with its subject matter, the result in some measure of her study of the history and traditions of the Ashanti people.

Laurence left the Gold Coast in 1957 with her two children, four-year-old Jocelyn and one-year-old David — the latter had been born in the Gold Coast — to return to Canada where her stepmother was dying. Her husband, who was to follow her later, saw her off at Accra airport, and he was moved by the sight of his wife walking away across the tarmac, "carrying one child while the other gamely trotted by [her] side" (Laurence, *Dance* 113). It was perhaps an omen for the future because their happiest years together, those spent in Africa, were over. The family spent the next few years in Vancouver, but Laurence's career was putting a strain on her marriage. When Jack Laurence left for Pakistan in 1962, he went alone, while his wife returned to England with the children. There she had to rely on her writing to earn a living and it was during this time that she wrote *Long Drums and Cannons*, a study of the Nigerian writers of the 1950s and 1960s. It was published in 1968.

Laurence's African writings represent an impressive variety of literary genres, and there is much to be gained from juxtaposing them. The exceptional quality of her West African fiction is not something that needs to be proved. What is not so immediately obvious is the wealth of reading and experience from which it was woven, and, when the corpus of her African writing is seen as a whole, it gives a clear indication of the extent of her knowledge of Africa and shows how well she interpreted the strangeness of foreign lands and unfamiliar customs. Her work allows her readers to share in her journey. If they are outsiders like herself, the journey is one of rewarding discovery. However, Africans as well as non-Africans have welcomed her careful definition of the territory through which she travelled.

Part I

Margaret Laurence of Hargeisa

1

Water and Shade

The Prophet's Camel Bell tells the story of a quest for water and for shade. Jack Laurence set out to improve the water supply in the desert by constructing a series of U-shaped retaining walls that would capture the rainwater when it fell and hold it in big pools. While he was occupied with the planning and construction of the first *balleh*, the term used by Somalis for a rainwater pool, Margaret Laurence began to collect and translate poems and stories, choosing her examples from the rich store of Somali oral texts. She noticed how much the Somalis enjoyed reciting poems and telling stories, especially at the end of each day. Their literature seemed almost as necessary for their well-being as water. She saw song and story as providing spiritual shade, in the way that a desert tree protects the traveller against the burning sun. Both water and shade are essential for survival, but scarce in the desert. There they constitute the goal of every pilgrimage, and, when Laurence decided to turn her Somali diaries into narrative form, she saw water and shade as the obvious symbols around which to design her story. *The Prophet's Camel Bell* is called a memoir, and it is, indeed, a detailed and factual account of Laurence's short stay in Somaliland. But the skill with which she tells her story is that of the practised writer of fiction.

There are two distinct desert regions in northern Somaliland: the coastal Guban (which means "burnt") and the inland Haud (which means "south"). They are separated by a high escarpment, where the mountain town of Sheikh and to a lesser degree the capital Hargeisa enjoy some relief from the desert climate. Most travellers used to land at one of the two old ports, Berbera or Zeilah. When Richard Burton made his remarkable journey in 1854 from Zeilah to Harar, he chose to start his trek as evening fell, crossing the Guban "towards a thin blue strip of hill on the far horizon." The Guban, he writes, is "a dull ochreish yellow" and shimmers in what seems "eternal summer" (117). In the 1920s the young English woman Margery Perham made a journey to Somaliland, a journey that led to a life-long interest in Africa. She landed at Berbera in 1921 on her way to stay with her sister whose husband, Major H. Rayne, was District Commissioner in Hargeisa; and so she, too, had to cross the Guban before reaching her final destination. In *Major Dane's Garden*, the autobiographical novel that resulted from her visit, her heroine, Rhona, travelled by truck to Hargeisa, leaving Berbera at the height of the dry season on the long journey inland. Rhona was paralyzed by fear as she made her way through the desert which "lay east and west, the warm sea drowning its northern rim, while to the south the mountains rose clear out of the limp sand. It was like the carcase of a land that had died of thirst; it was littered with rocks that lay on it, blanched like bones" (50). Like Rhona, the Laurences travelled from Berbera to Hargeisa in a "borrowed and bone-rattling truck" and their journey across the "scorched plains of the Guban" also filled them with fear because it "seemed to be no place for any living thing" (*Prophet's* 20).

Once the escarpment has been climbed and Hargeisa reached then the Haud is visible stretching south. In the dry season the Haud is as barren as the Guban, but when the rains have fallen this southern desert changes for a short time into a garden. It has been well described by Angus Hamilton, who came to know the area when he was sent there as Reuters correspondent to cover the early campaigns against the Sayyid. Writing in 1910, when it was still possible to move freely from the Haud into the Ogaden, an area now largely in Ethiopia, he drew attention to the importance of this region when the rains have turned it into good grazing. The Haud, he writes, is "a great elevated undulating plateau, waterless in the dry season" and ". . . it is probably the most valuable part of Somaliland, for on its pasturages the surrounding tribes are dependent for the summer grazing of their flocks, the source of their food and their wealth" (27).

The Laurences spent most of their time in the Haud, and they first saw it in the *Jilal*, the Somali word for the dry season. When Laurence describes her first impressions, the need for water and shade becomes obvious. She opens her chapter on the *Jilal* with a description of the Haud, where ". . . no rain had fallen for a year. No green anywhere, none, not a leaf, not a blade of grass. In stretches where the wind-flattened grass remained, it had been bleached to bone-white. The earth was red, a dark burning red that stung the eyes. The sun was everywhere; there was no escaping its piercing light" (51). It was a bad year, but such years were common and Laurence realized that the Somali Bedouin had learnt to cope with their harsh environment and were able to survive the seasons of drought and famine. Westerners visiting Somaliland have often asked themselves whether they would be able to survive even for a short time in the desert, spoilt as they have been by privileged lifestyles. Perham, who was profoundly moved and humbled by all she saw, sought an outlet for her feelings in her novel, which proposed the impossible dream of turning the desert into a permanent garden. Laurence was also deeply moved, but admitted that her feelings seemed pointless in the face of the dignified and independent way the Somalis faced their own fate. However she, too, saw the need to water the desert and she added her commitment to her husband's as he undertook in the only way possible to improve the supply of this precious resource.

The Laurences arrived in Somaliland shortly after John A. Hunt had completed a survey of the entire Protectorate for the Government, in which he paid special attention to water shortage. Laurence read his finely written report, the work of a man who knew and loved the country and its people. Hunt lists five possible sources of water for the Protectorate: 1) surface rainfall pools (*ballehs*), 2) wells in dry river beds, 3) permanent flowing streams, 4) rock pools, and 5) boreholes. In the waterless Haud, however, the *ballehs* provide the only water ever available, and most of these "are natural pools, but some have been dug or improved." Hunt adds that "many more artificial pools and storage cisterns are needed" (103). It was to meet this need that Jack Laurence was sent to the Haud.

In the dry season, the Haud becomes a burial ground, a place of death, bleached bone-white and littered with skeletons. The only signs of growth are the grotesque red termite-mounds, "some of them three times the height of a man" (*Prophet's* 51), which Burton thought gave the land "the appearance of a Turkish cemetery" (134). The region is haunted by vultures, birds that symbolize the horror of the landscape and humanity's precarious place within it. Burton, referring to the vulture by its Somali name, "gurgur," points out that it is hated because it "kills the dying and devours the dead on the battlefield" (156). To Perham the vultures "seemed like a company of vile old men, solemn and yet ribald, gathered for an obscene rite"

(156). Laurence, using the word "good" with chilling and ironic effect, made her revulsion clear in a passage of extended and horrific detail:

> The *Jilal* was a good season for the vultures. They swarmed and shrieked around the dead camels that had succumbed to the drought. They stuffed themselves with carrion until they were too full to fly. Their bloated black bodies would run a little, try to take off, fall back again to earth. Their beaks and dirty white ruff of feathers around their necks were crusted with red. Their snake-like necks craned interminably and their eyes searched for more dead flesh. Sometimes they could not wait for a camel to die before they descended, picking first at the greatest delicacy, the still-seeing eyes. (52)

The other animal that symbolizes the graveyard aspect of the Haud is the hyena. Hunt described the hyena as a "common and a serious pest." During periods of drought, the hyena has been known to attack people and ". . . Somalis sleeping out on the ground always cover their faces to prevent the 'snatch-and-run' tactics of the hyaena, which has taken many noses, or other uncovered parts of the sleeping human body" (117). Laurence, describing the graves of those "who had not reached the wells," notes that the bodies "were buried in a shelf jutting from the pit, in the hope that this might protect the bodies from hyenas" (52). She dwells at length on the nature of these animals. They are "scavengers, not fighters," with "strength but no heart." They used to come out at night and prowl round the camp but lacked the courage to "venture inside our brushwood fence unless our campfires died untended and all the humans slept" (56).

Those outsiders who have experienced a *Jilal* drought have been deeply moved by the suffering of the people and their domestic animals. Some of the finest writing in Perham's novel comes when she describes her heroine's reaction to the sight of the emaciated animals and starving people that are camped around Hargeisa at the end of the dry season, a scene that "bit itself into her mind to remain with her all her life, and often to enter her dreams" (151). Laurence also writes with passionate but more controlled emotion of her own anguish at what she saw. She found that she could not write out of pity but only in wonder and humility that humanity could bear so much with such dignity. "Despair keeps its own silence" (65), she wrote, as she recalled her encounter with a Somali mother and child, both in desperate need of water, a desert scene that she remembered all her life and which later entered her fiction. Her chapter on the *Jilal* closes as the Somali woman slowly moves on with her camels across the great plains of the Haud where "The red termite-mounds stood like tall misshapen towers of the dead. On the carrion of camels the vultures screeched and gorged themselves" (66).

With luck the dry season ends with good rains that ensure new pasture on the Haud plateau, turning it into the "flowering desert" that Laurence describes in the succeeding chapter. But the rains, too, cost the people dearly, because the "violence of them matched the depth of the *Jilal* drought" (67). The amazing force of the infrequent desert rains is a phenomenon that must be experienced to be believed. The magnitude of some of the recorded rainfalls has been questioned, but Hunt confirms "that astounding falls of rain do occur in the Protectorate" (56), as he proves from his own experience and that of others. He mentions "[t]he terrific storm in May 1945 at Bihen in the usually dry S.E. Nogal," which "was fortunately observed by Captain Gilliland who was making a botanical survey there, though he fled before the storm and did not actually read the gauge." He himself had experienced a storm in 1941 when his "transport was marooned for ten days to a half-mile perimeter by floods at Gardo" (55).

The Laurences were caught one night in such a desert storm, and they only found their way back to Hargeisa because of the tenacity and courage of their driver, Abdi. The violence of the rain called for dramatic language and imagery. "There could," Laurence felt, "be no darkness anywhere to compare with this darkness, unless in caverns under the sea where the light never reaches. The rain was a black wall of water before our eyes. Abdi hunched forward, glaring at the streaming windscreen as though hoping by sheer force of will to penetrate the dark rain" (71). Laurence saw the rain as one of nature's cruel ironies. To begin with, most of the water was wasted. The river-beds were dry for most of the year, but ". . . during the rains they flowed in spate, roaring briefly with their flood, hurling the water down to the sea, carrying it off where it could not be used" (67). It would be Jack Laurence's task to catch some of this water in his *ballehs* but nothing could be done about the "ultimate irony." "Two days before," Laurence writes, "men and animals were dying of thirst here. Now some of them would drown. Every year, Abdi told us, a few sheep and goats, a few children, were swept away by the *tugs* when they flowed in spate. This must be the ultimate irony, surely — to drown in the desert" (71).

In spite of the cruel seasons of drought and rain, most travellers become attached to Somaliland. One of the reasons outsiders are attracted to this country is the feeling of timelessness conveyed by the desert and its people. The pastoral nomads move with such regularity through their landscape that they become an inseparable part of it: ". . . the people would go on as they always had, herding their camels between the wells and the grazing, the grazing and the wells" (*Prophet's* 102). What appeals to the visitor is, for example, another line of camels crossing the horizon led by the patriarch of the herd from whose throat hangs "a Kor or wooden bell" (Burton 107), or the solitary figure that can suddenly appear in an empty land, perhaps a Somali camel herder "standing against the sky . . . very straight and calm . . . his spear across one shoulder" (*Prophet's* 20).

Time has no power to alter this landscape, and it is a landscape that western visitors can associate with the their own traditional beginnings. Douglas Jardine, who was Secretary to the Somaliland Administration from 1916 to 1921, found his idea of the Old Testament world exactly matched in Somaliland. "The natural state of a Somali," he writes in *The Mad Mullah of Somaliland*, "is entirely nomadic; and his life in his own country to-day must be exactly the same as it was 500 years ago. Indeed, we can go further back and say that Ibrahim, Ishaak, and Yakoub are supporting the same sort of existence in British Somaliland to-day as did Abraham, Isaac, and Jacob elsewhere in the Orient in the days of Genesis" (20–21). Laurence has explained how appropriate it was that, while waiting in Rotterdam on her way to Somaliland, she read "for the first time in [her] life the five books of Moses" (*Prophet's* 9). She knew the Bible from her childhood when, like Vanessa MacLeod in *A Bird in the House*, she had gone to the United Church every Sunday, but in Rotterdam she read the story of the Children of Israel as she might have read a novel, from cover to cover. "Of all the books which I might have chosen to read just then," she adds, "few would have been more to the point, for the Children of Israel were people of the desert, as the Somalis were . . ." (9).

She was frequently reminded of the Old Testament, of the Children of Israel and their wanderings, as she travelled through the Haud and encountered the Somali nomads. The scarcity of wells and grazing, the drought, floods, and locusts had been the traditional means whereby an omnipotent Old Testament God tested his people. The Somalis are devout and faithful Muslims and "hold steadfast in the belief that God is the ultimate source of causation, and conceive of their Creator as a largely impersonal power in whose sight man is helpless and impotent" (Andrzejewski and Lewis 28). Laurence knew she could never adopt the fatalistic attitude of the Muslims, but she came to see why survival in the desert was made easier with the support of such a faith. It was a faith that also looked back to Abraham and his pastoral people who were often tested during their wanderings in the wilderness. Old Testament mythology shaped Laurence's vision of the desert world and an extensive use of biblical imagery in her later writing followed this apocalyptical experience. In Rotterdam she read how Hagar alone with her son in the wilderness wept when their water was finished. In the Haud, when she faced the woman who was watching "her child's life seep away for lack of water" (66), she thought of Old Testament Hagar, and the name of her first Canadian heroine was ordained by this encounter.

The desert is a timeless place where people have remained true to the ways of their forbearers. It is also by tradition a place of purification, a refuge from the cities of the plain. Laurence's descriptions of Somali towns are revealing and they anticipate an attitude to urban settings that is found in all her fiction. She confessed in an interview with Graeme Gibson that she found it difficult in her fiction "to create the feeling of living in a city, because I hate cities" (196). With the exception of Sheikh, she found the towns she visited while in Somaliland repugnant, and she describes them with strong imagery, suggestive of disease and decay. Both Zeilah and Djibouti are described in the chapter called "Place of Exile." From afar Zeilah had the appearance of "a shining city," but nearer, the whitewashed mudbrick appeared "stained by rain and goat dung. The shops and houses were decaying, the soiled plaster falling away in shreds and chunks" (105). In Djibouti the contrast between the Somali *magala* and the European quarter was marked; the former was "a shanty-town" where "[t]he stench and the hordes of flies were indescribable" (112). Laurence had already remarked on the same distressing contrast in Hargeisa where only the moonlight could make the Somali quarter of the town look a pleasant place to live. "The Hargeisa *magala* looked best at night," she remembers, "when the milky moonlight was spilled over the town, blanching its stained daytime countenance. The festering gutters, the leprous whitewash of the mosque, the jaundiced mud walls of the tea shops that squatted around the market place — by moonlight the sores of all these places were made to appear sound" (23). Laurence returned to the desert after her visit to Zeilah and Djibouti with a sense of relief. "Re-acquainting myself with the desert," she tells her readers, "I had a feeling of homecoming" (123).

Laurence's respect for the desert was reinforced by her visit to the ancient ruined city of Amoud. Amoud is one of the group of ruined cities that lie in the mountain escarpment "roughly half way between the ancient port of Zeila and the walled town of Harar" (Curle 315). Burton visited them in 1854. When crossing the mountain range, he turned aside "to visit some ruins a little way distant from the direct road," probably the ancient city of Abasa. Burton was uncertain of their age, but he could see that "the substantial ruins" had "fought a stern fight with time." He made a note of all that was left of the mosque, namely twelve square pillars and a rounded arch that marked the *Mihrab*, or prayer niche. The sight inspired the crafted and impressive prose that Burton could produce when the occasion demanded. "But the voice of the Muezzin is hushed for ever," Burton lamented, "and creepers now twine around the ruined fane" (148).

Other travellers have described these ruined cities. Major H.G.C. Swayne criss-crossed the country in the closing decade of the nineteenth century in pursuit of its wild life, but took time off to visit the "ancient ruined town of Auboba" (23), which Burton inspected the day after his visit to Abasa. Aububah, as Burton spelt it, was the resting place of Sheikh Aububah [Au Boba] whose tomb was covered by "a little conical dome of brick, clay, and wood. . . . It is falling to pieces," Burton adds, "and the adjoining mosque, long roofless, is overgrown with trees, that rustle melancholy sounds in the light joyous breeze" (152).

The ruins were later examined and dated by archaeologists. In 1934 A.T. Curle, reporting for the journal *Antiquity: A Quarterly Review of Archaeology*, spent some time visiting all the ruined cities and excavating a number of the refuse dumps, so making it "possible to assign the period of occupation of the towns to the 15th and 16th centuries" (315). They were probably built as trading stations linking the port of Zeilah with the interior. Curle describes the mosque at Abasa and the tomb of Sheikh Au Boba, and he dwells at length on the town of Amoud. His findings were largely confirmed by the archaeologist A.G. Mathew, who in 1951 made a short report for the Colonial Office on the ruins of Amoud. He thought the ruins of an older city, which he called "Amud I," possibly pre-Islamic, lay beneath "Amud II." He believed the later city was a holding place for slaves. "This was," he writes, "obviously a slave route and around the edge of the town there are remains of a number of large pens built roughly from stones placed loosely one upon the other without mortar; it seems probable that these were slave pens" (31). These cities, however, have guarded their secrets over the years, and they remain "an unsolved riddle of Africa," which was how John Parkinson had described them in the 1930s. While working as a geologist for the Colonial Office on a scheme to develop the water supply in Somaliland, Parkinson visited the ruined cities. He ended an account of his impressions, written and published in 1935, with the remark that solving this African riddle was almost irrelevant in face of the great problem of British Somaliland, which was "the obtaining of water." He knew that "the prosperity and very life of the tribes" could depend on alleviating the water shortage (126–27).

Little had changed in 1951 when the Laurences went to explore the ruins of Amoud. While waiting impatiently in Borama for the arrival at Djibouti of the heavy machinery needed for constructing the *ballehs*, they realized they were close to the ancient city of Amoud. They went as tourists to visit it. Standing among the sand-covered ruins, Laurence conjured up Amoud's former greatness when the city "would have been a babble of noise, shouting and haggling, the scuffing of feet along the rough stone roads, the uproar of camels" (102). But ". . . Amoud had been dead a long time," and she was subject to the same feeling of melancholy that overcame Burton. In lyrical prose not unlike his, she described the scene:

> The candelabra trees had grown inside the houses, their bright green tapers looking as though they had been here always. Generations of the *galol* tree had grown old and fallen, and their boughs were strewn around the ground. Blue flowers the colour of kingfishers grew in the tangled grasses, and the trees cast long shadows on the skeleton of Amoud. (102)

Laurence has her own version of Amoud's history, based on her reading, but she may well have heard Mathew on the subject. She had been told that several cities had stood on the site, and one "might have been pre-Islamic." However, her account does not include mention of Amoud's possible links with the slave trade, but emphasizes instead the fact that Amoud has become an empty ruin. She found the name of the city apt since it means "sand": ". . . the city had returned," she noticed, "to the mountains and the desert" (101). Turning from the ruined city to look at the nomadic camp at the foot of the hill, a camp soon to be dismantled and moved once more to a new grazing ground, she was struck by the paradox that the wandering desert people achieved a permanence no settled city civilization had been able to equal. "Looking at Amoud," she mused, "and then at the nomads' huts crouched at the bottom of the hills, I could not help thinking of the western world with its power and its glory, its sky-scrapers and its atom bombs, and wondering if these desert men would not after all survive longer than we did, and remain to seed the human race again, after our cities lay as dead as Amoud, the city of the sands" (102–03). Perham had put similar feelings into words as she compared the way of life in the desert to the society she had left: " '. . . our top-heavy civilization will crash,' " one of her characters in *Major Dane's Garden* believes, " 'because, for all its great scientific achievements, its morals are clumsy, and it has no intention. And sometimes I wonder if the Somal will not then be found still walking the land, no better and no worse than he is now, only, because he has survived, proved perfect' " (198).

In *The Prophet's Camel Bell*, the Somalis are seen walking the land as a remote and independent people, at one with their environment, but they also walk through the pages of the book as individuals. In "Many Solitudes: The Travel Writings of Margaret Laurence," George Woodcock voiced the general feeling about Laurence's travel memoir when he argued that it has "many of the characteristics of fiction," and in particular her "character sketches often read like stories" (146). Some of the best character sketches come in the chapters devoted to the Somalis who lived with the Laurences in the desert: Hersi, Mohamed, Arabetto, and Abdi. These chapters do, indeed, read like stories, and they are the work of an accomplished writer of fiction. In them incident and voice are admirably handled with a sense of humour to lighten her thoughtful representation of the "other," of people very different from herself.

An excellent parallel to her gallery of Somali portraits can be found in Burton's book. Like the Laurences, Burton spent many days alone with the Somalis in the desert. In his book Burton gives himself the role of hero, but his supporting cast of Somalis comes close to stealing his limelight. Chief among them are the three who stuck to Burton throughout his journey. Mohammed Mahmud, a sergeant lent to Burton by the Aden police, was in charge of Burton's caravan and was known as *Al Hammal*, "the Porter." In spite of being somewhat overweight he was capable of matching Burton's extraordinary stamina. *Al Hammal* was still to be found in Aden thirty years later, recounting details of his adventures with Burton. A certain Langton Prendergast Walsh, Second Assistant Resident in Aden, was sent to Berbera in 1884 to establish an official British presence in Somaliland. In his colourful and lively record of his life there, *Under the Flag and Somali Coast Stories*, Walsh describes how before leaving Aden he spoke with "Mahomed Mahmud, a pensioned Havildar of the Aden Police, who had been the head-man of Burton's party and was generally known as 'the *Hammal*' (the Porter)" (127). Burton's second companion was Guled, also of the Aden police. He must have presented a striking contrast to *Al Hammal* since he is described as one of "those long, live skeletons, common amongst the Somal." Burton's third faithful companion was one Abdy Abokr whose nickname was "End of Time." In spite of End of Time's "prodigious rascality" he proved a pleasant companion and enlivened all conversations from his store of proverbs. Other smaller characters are well sketched in. There is One-Eyed Kalendar who was usually left to guard the baggage and the women. The latter were two "buxom dames" who worked with the camels and cooked the meals. They looked "each like three average women rolled into one," and Burton ironically named them after Shehrazade and Deenarzade of *The Arabian Nights* (101). Most readers are beguiled by Burton's lively descriptive powers, and it is not surprising that Shehrazade and Deenarzade particularly caught the imagination of Saul Bellow. Burton gives an ironic description of "jogsi," the means by which Shehrazade and Deenarzade relieve their fatigue, explaining that "they lie at full length, prone, stand upon each other's backs trampling and kneading with the toes, and rise like giants much refreshed" (102). In *Henderson the Rain King*, Bellow's Eugene Henderson, who takes Burton's book with him to Africa, is "given" two women, Tamba and Bebu, "to render him service." They demonstrate "joxi" for Henderson but fail to convince him that the treatment would prove therapeutic (205).

Though Burton's tone when describing his Somali companions is ironic and condescending, he seems to have enjoyed a happy relationship with them, not without affection on both sides. One-Eyed Kalendar and the women did not complete the journey to Harar, and when Burton, accompanied by *Al Hammal*, Long Guled, and End of Time, returned from the forbidden city there was much rejoicing. "Loud congratulations and shouts of joy awaited our arrival," Burton notes, adding that ". . . the Kalendar was in a paroxysm of delight," and "both Shehrazade and Deenarzade were affected with giggling and what might be blushing" (244). Burton's attitude to his Somali servants was uncomplicated. He regarded the Somalis, as many of his contemporaries would have done, as barbarians, while he saw himself as a member of a superior species. The role of master came naturally to him as can be seen when he is called on to resolve arguments. At one time or another he had to settle "disputes between the Hammal and the End of Time" (185–86) or compose "quarrels between Shehrazade, whose swains had detained her from camel-loading, and the Kalendar whose one eye flashed with indignation at her conduct" (161). Yet Burton's servants never behaved in a servile or dependent way even when accepting his leadership, and the relationship seems to have operated on more equal terms than Burton's patronizing voice suggests. Most importantly, it was a relationship that left neither side with a complex. After leaving Harar, Burton relentlessly drove himself, his companions, and the mules during a spectacular speedy ride to Berbera. End of Time and Long Guled arrived "completely worn out," Burton records, but the *Hammal* "retained strength and spirits: the sturdy fellow talked, sang, and shouted, and, whilst the others could scarcely sit their mules, he danced his war-dance and brandished his spear. I was delighted with his 'pluck'" (267). There is no doubt that Burton enjoyed the company of his Somali servants and appreciated their proverbs, songs, and stories.

The Prophet's Camel Bell has a similar cast of characters. The Laurences were as well served by the Somalis as Burton had been, but a century later the relationship between employer and servant was more complex and not always trouble-free. The Somalis have often struck outsiders as an excitable and theatrical people. Laurence saw them as an "extremely excitable people," with a "highly developed sense of the dramatic" (*Tree* 1). Others have agreed. Writing at the beginning of the century with the paternalistic attitude not uncommon at the time, in *The Mad Mullah of Somaliland* Jardine gave a summary of their "few vices and many virtues." He considered avarice, vanity, and excitability as their "besetting sins," the first being understandable considering "the Somali's terrible struggle for existence in his own country," and the second two being rarely of serious consequence. Jardine's readers are told how vanity will lead a man earning good wages to "spend most of them on the adornment of his person. Bright turbans, shirts, handkerchiefs, and coats, all of silk, and imposing walking sticks are most popular with the wage-earner of Berbera or Aden; and a Somali dandy will devote hours to combing his hair before a looking-glass. Nor are his efforts in vain: for the general effect of all this adornment is most attractive" (23–25).

Jardine could have been describing the Laurences' cook, Mohamed — "not the quiet sort" — who "liked to make his presence known to the world." Laurence has described his appearance when, dressed in "robes of royal purple," he set out for an evening visit to the city. He usually put on, she recalls, "his shoes of oxblood leather, tossed an embroidered kashmir shawl across one shoulder and tucked a small cane, like a swagger stick, under an elbow. He felt I was making a ridiculous fuss about nothing when I strongly objected to my brightly patterned linen tea-towels being used as turbans" (161). Jardine also blamed vanity for the Somali refusal to admit ignorance. "If you ask a Somali," Jardine declares, "whether he knows how to do anything, he invariably replies, *tout court*, that a Somali knows everything" (25). Mohamed "would never admit ignorance," Laurence has to agree, and so a precious cucumber, a vegetable rarely seen in Somaliland, was boiled as though it were a potato because Mohamed scorned to seek advice on how to prepare it (164).

While the Laurences enjoyed the company of such enterprising and lively people, they soon realized that an uncomplicated relationship with their servants was not possible. As employers they were unable to play the part expected of them. When she arrived in Somaliland Laurence found the very idea of having a servant unpleasant. "I could not face," she tells her readers, "the prospect of being called 'Memsahib,' a word which seemed to have connotations of white man's burden, paternalism, everything I did not believe in. Furthermore, I was not sure I would be able to cope with servants" (14). Her fears proved justified. The domestic peace of the household was often disrupted, and the Laurences did not know how to settle the disputes that arose. Ironically, Mohamed would perhaps have found it easier to play his part of servant with a colonial *memsahib* than with a young Canadian liberal who was kind and friendly but unpredictable. Certainly the reaction of Ismail, who was employed by the Laurences as a houseboy, would suggest this. Though Ismail was young, he had worked for the British for a long time, and he "had a fantastically strong sense of what was fitting. This insistence upon formality seemed to protect his own status. No Somali wanted to work for an Englishman who did not know the proper thing to do" (41). Laurence's problem has been clearly identified by Raja Rao, who comes from the land where the terms "sahib" and "memsahib" had their origin. In *The Serpent and the Rope* Rao's chief character Rama, a Brahmin from the south of India, observes that "[s]ervants like to obey those who really know what is right and what is wrong," and, Rama adds, "I cannot make a *pankha*-boy obey, for I cannot understand why anyone should obey anyone" (90). Both these aspects of the question troubled Laurence, who was unused to servants and who soon realized that she was always, as far as Mohamed was concerned, doing what was wrong. One of the first things she did in Hargeisa was, Mohamed considered, a very improper thing to do. Nevertheless, he accompanied her as she went on foot to the local market, shuffling "with some embarrassment beside [her] along the dusty road" (23). Mohamed's reaction to what she considered her laudable curiosity surprised and impressed her, and she was to return to this market visit in her fiction. Laurence was not unaware of the irony of the situation. She and her husband had expected that they would "be more likeable as employers than the majority of English" whom they referred to as " 'the sahib types.' " "Were we not," Laurence suggested, "more democratic? What a good thing that Mohamed appreciated this quality" (164). In fact Mohamed did not appreciate this quality because his own status as servant depended on the status of his master. Mohamed stayed with the Laurences until they left. They finally parted with regret but without ever having fully come to terms with each other.

Similarly, relations with Abdi, the driver, proved difficult. His story, which is told in chapter twelve and entitled "The Old Warrior," began in the days of the Sayyid, since Abdi was nearly sixty when the Laurences arrived. Laurence recreated his past with compassion as she imagined his days as a warrior, fighting for the British as a member of the Camel Corps, and the succeeding years of drought in the desert when his children and stock died. The Laurences owed Abdi their lives since his strength saved them from the floods, but his demands on their gratitude multiplied, and he caused trouble when they had to be denied. Abdi was a man of contradictions, "both humble and proud" (179), one moment "gentle, compassionate, courageous," the next "fierce, violent, raging" (184). The story of his association with the Laurences is one of a failure of comprehension on both sides, and there is a sense of loss that a man they admired for many reasons did not become a friend. The feeling of regret is movingly conveyed on Laurence's part, and, though she may have felt she never understood him, she was nevertheless able to sense intuitively a great deal about him. Her version of his story ends with an unusual prayer for this courageous warrior. ". . . I would wish," the prayer goes, "there to be battles somewhere in Paradise, for an old warrior who never knew — and who probably could not have borne to know — that his truest and most terrible battle, like all men's, was with himself" (189).

Laurence had no problems when she described Abdi as she first knew him, his appearance, his words and his deeds, but she puzzled for long over his enigmatic behaviour. When writing *The Prophet's Camel Bell*, more than ten years after leaving Somaliland, she thought she had found an answer to the riddle. She would, however, have been wise to trust in her own initial response, instead of trying to solve the problem in more general terms. In her chapter on Abdi, Laurence quotes directly from the diary on which *The Prophet's Camel Bell* is based, giving for once a tantalizing glimpse of this now unavailable document. "The Somalis," she wrote in the diary, "are proud, not grovelling, and in their own eyes they are aristocrats and warriors. But they are also terribly poor, their lives hounded by drought and disease. Many of them cannot treat Europeans as people. If we are sahib and memsahib, Abdi can do his job, and be polite, and try with a clear conscience to get as much as possible from us, secure in his basic hatred of us" (186). This explanation of Abdi's behaviour is logical and possible, even if it is not palatable. Some ten years later, she looked back with a changed attitude, one that had resulted from reading a book that greatly impressed her. Towards the end of her life, Laurence told an audience at Trent University that when she was planning *The Prophet's Camel Bell*, she read a book called *Prospero and Caliban: The Psychology of Colonization* by the psychologist Mannoni ("Books That Mattered"

244). O. Mannoni's work was originally published in France in 1950, but Laurence probably read the English translation that was made in 1956. Evidence indicates that she read *Prospero and Caliban* between 1960 and 1962. She was on her own admission influenced by this work, and it was fresh in her mind when she wrote *The Prophet's Camel Bell*. She thought that Mannoni's use of Prospero and Caliban as archetypal examples of the colonizer and the colonized could be employed to explain Abdi's behaviour. Mannoni's argument centres on the premise that a feeling of dependency is natural to Caliban or, the example Mannoni uses, the colonized Malagasy. Both, it is suggested, have an innate need for a master. This point in Mannoni's argument has now been challenged, most notably by Franz Fanon, but Laurence accepted it, and it allowed her to look back on Abdi with new eyes. Perhaps his need had been for a powerful friend, someone who could provide the protection that the ordinary warrior expected from the chief of his clan. As employers, she and her husband had failed in this respect. Though it is a factor that should be taken into account, this explanation when carried to its limit does not seem just to the man she had earlier described as "courage and pride and anger writ large" (188).

Prospero, autocratically ruling his desert island, is a more satisfactory archetype of the colonizer than Caliban is of the colonized, though the comparison may not always seem fair to Prospero. Mannoni distinguishes between a "colonizer," someone who is "of necessity a man of strong character," and the colonial, who comes later and "finds the relationship ready made." The latter will be able to exploit the colonial situation (97). It was with colonials that Laurence was concerned. As she readily admits, she arrived in Somaliland prepared to dislike the "imperialists." "I believed," she acknowledges, "that the overwhelming majority of Englishmen in colonies could properly be classified as imperialists, and my feeling about imperialism was very simple — I was against it" (16). Laurence met a good many of "the sahib-type" in Somaliland, and, when she was writing *The Prophet's Camel Bell*, she was still extremely critical of them as a class, expressing her dislike in vitriolic terms and finally dismissing them as not worth the invective she once thought they deserved. "I have never in my life," she writes, "felt such antipathy towards people anywhere as I felt towards these pompous or whining sahibs and memsahibs" (207). On the other hand she had sympathy for the previous colonial rulers of Somaliland, the Italians, who lived on in the country as sad and lonely exiles. One of them was a former Italian colonial known simply as *il Capitano*. He had surveyed the dangerous Danakil area of Ethiopia for the Italian Government and now, dependent in his turn on an imperialist master, found consolation in his huge tawny spotted "pet" cheetah (149).

Laurence opens her chapter on the imperialists with an explanation of her feelings about the British living in Somaliland, but she moves from her condemnation of them as a class to a survey of those she knew as individuals. Some of them can be clearly identified from the Colonial Office Lists of 1951 and 1952. The Governor who arrived unexpectedly one day to visit the Laurences' camp in the Haud was Sir Gerald Reece, who had come to Somaliland in 1948 from the Northern Frontier District of Kenya. Conscious of the dignity of his position, the Governor was a formal man, and Laurence describes him in his official uniform, wearing "the most distinctive piece of headgear I had ever seen" (204). Though she treated the Governor's plumed helmet with some disrespect by reporting a friend's opinion of it — " 'If he put these feathers on his bum . . . he could fly' " (208) — she had nothing but admiration for the Governor himself. When she recalls the day he turned up in his shiny Humber at their muddy desert camp, she acknowledges that the unease between them was largely the result of her shyness and her consciousness of her own bedraggled appearance in the face of his impeccable attire. Laurence remembers that when the Governor asked her "very directly" what she did with herself in camp, she had "stammered over a reply." She had hesitated to explain that she had begun "to translate Somali poems and folk-tales," but writing later she realized that she should have mentioned her preoccupation, "for it was a subject which interested him" (85).

Later, in Hargeisa, she met the Governor's wife, and again shyness on one side and formality on the other prevented the two drawing close. Lady Alys Reece wrote an account of her early married life in Kenya, *To My Wife — 50 Camels*, and it was published the same year as *The Prophet's Camel Bell*. It suggests that the two authors could have been good friends. Soon after her marriage in 1936 Alys Reece joined her husband in northern Kenya, where he was District Commissioner in an area close to the Ethiopian and Somali borders. There, his wife notes, he worked as "something of a one-man welfare band" (44). She, too, was soon involved in the lives of the local people, and her experiences were not unlike Laurence's. Some examples will show how happily the two might have reminisced together.

Many Somalis lived in northern Kenya, and the Reeces were served by someone not unlike Mohamed. Ibrahim was a Somali from the Wajir district. He liked to wear "the gaudiest embroidered waistcoats . . . and he had a particularly nice taste in turbans." Reece adds that she particularly admired his turban "of fine orange wool embroidered in peacock blue and green" (53). Later in her book, Reece describes the day when her husband was bitten by a snake. Her feeling of absolute helplessness in an emergency of this sort was a dreadful experience. "There was," she recalls, "so little I could do and I badly needed to feel I was doing something that might help. The do-it-yourself doctoring book we kept on the shelf had nothing to say on the subject of snake bites" (70). Laurence would have sympathized with such feelings. Even when making preparations for departure, she had foreseen them. "There you go," she writes, "anxious, as you may well be, for anything might happen and so you furtively reassure yourself with pages from the first-aid book in which it says the best thing to do for snakebite is to keep the patient quiet until the doctor arrives — luckily, you do not notice that it does not tell you what to do if there is no doctor within a hundred miles" (1). When Laurence met Reece, she realized with delight that here was someone who shared her interests, but "[o]ne does not ask the Governor's wife to drop over for a beer" (234), and so what would in all likelihood have proved a happy friendship did not develop.

Laurence felt more at ease with other members of the administration, some of whom she vividly portrays. Many of them were "uncommon" people (208). Ernest, who can be identified as E.F. Peck in the Colonial Office List, was Director of Agriculture and Veterinary Services. He was blessed with "the ability to travel hopefully, and here, where the earth was about as hard and unyielding as it is possible for earth to be, and where setbacks were not the exception but the norm, this ability was a great gift indeed" (211). Laurence often listened to Lieutenant Colonel A.D.M. Lewis, Aide-de-Camp to the Governor, known simply as the Colonel, who had read everything he could find on the campaigns against the Sayyid. He told Laurence many stories about the gallant deeds performed by the British and their Somali allies. Laurence was also indebted to James Martin, the Information Officer, because she used his photographs along with her own to illustrate *The Prophet's Camel Bell*. But Laurence owed most to the Chief Secretary and Commissioner for Native Affairs, Philip Shirley, who was an exceptional civil servant. He knew the Somalis well and had great respect for their culture. He was also responsible for the publication of A *Tree for Poverty*.

Imperialists such as these were redeemed, Laurence recognized, because they loved Africa, but their love did not win them the right to belong there. She concludes by questioning the reasons that took them to a continent where, in spite of their goodwill, they would always be strangers. She argues, once more drawing on Mannoni's work, that they, no less than the "sahib-types" who hated Africa, had felt a need to escape from their place of belonging and, like Prospero, settle on a desert island, where they could establish an empire, "a mythical kingdom and a private world" (228). Finally, therefore, she must recognize herself as an imperialist since she has been searching in Africa for a world made to her own pattern. She certainly used her experiences for her own ends, exploiting them in her writing, but her relationship with Africa extended beyond one of selfish interest. Laurence, like many of the British she met in Somaliland, was prepared to give as well as take, not always easy since she soon discovered she was not in control of this desert island. She was living in a real, not a mythical, world as she acknowledges when she agrees that ". . . the real world did impinge upon our consciousness, and portions of the secret empire of the heart had to be discarded, one by one" (228). The British in Somaliland, many of whom she singles out, lived, as her descriptive powers have only too well attested, in the real world, which was sometimes terrifying and sometimes beautiful. She and her husband also worked there with dedication. They could, perhaps, never be anything but strangers in this desert world, but they respected its customs and worked there on behalf of its inhabitants. When Laurence recreates the imperialists as she remembers them, be it a racist *sahib* in the Hargeisa Club or a dedicated Veterinary Officer in the Haud, they are understandable as living individuals and not as variants of a mythical Prospero figure.

Laurence became especially aware of her status as a stranger in Somaliland when she considered the differences between the traditions of the land she had come to and the one she had left. These differences raised questions, but they were questions that did not need to be, perhaps could not be, resolved. One of the themes of *The Prophet's Camel Bell* is that of loneliness, a theme that, as Woodcock realized in "Many Solitudes," is central to all her work. The feeling of solitude that arises from "the experiences of foreignness" makes it all the more important to communicate across cultural barriers (144). Laurence recognized the limitations to her understanding of the Somalis, but her attempts to set up lines of communication were not always unsuccessful.

Perhaps the difference that most disturbed her — it brought home her own foreignness — was the place of women in a Muslim world. Arranged marriages, circumcision, and child prostitution were subjects that Somalis were unwilling to discuss, above all with a western woman, and Laurence learnt not to raise them directly. She does, however, find effective means to make her own viewpoint clear in her writing. Take, for example, two young girls who fleetingly entered her life but whom she found impossible to forget. Hawa, fifteen or sixteen years old, gauche like a child, but dressed in splendid robes of blue and white, with gold bangles on her wrist, came to visit Laurence in Sheikh. Hawa was married to an elder, a man old enough to be her grandfather, maybe too old to give her the children she longed for. Laurence could not question Hawa about her feelings but "the look of resignation in her eyes said that her life was a bitter one" (45). Also sad and remote was the eight-year-old child-prostitute, Asha, unkempt and unwashed, with "a curiously vacant and withdrawn look." She made daily visits to the camp, but "We did not talk much," writes Laurence, "for I did not know what to say to her." Hawa and Asha continued for a long time to haunt Laurence, as "a reproach and a question" (142). As ghosts, they were partly exorcized in *The Tomorrow-Tamer*: Hawa as Sunday's child-wife in "A Fetish for Love" and Asha as Ayesha in "The Rain Child."

The circumcision and infibulation of young girls, an operation that has worried succeeding visitors to Somaliland from Burton on, is a closely guarded tradition that encourages the virginity of a girl until she marries, but it seems to many westerners a truly barbarous practice. Burton's thoughts on the subject could not for conventional reasons be included in his book. He restricts himself to the comment that ". . . the Somali women are of cold temperament, the result of artificial as well as natural causes" (93). According to Fawn M. Brodie, Burton wrote an appendix in Latin on the matter for *First Footsteps*, but the publisher removed it (110–11). Laurence, at first over-eager to investigate the nature of the operation, soon realized that there were things she could not openly question in the manner she had employed when she had been a journalist with *The Winnipeg Citizen*. "Somali girls," she reports, "underwent some operation at puberty, the exact nature of which I had been unable to determine, partly because in our early days here every Somali to whom I put this question gave me a different answer, and partly because I no longer questioned people in this glib fashion" (63).

Such self-discipline was not easily acquired, as she admits. She discovered this when she began "playing doctor" for the camp workers with her first aid kit. Exaggerated word of her powers spread into the surrounding desert and the sick, some of them in urgent need of skilled medical care, came in search of healing. Stunned by the suffering and shamed by her inadequacy to cope with it, Laurence put away her medicine chest in almost childish pique. Then Mohamed's young assistant cut his finger with a butcher's knife, and the first-aid kit came out of its hiding place, and Laurence acknowledged her mistake. "Would I do nothing," she asks herself, "simply because I could not do everything?" (63). The important thing was to be ready when there was something she could do and to recognize those situations where she could do nothing. So when a group of women came to her to ask if she could give them something for their menstrual pain, she turned them away without comment. She knew that she must remain silent. Laurence had learnt that as a direct result of circumcision and infibulation ". . . many women had considerable pain with menstruation and intercourse, and the birth of their children was frequently complicated by infection," but there was nothing she could do to help them. Somali women lived according to customs totally different from her own, and she would never understand the reasons for circumcision and infibulation. It was not, indeed, right that she should criticize the practise openly. There were some Somalis who questioned the tradition. "In the opinion of an educated Somali friend of ours," she notes, "this operation was one custom which would take a very long time to die, for the old women would never agree to its being abandoned, he believed, even if the men would" (64). In later years a Somali writer would raise the question in its rightful place. In *Sardines* Nuruddin Farah allows Medina, a modern Somali woman, to express her feelings about circumcision and voice her determination that her daughter be spared its cruelty.

Prostitution, child marriage, and circumcision raised questions that Laurence could not pursue while she was in Somaliland, but the suffering they caused could not be forgotten. In her West African fiction, Laurence did not feel bound by the restrictions placed on her in Somaliland. In her novel *This Side Jordan*, she gives fictional expression to her own horror when she describes Johnnie's reaction after he has raped the innocent Emerald, causing great pain:

> He remembered having heard that some tribes still practised female circumcision. It was one of those scraps of information about Africa that every white-man picks up. He had always thought it exaggerated. But it was not. Among certain peoples, the clitoridectomy was performed at puberty. By a bush surgeon — some fetish priestess, perhaps. Some of them were said to use the long wicked acacia thorns as needles. The wounds often became infected and did not heal for a long time. (232–33)

The young liberal from Canada also had a problem accepting the traditional Somali attitude to the non-Somali clans, in particular the Midgan, Yibir, and Tomal people. Laurence's questions always met with evasions when she asked Somalis about them. It had been customary in the past to treat these people as outcasts and heretics. The Midgans had been given work that the Somalis would not do, and the Yibirs had been abhorred by true Muslims because they practised magic. Laurence approached the non-Somali clans on equal terms, and was rewarded by their trust, as can be seen from her relationship with Said the Midgan, sandal-maker of Hargeisa, whom she describes in her final chapter of farewell. Said was "somewhat temperamental" and "worked only when he felt like it," but he made many pairs of sandals for Laurence and told her tales of the Midgans while he sat under the *galol* tree in her yard (233).

There was one area where Laurence was able to override all barriers and find herself at one with the Somalis and that was in the sphere of literature. Running parallel to the story of her husband's Herculean labours as the dams took shape in the Haud is the account of her own successful achievement: the writing and publication of *A Tree for Poverty*. She devotes a chapter of *The Prophet's Camel Bell* to extracts from her translations. The most important barrier she had to overcome to achieve her goal was that of language, and she acknowledges the help given her by Bogumil Andrzejewski and Musa H.I. Galaal, who provided her with literal translations of Somali poems and stories. Her "sincere thanks" also went to Hersi Jama, "who spent many hours of his own time in gathering material from other storytellers" (*Tree* [ix]).

Laurence's chapters on Mohamed and Abdi tell of misunderstandings that are never resolved. In her chapter on Hersi, she explains that here, too, her overtures of friendship were suspect, at any rate to start with, since it was some time before he trusted her enough to tell her the folk stories she was eager to hear. However, when Hersi realized that her interest was serious and sympathetic, things changed. "From that day, we never looked back," she recalls happily (159). Hersi, the teller of tales, becomes the subject of the best character sketch in her book, and, as she tells his story, her voice takes wing, as so often his must have done, "rising excitedly in a lengthy recitation" (158).

She tells of a man cruelly used by fate since he was born with a stammer, but who used his wits, like many of the heroes of his own tales, to overcome his deficiency. She tells of a man born for the stage, who throws himself into the role of camp peacemaker. His moods fluctuate from despair, when his wife produces yet another daughter, to triumph, when one of the completed *ballehs* is named after him. She can see with understanding that he is a man caught between yesterday and today, one who has lost touch with his clan but is at a disadvantage in a changing world where younger men with better educations will take his job. But she finally pays tribute to a man who can tell a good story and will always be honoured, "for he was an artist and he gave to each performance the very best of which he was capable" (160). Hersi's imperfect but imaginative use of English is vividly recreated, his powers of acting are described in detail, and he lives on as the story-teller out in the Haud, his listeners sitting around him, "pulling their robes close against the chill of the night, and urging him on" (160).

Laurence shared the Somali enjoyment of story-telling and, as Clara Thomas observes in her afterword to the *Prophet's Camel Bell*, ". . . their story-telling inspired the story-teller in her" (268). Westerners in Somaliland have found themselves, often to their satisfaction, the subject of camp-fire tales. Burton can hardly hide his delight that his mad ride from Harar to Berbera will not be forgotten. He describes the night of his arrival and how he eventually "fell asleep, conscious of having performed a feat which, like a certain ride to York, will live in local annals for many and many a year" (267).

The Laurences, too, become part of an exciting story. One night out in the Haud, their truck was ransacked and many items were taken, including a large wooden box in which Jack Laurence kept his theodolite, a practical surveying instrument that measures horizontal and vertical angles. The thieves were disturbed and fled, but one of them dropped a spear, thus enabling Hersi and Abdi to track down the villains and recover the loot, which had in fact proved a disappointment since the thieves had believed the theodolite case to be a chest full of gold. Hersi was quick to develop the story, and Laurence too helps transform it, imagining that the theodolite case may well suffer an Arabian Night change into "some rare carved chest laden with golden coins and necklaces like the sun." She is sure at any rate that the tale will live on and lose "nothing in the telling." "For all we know," she concludes, "fifty years from now the Eidagalla in the Haud may be chanting a *gabei* called *The Thief Of Selahleh* which tells how Abdi the warrior and Hersi the orator outwitted the enemy and vanquished him utterly . . ." (96–97).

The Prophet's Camel Bell is itself a good story. When he reviewed the book, Robert Fulford wrote, "Mrs. Laurence has a first-class talent for narrative and description, and in *The Prophet's Camel Bell* she uses it well" (81–82). The characters in the story have not been invented, but their deeds and words are presented in a fictional manner. Abdi plays his part of warrior and Hersi that of orator, but the narrator and her husband are the two central figures, and their quest is the subject of the plot. Jack Laurence is the hero of the book, and the slow but finally successful achievement of his goal is the thread that links the separate and distinct chapters. As a hero he labours mightily and against great odds, but slowly the first *balleh* is built, and he moves to the next site. His progress is linked to the Somali year; he moves on as another dry season comes in the Haud: ". . . the *Jilal* began again," the story-teller declaims, and "On the great plain, what was left of the grass lay wind-flattened and white. The vultures could be seen again, on the thorn trees, waiting" (142–43). Jack Laurence must wait, too, for the rains. As he starts the construction of the second *balleh*, he still does not know if the first will hold the rains.

By using her narrative talent to tell her husband's story, Margaret Laurence pays him, the Somalis would consider, the best possible tribute. It is a story she tells with great attention to detail. The story was told elsewhere in official terms. The Colonial Office *Report on the Somaliland Protectorate for the Years 1950 and 1951* noted that the pastures in the Protectorate had been "deteriorating rapidly through indiscriminate grazing," and to tackle the problem thirty *ballehs* were being constructed "with the object of spreading the livestock over a wider area in order that the land around the existing permanent wells [might] be rested." The Colonial Office could report that two *ballehs* had been completed, and each was expected to hold 2,000,000 gallons (6).[1] Laurence added drama and colour to these plain facts as she gave the story shape, finally bringing it to a happy ending. It was the completion of the first two *ballehs* that required the greatest effort because of the pioneering nature of the work and the initial distrust it caused. When the time came for the Laurences to leave, the Somalis themselves, trained by Jack Laurence, would take over the work. Jack Laurence won the respect of the Somalis because he was himself prepared to "tussle with the desert," and he was given the title *odei-gi rer-ki*, which means "the old man of the tribe" (121). Laurence describes the difficulties her husband overcame in winning Somali support for his work. She conveys the sense of fulfilment as the line of *ballehs* began to take shape across the waterless Haud. A fitting end to her husband's story came when a young, handsome Eidagalla chieftain, Ahmed Abdillahi, arrived at their camp with "an outsize camel bell, which he had made himself, out of *galol* wood. . . . This camel bell," Laurence recalls, "ranked as Jack's first, last and only presentation. It was a strange and unwieldy creation, with a hank of handwoven rope at the top. But we valued it greatly, for it signified the first real acceptance of the *ballehs*" (144).

When the time came to leave, the Laurences made a farewell visit to their first *balleh*, Balleh Gehli, "the Balleh of the Camels." Laurence as story-teller can still control the narrative, adding one final moment of tension: would the rains come in time to fill the *balleh* before they had to go? Their wish was granted because "Miraculously, the *Gu* rains fell early . . ." (234). The Laurences drove out into the desert. The *balleh* was full of life-giving water, and the Somali nomads, who had previously regarded Jack Laurence's work with deep suspicion, were watering their camels with all the confident rights of ownership.

The Prophet's Camel Bell also tells of a personal voyage of discovery. Travelling for the first time east of Suez, Laurence came upon a land of marvels, such as had been pictured in her father's *National Geographic* magazines. Her talent for description rose to the challenge of this unknown and fascinating land. Her book is full of the details one expects to find in a travel guide, laying emphasis on those things that struck her as foreign. She discusses the Muslim faith and the holy month of Ramadan. She describes the way the women dismantle their houses of sticks and mats each time the camp is moved. She comments amusingly on the habits of camels and tells her reader how the young animals are weaned. She writes of many wild and domestic creatures that are of interest, among them the ferocious black jinna or stink ants "with an odour that verified their name" (79) and the distinctive Somali sheep that are "white with ebony heads" (20).

While her journey is one of geographical exploration, it is also one of self-discovery. When Joseph Conrad fashioned from his own experience on the river Congo his allegory of an inner voyage into the heart of darkness, he designed a metaphor that became a pattern for other writers, the darkness being the one that lies within ourselves. Graham Greene, who has traversed the world, was particularly attracted to Africa, "the Africa of the Victorian atlas, the blank unexplored continent the shape of the human heart" (*In Search of a Character* 123). Greene recognized that he explored Africa in order to find his own identity, as others had done, though the purpose of the journey had been variously expressed. In *Journey without Maps* Greene writes, ". . . there are a thousand names for it, King Solomon's Mines, the 'heart of darkness' if one is romantically inclined, or more simply, as Herr Heuser puts it in his African novel, *The Inner Journey*, one's place in time, based on a knowledge not only of one's present but of the past from which one has emerged" (7).

This western allegorical use of Africa as a dark and primitive continent represents a colonial exploitation sometimes as unjust as the imperial acquisition of territory itself. Laurence recognized that in searching for her own identity within the African continent she was guilty to some degree of imperialism because she, too, had been looking for the answer to an inner need, but she was less guilty than most since she did not allow her need to influence her reporting. Her figurative use of the landscape and its inhabitants is an objective one and avoids the subjectivity of Conrad's literary exploitation of the Congo river world. Nevertheless, Laurence uses geographical features to symbolize her own journey of self-discovery. Her landscape has cities and deserts and high mountains. In Sheikh she lived in a house in the clouds and on the mountain tops she found the spiritual strength to see her through the places of exile and the burial grounds, places she must pass through before completing her inner journey and accepting the desert as home. "When can a voyage be said to have ended?" asks Laurence (2), who, like Burton, could be described as a "compulsive traveller" (*Prophet's* 16). The simple answer may be that it ends when you stop travelling, and more than once in *The Prophet's Camel Bell* Laurence is surprised into moments of self-revelation when she ceases her busy search and catches a startling glimpse of herself. The Margaret Laurence who arrived in Somaliland had thought it important to be continuously active, but in Sheikh she suddenly noticed the calm of the land. She had to accept that the land was not aware of her. "I might," she acquiesced, "enter its quietness or not, just as I chose. Hesitantly at first, because it had been my pride to be as perpetually busy as an escalator, I entered. Then I realized how much I had needed Sheikh, how I had been moving towards it through the years of pavements, of doom-shrieking newspapers and the jittery voices of radios" (27). The closest she came to ending her journey was when she accepted the desert as a place of rest. Strangely this happened as the cruel *Jilal* started again and the Bedouin, who accept without complaint whatever Allah may send, prepared once more to endure the worst until the rainy season ended the drought. No human act could make that "happen sooner, nothing could hasten the day, neither rage nor tears, neither curse nor prayer. It would happen when Allah willed it, and not a moment before" (143).

Something of the peace that comes with such submission had come to the Laurences' camp, too. "Whatever the day's difficulties, the arrival of dusk brought a feeling of peace to the camp," a camp that "was related, after all, to the camps of the Somali tribesmen through-out the whole land" (140). Laurence had come to understand why the Somalis found peace in their submission to Allah's will, and, in a poem called "Gates of Damascus" by James Elroy Flecker that she quotes as an epigraph to her book, she found the spirit of this faith truthfully expressed. It was this poem that provided the title for her book:

> God be thy guide from camp to camp
> God be thy shade from well to well.
> God grant beneath the desert stars
> Thou hearest the Prophet's camel bell. ([viii])

Laurence learnt from this faith. She could now accept her inadequacy in the face of poverty and suffering and admit that anything she had been able to do for the Somalis had been "only slightly more than nothing" (63, 66). What the Somalis had given her, on the other hand, was immeasurable. During her time in Somaliland, she discarded the unnecessary baggage with which she had arrived and replaced it with things of more value. In the days ahead, unpacking in a new home, she would find treasures to remind her of the Haud: the spear the thief dropped and the camel bell that Ahmed Abdillahi gave her husband. Both the spear and the bell had become part of her story.

But she would also have with her less tangible and equally precious souvenirs in the form of memories, and as she closes her last chapter, she indicates the form they will take:

> Whenever we think of Somaliland, we think of the line of watering places that stretches out across the Haud, and we think of the songs and tales that have been for generations a shelter to nomads on the dry red plateau and on the burnt plains of the coast, for these were the things through which we briefly touched the country and it, too, touched our lives, altering them in some way for ever. (237)

And in the end she did not leave without giving something in return, and it was a gift worth a great deal more than nothing. She left in Hargeisa, in the safekeeping of the imperialists, the manuscript of *A Tree for Poverty*.

2

Something More Than Nothing

In her introduction to *A Tree for Poverty* Margaret Laurence summarizes the traditional characteristics of Somali oral literature, a literature that occupies a central place in the lives of the desert people of northern Somaliland. In her lengthy introduction, Laurence depicts the hard and unsettled existence of the Somali Bedouin, who are always on the move, travelling with their flocks from the wells to the grazing grounds. Others besides Laurence have been impressed by this way of life. One of the Assistant District Commissioners in the region during the days of the Sayyid, Ian Ross, used the pen name of "Zeres" to describe his impressions of the Somalis. He quotes the words of an old Somali tribesman who explained that the northern Somali Bedouin were known as "the people without a pillow" because no rest was ever granted them in the whole of their country (257). Laurence thinks that "[t]he interminable trek with the herds to find grazing and water" was made bearable by "the sessions of singing and story-telling" (*Tree* 2). At the end of a difficult day the Somalis would gather round the camp fires and enjoy the welcome relief to be found in the songs and stories that cost them nothing. She thought of the literature as a tree that provided welcome shade for all travellers, rich or poor, beneath its great branches, and her title expresses this chosen metaphor. It was the ideal metaphor because, as Said Samatar has pointed out, trees have important significance in Somali life. Gatherings of herdsmen for any purpose are "invariably held under the shade of a tree," and "so important is the refreshing shade of a tree in the barrenness of the land, that the term 'tree' (*geed*) has come to assume a synonymous meaning with 'assembly' (*shir*)" (28). In her introduction, Laurence discusses in practical terms the main features of the oral songs and stories. It was, however, the argument for her metaphor that first attracted Philip Shirley.

Towards the end of her time in Somaliland when Laurence realized to her joy that she was pregnant, she moved in from the desert to Hargeisa leaving her husband to finish his work in the Haud. Laurence took a job with the administration, working for the Chief Secretary of the Protectorate Government, Philip Shirley. He saw her collection of poems and stories, and his attention was particularly caught by one of the passages in her introduction, describing the hardships endured by the Somali herders. He undertook to get her work published with official funds. Eventually in 1954, after the Laurences had moved to West Africa, *A Tree for Poverty* appeared, printed in Nairobi and published by the Government of the British Protectorate of Somaliland.

This was Laurence's first published book, and it earned her a place in the British Library General Catalogue as "Margaret Laurence of Hargeisa." She is now, of course, better known as the first lady of Manawaka, but her entitlement to this African identification should not be forgotten. Her first book, African by virtue of its theme and its production, is a valuable individual contribution to the general study of oral literature. It also contains constructive guidance on the question of translating literary works, and Laurence's considered and polished English versions of the Somali originals illustrate one way of tackling this difficult problem.

The richness of Somali oral literature had impressed earlier visitors to the country. Burton's remarks are often quoted because of their enduring truth. "The country," he reports, "teems with poets, poetasters, poetitos, and poetaccios." He adds that ". . . every man has his recognised position in literature as accurately defined as though he had been reviewed in a century of magazines." Above all Burton commends the "fine ear of this people," which allows them "to take the greatest pleasure in harmonious sounds and poetical expressions, whereas a false quantity or a prosaic phrase excite their violent indignation" (91).

During the second half of the nineteenth century, the British became regular visitors to the area as they took control of Zeilah and Berbera to safeguard their interests in Aden, their important staging post on the route to India. By the end of the century, the British claim to northern Somaliland was accepted by the outside world, though their right to be there was vigorously challenged by the Sayyid. Among those who served the British crown as soldiers and administrators during these years were some who found time to study the language and literature of the Somalis, and they ensured the preservation of some valuable reference material. Laurence was familiar with two books written during the campaigns against the Sayyid. The first was *A Grammar of the Somali Language*, published in 1905 and written by J.W.C. Kirk, a lieutenant in the King's African Rifles, and the second was *British Somaliland*, a comprehensive description of the country and its people, published in 1912, by a medical officer, Ralph E. Drake-Brockman.

As the twentieth century progressed, scholarly interest in the language and literature increased. The 1920s and 1930s saw Enrico Cerulli travelling in Italian Somaliland, studying oral literary traditions and collecting many examples of the poetry, though the result of his studies was not generally available until 1957 when his important work *Somalia: Scritti vari editi ed inediti* began publication in Rome. Meanwhile, in the British Protectorate, a young Polish poet, Bogumil Andrzejewski, who had been given a Colonial Office research grant, began to study Somali language and literature. He had a Somali assistant, Musa H.I. Galaal, also a poet, who was to devote the rest of his life to the promotion of his people's traditions.[1] When she arrived in Somaliland in 1951, Laurence met Andrzejewski and Galaal, and she joined them in the task of winning an outside audience for Somali oral literature, already held in great honour in its homeland. Laurence rightly describes her meeting with Andrzejewski as "A stroke of luck" (*Prophet's* 33). He was to become "a foremost authority on Somali language and literature," as Laurence acknowledges in the preface to the 1970 edition of *A Tree for Poverty* (v). When she began collecting Somali poems and stories, he and Galaal gave her their help and encouragement, and *A Tree for Poverty* is the result of a close and happy collaboration. Together, they made a wide range of Somali oral literature available to a foreign audience.

Burton's comments relate to an unwritten literature, and in 1951 the Somali language was still without an orthography. The Somali scholar Said Samatar commends Burton because he "correctly noted the prominent place occupied by poetry among the pastoral Somalis," but rebukes him for being surprised that "the unlettered Somalis" had a "developed literature." Burton's reaction, Samatar argues, "reflects a widespread, if complacent, assumption, especially in the West, that equates literature and literary perfection with writing" (55).

It was perhaps a natural reaction for someone accustomed to the written word, and Laurence was also misled by the same assumption. She is surprised by the literary fertility of an illiterate people. "Although they have no written language," she comments, "the Somalis are a nation of poets. There is no sign of this art dying" (*Tree* 1). One of the results of the work of Andrzejewski and Galaal was the final choice in 1972 of a modified Roman script as the official orthography. But Laurence was concerned entirely with oral traditions.

She began her study of Somali oral literature before Albert B. Lord published his influential book, *The Singer of Tales*. Lord's book, which appeared in 1960, was the direct result of Milman Parry's earlier study in *SerboCroatian Heroic Songs* of the formulae used in the 1930s by Yugoslav epic oral poets who performed their lengthy works without recourse to written texts. Lord demonstrated that the use of formulae made it possible for the Yugoslav poets to compose as they performed, and he argued that similar formulae used by Homer meant that he too should be regarded as an oral poet. Supporters of the Parry-Lord formulaic theory were then inclined to insist that all oral poetry was composed as it was performed. Lord's work produced a fundamental change in attitude to oral literature, but it was a change so dramatic that a reaction to his revolutionary work inevitably followed. As the formulaic theory was applied to other supposed oral literatures, such as Old English, the flaws in its argument became obvious; but Lord sparked off a lively debate on the techniques of oral composition, which served to draw wide attention to unwritten literatures.

For example, Jeff Opland, working from Lord's conclusions, has studied another living oral tradition, that of the Bantu praise singers, or *imbongi*, whose spontaneous compositions depend on known and memorized phrases. Opland argues that an appreciation of the Bantu traditions can be used to flesh out our meagre understanding of the Anglo-Saxon people and their poets. In both societies, loyalty to the king or chief, whose praises must be sung, is of primary importance, and Opland feels that ". . . societies similar in structure will produce literatures with strong similarities" (173). He sees the Bantu example as indicating that Old English poetry was also in origin an oral art. Opland, however, undermines his own argument by drawing his reader's attention to the chief flaw in the formulaic theory: formulae could also be used by literate poets and were not necessarily a prerogative of oral composition.

Another important point missed by Lord's followers is that oral literature is often composed in advance of its performance. Indeed, it may well be performed by someone other than the composer. This is certainly the case with Somali literature. In fact, Opland could have found more convincing corroboration of the oral character of Old English poetry if he had used the Somali example. He would have been able to argue again that societies with some characteristics in common may produce comparable literatures, but he would have had to acknowledge that oral literature is not of necessity a spontaneous art.

The Anglo-Saxons may seem at first consideration to have little in common with the Somalis. Theirs was a monarchical society while the northern Somali Bedouin have been aptly described as "a fierce and turbulent race of republicans."[2] However, kinship or clan loyalty is important to both these warrior races, and they alike honour the singer of tales because the task is to record the history and preserve the honour of the family or clan. The formal and measured alliterative lines of Old English poetry have their parallels in the classic Somali *gabei*, not only in their stylistic characteristics but also in their favoured themes of loyalty, honour, and courage. It is, however, generally agreed that the Somali poets do not compose as they perform. Their work is complex in thought and imagery and requires long preparation. The often lengthy completed poem is committed to memory before performance. The Old English poems that have been preserved may or may not qualify now as oral literature, but a strong argument could be made that these poems were composed in the Somali manner.

Ruth Finnegan's balanced and comprehensive book *Oral Poetry* is indebted to the study made of Somali literature by Cerulli, Andrzejewski, and Laurence. While Finnegan is grateful for the respect won for unwritten song by Lord's *The Singer of Tales*, she points out that oral poetry is a subject too vast and too complex to be submitted to one grand theory. She uses Somali examples to show that ". . . memorisation and near-word-for-word reproduction sometimes *are* important in oral literature" (73). When Nuruddin Farah recalls his childhood, he relates how one Somali poet in particular composed her work. In an interview he describes a scene that had been a commonplace one in his early life. "My mother," he says, "was an oral poet so she used to pace up and down, wherever there was some space in the courtyard, thinking about her poems, and all I could actually hear were murmurs of her own whispers to herself. And then I used to be amazed with the final result: a poem to be sung, chanted to music." When Samatar comments on the debate, he points out that ". . . its practitioners would only too painfully remind us" that "Somali oral poetry is both individually created and chiefly transmitted through verbatim memorization. Composition and performance," he adds, "seldom, if ever, occur simultaneously and in fact composer and performer are often separate individuals" (74). Summing up the importance of the work that had been done on Somali poetry, Andrzejewski claims in "The Literary Culture of the Somali People" that ". . . the poetry of Somalia has some special characteristics which are highly relevant to the current debate on the mode of composition, memorization, and transmission of oral poetry" (35). In *A Tree for Poverty*, Laurence describes and illustrates many of these characteristics, and her work helped to make their importance understood.

Somali poetry can be divided into a dozen or so genres, but Laurence concentrates on two of them: the classic *gabei* and the modern *belwo*. When she was writing, they were the oldest and youngest of the recognized forms of Somali poetry and provided an effective contrast of content and style. Cerulli referred to the *gabei* as "la piu elevata delle forme poetiche per i Somali" ["the most elevated of the poetic forms for the Somalis"] (3: 7), and Laurence is of the same opinion:

> The Somali gabei is considered to be the highest literary form in the culture. Gabei may be on any topic, but the rules of gabei-making are strict and difficult. A gabei poet must not only have an extensive vocabulary and an ability to express himself fluently and in terms of figures of speech. He must also possess considerable knowledge of the country, its geography and plant-life, Somali medicine, and animal husbandry. (*Tree* 12)

One of the main features of the *gabei* is the use of alliteration, undoubtedly a memory aid, as it may well have been for the Anglo-Saxon poet. The demands made on the Somali poet are heavy, since alliteration is not confined to one line, as in *Beowulf*, but is carried through the whole poem, which is often of some length. Andrzejewski believes that "... the exacting demands of alliteration, maintained throughout the whole poem, have had a profound influence on Somali poetic diction. The poet, to supplement his store of words, has to resurrect archaic words, enliven obsolescent ones, and even create new ones, and many arguments arise among Somali audiences as to the precise meanings of such archaisms" (Andrzejewski and Lewis 43). It follows that the *gabei* is difficult to translate.

A Tree for Poverty has one complete *gabei*, an unusual one on the subject of love, composed by Elmii Bonderii, the poet who is said to have died of a broken heart. Otherwise the *gabei* is represented in Laurence's book by extracts, including one by the Sayyid, generally considered by his compatriots to be their greatest poet. Laurence felt that, while it was impossible to capture fully in translation the chanting tones and alliterative sounds of Somali poetry, it was important to create an impression of their effect in the English version. Her short extract from the Sayyid's *gabei*, "To a Friend Going on a Journey," manages to suggest the Sayyid's melodious but commanding epic voice without attempting to reproduce the alliteration. The extract she translated has found its way into other anthologies, including Ruth Finnegan's *The Penguin Book of Oral Poetry*, because it demonstrates her understanding of the poetic effect of the original. The following lines, which, incidentally, reinforce *A Tree for Poverty*'s guiding metaphor, are a good example of her work:

> And in a random scorching flame of wind
> That parches the painful throat, and sears the flesh,
> May God, in His compassion, let you find
> The great-boughed tree that will protect and shade. (*Tree* 36)

Suggesting the alliteration of a Somali *gabei* is something that can only be lightly done but Laurence's restricted use of "f" (a consonant favoured by English poets for alliterative effect) works well in the extract she translated from the war *gabei* "Battle Pledge." This *gabei* was composed by an unnamed Ogaden chieftain, as a vow of vengeance for the death of his son. The Chieftain praises his war horse, his "fleet and fiery horse," with its "shining flanks and finely arching neck" (38). The archaic quality of the *gabei* vocabulary is also difficult to imitate, but Laurence achieves this in "Battle Pledge" with inverted constructions and melodic phrasing (with the alliteration kept up):

> And if the sky in future does not its colour change,
> Filled with the dust of death, reflecting the flare of the fray;
> And if all that I swear does not, as I swear it, come to pass —
> Then the warrior son of my father has become a witless fool. (39)

In the oldest poem in the collection, "The Bond between Kings," in this case a *giiraar* not a *gabei*, an archaic formality is suggested with the use of "thee" and "thy."

Laurence worked in most cases from literal translations provided by Andrzejewski and Galaal, and her aim was to render them into a literary English that was faithful as far as it could be in letter and in spirit to the original. She soon found she had to expand compressed one-word images in order to suggest their complexity of meaning. A letter she wrote in 1951 to Adele Wiseman shows how much thought she gave to the work:

> I have tried all along to be as true as possible to the original, and yet not to be too hidebound and thereby lose the implied meaning in the original. In some of the poems I've added a line, in order to explain something that was implied in the Somali, or perhaps phrased something in 6 words instead of one, because often a Somali word is very compressed and there is no single counterpart for it in English. It is very difficult to resist putting one's own bits and pieces of thought into the poems, but I think I've avoided that, in the main, by not adding one single word that was not either there in the Somali or directly implied.[3]

Her commitment to the original is expressed more formally in her introduction:

> My translations are, in most cases, by no means literal, but they do remain true to the thought and imagery of the original. Although in some poems phrases have been added to make clear a concept contained in one or two Somali words, I have in no sense embroidered the original text or developed the thought of any poem. (4)

In 1964 Andrzejewski and Lewis illustrated their introduction to Somali poetry with their own translations, which included some lengthy poems, among them a number of fine *gabei* by the Sayyid. It is interesting to compare their translations with Laurence's, bearing in mind that their objectives in making the translations were not the same. Laurence's aim was to construct independent poems, faithful to but detached from the original. Andrzejewski and Lewis were fluent Somali speakers, and Laurence acknowledges that their work was of a "much more scholarly and accurate nature" than her own (*Tree* v). She had only a smattering of Somali but considerable practice at writing her own tongue, and her translations have an elegant literary style that compensates for any slight loss of accuracy. The translations made by Andrzejewski and Lewis were not designed in themselves as literary works but to accompany a written Somali text of the poems, in order to make them intelligible for non-Somali speakers.

However, Laurence could only produce an independent English version of a poem, one that made sense to a western reader, if she added essential background information. In her introduction, Laurence says that ". . . the gabei poet must be, in terms of his own culture, a learned man" (12), but non-Somalis may have difficulty following this knowledge. Laurence felt her translations should be accompanied by explanatory notes. Sometimes notes were also needed to explain the imagery used by the poets. A *gabei* writer will often open the poem with a striking image, using it like a chapter heading to indicate the theme. The image may be condensed and its connection to the theme may be difficult to detect by those unused to this practice. In a note Laurence explains that ". . . it would be considered unsubtle and unpoetic to plunge directly into the poem without first preparing the way. The introductory figures of speech, from the point of view of style, serve the dual purpose of providing a striking and dramatic opening, and of strengthening the poet's argument in advance" (Papers). It therefore became necessary to annotate and sometimes expand the Somali originals in order to make viable independent poems in English.

Among the *gabei* poems chosen by Andrzejewski and Lewis are "An Elder's Reproof to His Wife" by 'Abdillaahi Muuse and "Ingratitude" by Salaan Arrabey. Translations by Laurence of these poems exist, but they were not included in *A Tree for Poverty*. They can be found among her papers in the Archives of York University, together with the literal translations supplied by Andrzejewski and Galaal. Salaan Arrabey's poem, to which Laurence gave the title "To a Faithless Friend," is of considerable length.[4] Laurence included a short extract from it in *A Tree for Poverty*, and, when she wrote *The Prophet's Camel Bell*, she took the opportunity to publish further passages from the poem; but her complete and impressive version, which conveys the epic effect of Salaan Arrabey's *gabei* voice, has never been published.

There is, therefore, sufficient material available to illustrate the way she worked. She encountered some problems translating 'Abdillaahi Muuse's poem, "Reproof from an Elder," in which the poet addresses his wife, complaining about her insolence and disobedience. To appreciate his principal grievance it is necessary to understand the Somali custom that requires a prospective husband to pay a *yarad* or bride-price for his wife. Laurence's note explains that when the bride-price has been paid "something is usually returned as a gesture of goodwill" (Papers). The poet complains that he has received nothing in return for his outlay, and he feels that his bride-price has proved a fruitless investment. To indicate his feelings, he describes those of a merchant who has lost all his wealth as the result of a shipwreck. The comparison is expressed tersely in the original. This terseness is matched in the literal translation of the Somali, which Laurence used as her guide, and which was presumably given her by Andrzejewski and Galaal. It is a model of compression but it is also extremely cryptic:

> A dhow full of cargoe [sic] sometimes sinks, a great loss to men.
> Of the firearms and the camels not even a little was returned.
>
> (Papers)

In their translation for *Somali Poetry*, Andrzejewski and Lewis see the necessity of adding to this brevity and they use parentheses to indicate their, undoubtedly reluctant, addition:

> Sometimes a fully laden vessel founders with great loss of property,
> And certainly I received no return at all for the rifles and camels I gave (as bridewealth). (104)

Laurence's translation is not wholly satisfactory. Since it was never published, we cannot assume that she was satisfied with it either. As her translation stands, however, it illustrates her working method. The original is developed freely, losing its conciseness in the process, but its meaning becomes clearer:

A laden dhow, storm-harried, sometimes sinks,
With all its cargo — a great loss to men.
No sunken dhow could have more surely lost
My wealth, than the bride-price which I gave for you.
The shining rifles, the camels — all are gone,
Nothing returned as ancient custom decrees.

(Papers)

While "Reproof from an Elder" proved difficult to translate, Arrabey's poem "To a Faithless Friend" seems to have presented fewer problems, and it is unfortunate that Laurence's complete and flowing version has not yet found its way into print. Arrabey, a well-travelled and knowledgeable man who died in the early 1940s, was "one of the most versatile Somali poets" (Andrzejewski and Lewis 58). As Hersi told Laurence, ". . . he could turn out gabei 'like the rain'" (*Tree* 38). In *The Prophet's Camel Bell*, Laurence recalls an evening she spent with Galaal discussing "a long *gabei* by Salaan Arrabey, who was reckoned to be one of the best Somali poets" (100). The *gabei* they discussed was almost certainly Arrabey's "long anguished outcry against a faithless friend," which is "one of the classics of Somali literature" (*Heart* 80).

This *gabei* was composed when Arrabey was visiting Nairobi. Finding himself in financial difficulties, he looked for assistance from a cousin whom he had helped in earlier days when they both lived in the Ogaden. When his request was turned down, he composed a lengthy and passionate declamation condemning his kinsman's ingratitude. The poem takes the form of a speech to the assembly of the speaker's kinsmen gathered in Nairobi, among whom his faithless friend was sitting when the poem was first performed. The poet addresses himself to his audience, turning from time to time to speak directly to his cousin.

The ungrateful man had been only too ready to accept the poet's assistance on three occasions. The poet recalls how he rescued his cousin, who had been captured by another clan, then helped him in a fierce battle to avenge the loss of his camels, and finally rescued his bride who had been abducted by the warlike tribesman Qasaal.

A separate section of the poem deals with each incident and the whole is linked with a refrain.

Laurence uses this refrain to great effect. It is translated by Andrzejewski and Lewis thus: "But amazing is the wickedness of he who disclaims great deeds wrought for his sake" (122). As was her custom, Laurence produces a longer version, and, when the refrain is repeated for the last time, she changes the pronoun from he to you, departing from the letter of the text, but capturing the spirit of the first live performance of the work, allowing the poet at this point to address his cousin directly:

> No — you forget your anguish of the past,
> Deny remembrance of the help I gave,
> And in my dire need you turn from me —
> Exceeding is the evil in such a man! (Papers)

The poem is rich in the kind of imagery that is typical of the Somali *gabei* and the poet's allusions would have reminded the assembled clansmen of their homeland. There are references to the birds and plants of the Ogaden, horses and camels, the desert climate, and the customs of nomadic life. The imagery also comments cryptically on the poet's theme. In Laurence's version the imagery, imaginatively and skilfully translated and interpreted, has a pleasing effect. Some examples will indicate this. To illustrate his argument that even the strongest man needs help from his kinsmen, Arrabey uses an image that would be immediately understood by people used to sitting round the campfire in the cool desert evenings. Andrzejewski and Lewis's literal translation is confined to one line: "Kindling is necessary to set ablaze a log of wood" (122). Laurence interprets this as

> A heavy log cannot be set ablaze
> Without the assisting fire of tinder straw;
> And no man lives who will not one day need
> His brother's help to lighten his distress. (Papers)

Another effective image that conjures up life in the desert is that of the fence of thorny boughs that is built as a protection round the Bedouin camp every time it is moved, and it helps the poet stress again the need for kin to support each other. Andrzejewski and Lewis as always are brief: "Kinsmen should be as the thorn fence protecting the encampment" (126). This is broken into Laurence's usual two line pattern as

> Kinsmen should be a protection each to each,
> Like the thorn-bough fence that keeps a village safe. (Papers)

Throughout her translation Laurence finds the declamatory voice. She does not hamper herself by attempting to reproduce the effect of Arrabey's alliteration, but she renders his vivid descriptions of battle scenes and his striking imagery with suitable formality and power. She suggests the oral performance with rhetorical questions and exclamations. The poet ends on a note intended to move his listeners. Disowning his kinsman and leaving Allah to judge the case, he describes his plight in moving terms, comparing himself to an emaciated and old camel, a sight that must have been familiar to his audience. Laurence's rendering of these lines is masterly:

> I am decrepit now, and sad with age,
> Like a burden camel that has borne the pack too long.
> The skin which was silken has now turned rough and hard.
> The throbbing veins now stand out along my neck
> And my wasted body betrays its framework of bone. (Papers)

The complex *gabei* poems are, Laurence notes, the work of skilled and mature composers. The *belwo*, however, "is considered to be the normal literary activity of the young" (*Tree* 7). It is a poetic form invented comparatively recently. It was enjoying considerable popularity while Laurence was in Somaliland, and the examples she preserves are from the period when the form was at its peak. The history of the *belwo* has been extensively documented since the publication of *A Tree for Poverty*, first by Andrzejewski (in *Somali Poetry* and in an article, "The Art of the Miniature in Somali Poetry") and then by John W. Johnson in *Heellooy Heelleellooy: The Development of the Genre Heello in Modern Somali Poetry*. Laurence gives only a sketchy history of the *belwo*, but Johnson, whose comprehensive study of the genre gives an account of its recent development, acknowledges the importance of her record of the form during its early flowering.

It is now generally accepted that the *belwo* was invented about 1944 by 'Abdi Deeqsi, a lorry driver. He composed his first *belwo* when his truck broke down in the desert. In "The Art of the Miniature,"Andrzejewski describes the new form, explaining that the ". . . new genre was called the *balwo*, a loan word from Arabic meaning 'calamity' or 'sorrow,' and it was, at least at first, a very short poem of two lines, or even one, though longer ones were not unknown; each *balwo* constituted a complete and self-contained artistic unit. Initially the subject matter was always love, and the favourite themes were unrequited affection, the sorrows of separation and the agonies of passion" (5).

The *belwo* was often sung, and its popularity was helped along by the newly established broadcasting service, Radio Hargeisa. Johnson describes how in the 1950s the *belwo* developed into the longer *heello*, by forming a string of *belwo* linked by a refrain "heellooy, heelleellooy," from which the new name was derived. The love motif of the *belwo* was frequently displaced in the *heello* by new and political themes marking the country's progress to independence. In *The Prophet's Camel Bell*, Laurence brings the *belwo* vividly and delightfully to life when she describes Mohamed:

> "*Helleyoy, helleyoy —.*"
> Mohamed was always singing *belwo*. He was fond of voice tricks — the song would rise weirdly to falsetto and plummet to bass within the space of a few notes, and the *yerki*, the small boy who was cook's helper, would applaud with a wooden spoon on a saucepan. (161)

Laurence translated a score of *belwo* for her collection, many of them lyrics of four short lines. Wiseman reviewed *A Tree for Poverty* when it made its way to Canada, and, while admitting that as "one unfamiliar with the Somali tongue" she cannot judge the quality of the *belwo* as translations, she considers them "very fine and sensitive lyrics in English" (610). Finnegan was of the same opinion and chose a selection of Laurence's lyrics for *The Penguin Book of Oral Poetry*. Finnegan contrasts Laurence's *belwo* with some translated by Andrzejewski. Commenting on the *belwo*, Finnegan says that the form presents special difficulties for the translator because it is "characterized by condensed imagery and 'miniature' form," and she points out the different methods employed by Laurence and Andrzejewski. While Margaret Laurence "felt forced to lengthen the translations slightly in her attempt to convey the images involved," the translations by Andrzejewski "approximate more nearly to the length of the originals" (110). There is no sense of strain, however, in Laurence's elegant four line lyrics. Wiseman chooses the following as an example in her review:

> All your young beauty is to me
> Like a place where the new grass sways,
> After the blessing of the rain,
> When the sun unveils its light. (*Tree* 33)

This *belwo* was also translated by Andrzejewski in Finnegan's *The Penguin Book of Oral Poetry*, and the contrast in style can be clearly seen:

> You are like a place with fresh grass after a downpour of rain
> On which the sun now shines. (112)

Andrzejewski's version is uncompromisingly direct; it exists as virtually a mirror image of the original. His aim was to produce a literal translation for those who wanted to study the poem in Somali. Laurence worked with a different audience in mind, and she redefined and explained a difficult image or removed an awkward grammatical transition, though she always respected the original, honouring her responsibility to remain faithful to it.

The *belwo* poets follow the traditions of classic Somali poetry in the use of condensed imagery, and their work often needs textual notes. When elucidating one of her translations, Laurence explained that it was "longer than the original, since some of the Somali words are rich in implication" (*Tree* 33). In the letter to Adele Wiseman already referred to, Laurence gave a specific example from the *belwo* "So perfect are her teeth" (*Tree* 33):

> In one poem, the word "place" occurs, but in Somali, a special word is used, which means "place" and also means "the grace of God," implying that the place referred to was highly blessed or particularly fortunate in some way. I've translated that by including the second meaning . . . "a place of Allah's kindly grace" . . . which is really what it means, altho' only one word is used in Somali.

In spite of the difficulties involved, Laurence considered the effort worthwhile, because ". . . there is nonetheless a good deal that comes through translation amazingly well." Laurence felt that the *belwo*, "the short love poems, have a freshness and a lyricism that cannot fail to be observed. Many of the images used are original, apt and lovely" (*Tree* 5). Her own translations are sufficient confirmation, and Andrzejewski and Galaal speak highly of them. In their article "A Somali Poetic Combat," they single out *A Tree for Poverty* by Laurence, "a Canadian novelist," who "through her translations gives an intelligent and sympathetic insight into Somali poetic diction and imagery" (15).

Andrzejewski divides Somali oral literature into two streams, which he calls time-bound and time-free ("Somali Literature" 38). The poetry is time-bound, and it alters remarkably little during transmission. The prose, generally stories that have been told many times, is time-free. Through many repetitions, folk-tales will keep a stable story-line but successive story-tellers will add their own colour and detail, having in mind their own audience.

When translating the poetry, Laurence, as she told Wiseman, restricted as far as possible the addition of her own "bits and pieces." When she retold the stories, she would have been justified in allowing herself a more personal contribution. Even here, however, she attempted to convey a Somali voice rather than her own. The stories in *A Tree for Poverty* are divided into two groups. Some are based on direct translations given to Laurence by Andrzejewski and Galaal; others are paraphrases of stories "performed" for her in imperfect English, which she had to interpret as best she could. The paraphrased stories are further divided into those of Arabic and those of Somali origin. The Arabic stories were told to Laurence by Ahmed Nasir and most of the Somali stories — the crowning glory of the collection — were told to her by Hersi, a story-teller par excellence. Laurence had discovered, as Burton had done, that the Somalis as a race were natural poets and story-tellers "with a highly developed sense of the dramatic" (*Tree* 1), but Hersi stood out even among his peers and could entrance an audience made up of his own critical countrymen. The dramatic strength of Laurence's rendering of the Somali stories is partly the result of Hersi's interpretive gifts that could transcend language barriers, as Laurence testifies: ". . . his acting," she recalls, "had tremendous value. It compensated to some extent for the fact that I was not hearing the stories in Somali, in which he would have been able to express them with better style. Hersi belonged to that ancient brotherhood of born story-tellers" (*Prophet's* 159). The narrating voice in her translations reflects Hersi's dramatic talents, and Laurence never intrudes as a story-teller. She is careful to suggest the original locality and character of these stories with images of desert life.

Some of the stories have travelled far and are recognizable from other sources. "Right or Wrong," for example, one of the translated stories, is an alternative version of Aesop's fable about the miller, his son, and his ass. The stories that are most effective are those that come in groups centred upon a single character. With the Arabic tales, Laurence is able to contrast the moral legends about the saintly Prophet Nebii Hhudur with the humorous stories in which the rogue Abana Wys always triumphs — "a worthless sort of creature in some ways. . . . But he had the great gift of a nimble wit . . ." (*Tree* 78–79). However, the local stories about the legendary Somali figures such as Sultan Wiil Waal or Queen Arawailo are the most memorable because their historical and national reference gives them mythic importance. As Laurence wrote down these stories from Hersi's dramatic performances, she became aware of their importance to the Somalis. These stories with their local reference were valued by Hersi and his compatriots because they were entertaining and also because they told of mythic figures of the past that could support the pride and honour of the Somali people.

Wiil Waal, the ruler or *gerad* of the sultanate of Jigjigga, is one such legendary figure. "Sultan Wiil Waal is supposed," writes Laurence, "to have lived in the 16th century . . ." (*Tree* 106). Andrzejewski in *Literatures in African Languages* tries to separate the man from the legend. This national hero, who is reputed to have driven the last of the Galla kings from the Ogaden and been a bitter foe of the Ethiopians, actually died, Andrzejewski believes, in the middle of the nineteenth century. He came from a long line of *gerads* and "had a very strong and colourful personality, immense courage and ruthlessness and, at times, great wit, and it was probably these qualities which gave rise to the many legends about him" ("Somali Literature" 391). Doubtless some of the legends now told about him relate to his ancestors. The fact that he governed the region between Jigjigga and Harar has added to his continuing importance to the Ogaden people since, as I.M. Lewis notes in *The Modern History of Somaliland*, that area was handed over to Ethiopia by Britain in 1954 against the wishes of the Somalis, and it became bitterly disputed territory (150 ff.).

Wiil Waal was also by reputation a poet, described by Samatar as "the earliest recorded poet-leader to have used his verse to achieve political ends" (88). The oldest poem in *A Tree for Poverty*, "The Bond between Kings," is said to have been composed by Wiil Waal. The poem is a *giiraar*, the only example Laurence gives of one. The *giiraar* is particularly associated with the northern Somali, and it has been well defined by Cerulli who contrasts it with the *gabei*: "Gerar e un canto in versi brevi ed in tono concitato che, quindi, si oppone nella forma e nella sostanza alla gabay cantata in versi lunghi ed in tono pacato e discorsivo" ["The *giiraar* is a song with short lines and an impassioned tone; whereas, in contrast, the form and the mood of the *gabei* is that of long lines and a calm and discursive tone"] (3: 24). The impassioned *giiraar* was originally chanted on horseback and traditionally included praise of the warrior's steed as well as his words to the enemy. The *giiraar* by Wiil Waal appears to be addressed to a defeated ruler and is a fine example of Wiil Waal's legendary wisdom, since he remarks that all power is temporal, including his own:

> And if thy kingdom is lost to thee,
> I tremble for my own. (38)

The group of five Wiil Waal stories in *A Tree for Poverty* make abundantly clear the qualities of this legendary hero. In these stories Wiil Waal, all too aware of his own wisdom, delights in testing the intelligence of his followers. The few who are as clever as he is are not found among his wealthy subjects. Wiil Waal's subtle riddles are solved by such people as the poor shepherd's daughter, who becomes his wife, and a quick-witted but lowly Midgan.

"Wiil Waal and the Sheep's Gullet" is a dramatic and well told story, and it captures the dry dusty world of the desert nomads. Wiil Waal summons his people and tells them that each man must kill a sheep and bring to council the part of the carcase that "makes men either brothers or enemies" (107). Desperation teaches a poor shepherd's daughter how to solve the riddle. She knows it is beyond their means to give away a leg or a saddle of mutton, so she persuades her father to offer Wiil Waal the sheep's gullet. The others view the poor man's offering with scorn, but his daughter has advised him well. Wiil Waal explains that it is material wealth — of which having food is a sign — that makes men friends if it is shared, or enemies if it is fought over. "The gullet receives the food. It alone makes men brothers, and it alone makes men enemies" (109).

Laurence tells the story mainly through the words of Wiil Waal, the poor shepherd, and his daughter, all parts that Hersi surely played to the hilt, emphasising the alarm of the poor girl, her father's roar of outrage when she makes her suggestion, and the mighty Wiil Waal's laughter when the gullet is displayed. The suspense is admirably held because the daughter refuses to explain her advice, requiring her father to trust in it blindly, and doubtless Hersi's audience shared the old man's ordeal until its happy end.

In another of the Wiil Waal stories, the listener is held in the same suspense while the autocratic ruler again tests the wisdom of his people. Wiil Waal on his "brave horse," holding a "white scarf of thin silk," rides to the outskirts of town where the clansmen own individual wells (121). Blindfolding himself he declares that he intends to let his black stallion gallop at will among the wells but if the horse falls into one of them, then the owner of that well will be beheaded. Mighty is the groaning and weeping of the clan as they try to steer the horse away from their wells, and only a humble Midgan is shrewd enough to call the Sultan's bluff. The Midgan takes no action since he knows full well that Wiil Waal is not likely to risk his own neck and that of his horse, and he has also noticed that the silk scarf tied around the Sultan's eyes is very thin. Hersi would surely have enjoyed delivering Wiil Waal's final ringing words:

"The Midgan saw that this scarf was thin, and he guessed that I could see through it. The rest of you were ready to believe me a fool, but he knew that I would not risk my own bones and those of my fine steed. The Midgans are a low people, and ye are Somalis, and high-born. But this Midgan, I say to you, has a wisdom from which you could learn much. Observe, ye tribesmen, and profit!" (122)

Obviously the stories about Wiil Waal have been told to many generations of Somali. The stories about Queen Arawailo also have a wide circulation and are especially popular with Somali women. When the story-teller is male, Arawailo is seen as a wicked and unnatural woman. Laurence, who has translated two of the folk-tales about Queen Arawailo, was aware of the many versions of them. "The Death of Arawailo" is one of the stories she had read in Drake-Brockman's book, but she chose to follow Hersi's version, appropriately relying on an oral source: "I have taken Hersi Jama's version of the tale, as it is the one I actually heard myself." Drake-Brockman's transcript then becomes valuable as an example of the modifications that can occur as the story is retold. "Here," observes Laurence, "as in other cultures, one frequently finds many versions of the same story" (123).

Certain elements of the story remain constant through the different versions, most importantly the belief that Arawailo lies buried under a huge mound of stones at Mait, which was the capital of her ancient kingdom. Consequently, all the distinctive piles of stones that dot the desert country are associated with her. Of the many legends attached to her, the story of her death is the one most often told. Arawailo is a cruel counterpart of Wiil Waal since, having conceived a hatred for her male subjects, she delights in setting them impossible tasks. Only an old magician is able to outwit her, and he finally engineers her death with the help of her "gentle copper-skinned daughter" (125). The magician, eluding Arawailo's guard, gets the Princess with child. When a boy is born, the wicked Queen determines to castrate her grandson. The child's mother successfully pleads on behalf of the boy as each stage of his childhood passes, thus enabling him to grow into manhood. Then with the magician's help he is able to kill his wicked grandmother.

Drake-Brockman's version of the story is the same in outline but differs in some essential details. Laurence explains that in Drake-Brockman's account ". . . the old magician, for example, is not mentioned at all, and the ritual leading up to Arawailo's death is somewhat different" (122–23). They agree, however, on certain interesting ingredients of the myth. One is the question of Arawailo's sex. Her male subjects find it difficult to believe she can be a woman, and only at her death is there conclusive proof that she is. Another point of interest is the attitude of Somali women to this mythic figure. Laurence describes how the women mourned Arawailo's death and put green branches on her grave, while the men rejoiced and threw stones on it. This tradition has not died and men and women continue to lay their different offerings on the roadside cairns that are thought of as "shrines to Arawailo" (128). Drake-Brockman ends his story outlining the same tradition, describing how "[t]o this day every Somali, as has been the custom for centuries whenever their caravans pass the supposed last resting-place of Arawailo, throws a stone on the pile, while the women, to show their respect for her memory, tear off a small portion of their skirt and place it among the stones, or sometimes they merely break a small twig off the nearest green bush and place it there" (171).

A completely different, somewhat garbled, but nevertheless interesting explanation of the legend is given by Major H.G.C. Swayne, who travelled widely through the British Protectorate. After describing the many cairns in the country, "crowning nearly every prominent hill," he recounts the "curious legend" that explains their origin. A wicked and powerful Queen, "Arroweilo," the source of all "evil in women at the present day," persecuted all male children in her kingdom. One mother fled with her baby boy who, when he grew up, returned in search of his grandmother. Swayne's informants believed that the young man "then attacked Arroweilo in a lonely pass, and hacking her to pieces, tied her remains on a camel, and sent it off with a parting cut. The camel trotted in mad career all over the country, and where-ever a piece of Arroweilo fell, the pious native as he passed said a prayer and threw a stone 'to keep her down'" (24–25).

To close *A Tree for Poverty*, Laurence chose the legends of the founding patriarchs of the Somali nation, legends of local importance, well documented by Drake-Brockman. The Somalis are a Hamitic race and, I.M. Lewis says in *A Pastoral Democracy*, ". . . they do not think of themselves as Arabs," though they do claim some Arabian ancestry, "which traditionally is their greatest pride" (11). Lewis goes on to describe the importance of the legends testifying to this traditional lineage:

> More circumstantial are the traditions which record the arrival from Arabia of the patriarchs Sheikh Isaaq and Sheikh Daarood, founders of the corresponding clan-families. The Daarood are regarded as older than the Isaaq; and Sheikh Daarood is supposed to have crossed from Arabia about the tenth or eleventh century, and Sheikh Isaaq to have followed some two centuries later. Whether or not these traditions are historically valid, they have great social importance since they provide a charter for the existence of the clan-families descended from the two sheikhs. (23–24)

The legends of Sheikh Darod and Sheikh Ishaak were ideal stories with which to close *A Tree for Poverty*, but inserted between them is a story of different significance: the tale of Sheikh au Barkhadleh who converted many Somali to Islam but was himself childless. Part of his story explains the special role played in society by the Yibirs, a role that resulted from Sheikh au Barkhadleh's encounter with Mohamed Hanif, the founder of the Yibir clan. Mohamed Hanif challenged the authority of Sheikh au Barkhadleh, boasting of his magic powers, which he demonstrated by walking not once but twice through a hill. "The Yibir walked into the hill for the third time. But this time Sheikh Au Barkhadleh prayed aloud to God to let the earth hold the Yibir so that he might never emerge" (142). His prayer was answered but the Sheikh admitted that an injustice had been done to Mohamed Hanif, and he made an agreement with the Yibirs that allowed them to exact a toll of the Somali people whenever a son was born or a marriage took place.[5]

One of the best accounts of the Yibir and Midgan clans is found in Kirk's *A Grammar of the Somali Language*. Kirk chose a number of Somali poems and folk-tales to illustrate Somali grammar, accompanying his Somali transcriptions with English translations. He has some fine examples of *giiraar* poems, but his most interesting contribution to Somali scholarship was his study of the Yibir and Midgan people and their secret languages. His book includes a Yibir version of the story of Sheikh au Barkhadleh and Mohamed Hanif. Kirk writes that the Yibir "are said to be sorcerers, and to have prophetic powers and the power of cursing. They live by begging, but especially by the levy of a tax on Somalis, at a marriage or the birth of a child, according to an old tradition told in a story which is given here in *Yibir* dialect" (184).

Laurence knew Kirk's book, but as was her custom she uses Hersi's version of the story, "which he obtained from a number of local elders," though she admits that Kirk's Yibir version "differs a good deal from the Somali version which is given here" (*Tree* 139). The attitude of the high-born Somalis to the Yibirs and to the other non-Somali clans, the Midgans and Tomals, was at one time less than generous, and Hersi is on record as saying "We have no use for bloody these people" (*Prophet's* 39–40). He tells the story with little sympathy for Mohamed Hanif. Laurence questioned the attitude of the high-class Muslim Somalis to these clans, but she came to realize that her critical queries on the matter were resented. She, therefore, held her peace because "[p]eople are not oyster shells, to be pried at" (*Prophet's* 40). She did, however, include this Yibir story, albeit the Somali version, at an important juncture in her book.

The stories of the two great founding fathers, Sheikh Darod and Sheikh Ishaak, are dramatically told, as all Hersi's stories are, but Laurence was also familiar with the accounts given by Drake-Brockman, whom she uses as an authority for some of the clan nomenclature. There is, she adds, considerable consensus between Hersi and Drake-Brockman about the details of these legends, reflecting perhaps their national and sacred importance. Both Sheikh Darod and Sheikh Ishaak came to Somaliland from Arabia, bringing the faith of Islam with them. Sheikh Darod survived in hostile country with Allah's help and married Donbirro, a local girl. By her he had five sons from whom the clans of Darod are descended. Sheikh Ishaak travelled widely in Somaliland preaching the faith until Allah led him to the coast at Mait. He married three times and produced many sons. Though the story of Darod is the more dramatic of the two, Laurence ends the book with an account of Sheikh Ishaak's missionary work and of the conversion of the people of Mait who "were a wild people who worshipped idols" (145). She concludes with the traditional list of the Sheikh's wives and children, and she gives the founder of the Ishaak people the final word, perhaps because she lived among his descendants in the Haud of northern Somaliland, whereas Darod's offspring inhabited areas to the south and east. So the closing lines of *A Tree for Poverty* are a splendid tribute to the patriarch of the people whose songs and stories she had translated. Sheikh Ishaak "was a great teacher, and brought the wisdom and the light of the Prophet's words to this country. And he founded a new race of people, as it had been revealed to him, and his sons inherited the land" (146).

Considerable research lies behind *A Tree for Poverty*, which has an authority that is based on written and first-hand knowledge of the Somalis, their country, and its traditions. The book also derives its strength from Laurence's admiration for the people and their literature. Many of her comments were anticipated by earlier visitors, who have successively found much to respect in the Somali way of life. The repeated testimony to the fortitude and faith of the nomadic pastoralists underlies the value of recording their songs and stories. Drake-Brockman, for example, expresses his admiration for "these people who will face the dangers of the waterless desert for days, full in the faith that God will provide their next day's meal, and should this not be the case, consoling themselves with the thought that He alone knows what is best for His children" (109–10). Perhaps the finest passage in Laurence's fine introduction is her explanation of her metaphor. Their poetry and folk-tales can console the people for the "hardships of drought, disease and hunger," and they "are as free to the impoverished nomad as they are to the Sultan." Somali literature Laurence affirms, quoting a line from a *gabei* by Ali Hammaal, "is, in its way, 'a tree for poverty to shelter under' " (2).[6]

This explanation of the place of poetry in the pastoralists' world has been questioned. Samatar has Laurence in mind in the following passage:

> The life of Somali nomads, it is said, is a life of wandering and danger, devoted as it is to eking out a living in a demanding environment. In the great boredom and bleakness of their surroundings, the theory goes, the Somali nomads turn to their poetry, the one thing which does not cost them anything and provides them with drama and entertainment. According to this view, without the twin inspiration of their faith and verse, the Somalis would waste themselves in fury and desperation.

Samatar considers Laurence's view a "quaint argument," though "it may have some merits" (3).

Samatar, on the other hand, sees Somali poetry as a medium of mass communication, serving a functional and political purpose, with the poet addressing vital community concerns. His view, however, does not invalidate Laurence's. Andrzejewski and Galaal point out that while Somali poetry has aesthetic value, it also plays "an important, and sometimes sinister, part in public life" (15). The fact that the Somalis used songs and stories for practical purposes such as communication and propaganda does not mean that they did not also turn to them for relief and enjoyment in a dreary world. There was no need for Samatar to dismiss the power of song to console and cheer in order to demonstrate the spectacular political use made of poetry by the Sayyid. Laurence herself discusses the Sayyid's employment of verse as a weapon to fight the British in her essay "The Poem and the Spear" in *Heart of a Stranger*.

A Tree for Poverty, like the literature it celebrates, represents more than just functional work. It was conceived as an artistic whole and bears the mark of literary excellence not only in the standards set for the translations but in the visionary concept that gives unity to a varied collection of individual songs and stories. Because *A Tree for Poverty* was the work of an obscure author, it was not widely reviewed. Wiseman, who had followed from a distance the author's hopes and difficulties as the book took shape, could speak with limited authority. The reviewer chosen by *Africa*, the journal of the International African Institute, could speak with more authority. I.M. Lewis finds much to commend in the work. He speaks of its "high literary quality" and the author's "unusually informed insight into the life and culture of the Somali people." He testifies to the book's "favourable reception among those Somali poets whose knowledge of English is sufficiently good for them to judge of the quality of the translations" (305). In 1970, when the book was reprinted, Laurence's commitment to her vision of the literature and its importance to the Somalis had not altered: "I would still stand behind most of what I said in the Introduction" (v). She spoke with affection for her first published book, but with modesty about the value of the translations it contained. Yet their value has never been questioned by the acknowledged authorities on the subject. *A Tree for Poverty* is a work Laurence thought of with affection. She would also have been entitled to think of it with pride.

3

"Bits and Pieces"

Some ten years after leaving Somaliland, Margaret Laurence wrote about two of the poets whose work she had included in *A Tree for Poverty*. The result was two interesting essays, "The Poem and the Spear" and "The Epic Love of Elmii Bonderii." Both these pieces were included in the 1976 miscellany *Heart of a Stranger*. All the pieces in this collection were written between 1964 and 1976, and the best of them look back to her years in Africa when, like the children of Israel in Egypt, she was a stranger living in a strange land. The most important essay in the collection is "The Poem and the Spear," important because of its length and the extensive research underpinning it, and important also because it appeared for the first time in *Heart of a Stranger*, which is mostly composed of previously published pieces. In "The Poem and the Spear" Laurence attempts to unravel the Sayyid's story and explain his role as a warrior and as a poet. "The Epic Love of Elmii Bonderii" is a shorter essay, and it was first published in the magazine *Holiday* in 1965. It tells the story of the Somali poet who died of love. When introducing her account of Elmii Bonderii's short and tragic life, Laurence admits, and it is not something she regrets, that the "tale may be myth, . . . myths contain their own truth, their own strong reality" (77). It is the mythic qualities of both poets that attracted Laurence.

Myth and history are certainly entangled in the stories that are told of the Sayyid. He was a fierce warrior and a fine poet. Even during his lifetime, which he spent trying to drive the infidel foreigners from Somaliland, he assumed mythic proportions, especially in the minds of his British enemies. For his followers he was always a hero, and after his death his legend spread even among the clans that had never supported him until he became the obvious choice for a national symbol in the run-up to independence.

His story has been told many times and from various viewpoints. One of his earliest biographers, and one who clearly recognized the Sayyid's legendary qualities, was Douglas Jardine. His book *The Mad Mullah of Somaliland*, published in 1923, was written when information about the Sayyid was scarce, but its strength lies in Jardine's first-hand knowledge of the British position. Andrzejewski and Lewis warn that the biography "is not always accurate" in matters of historical detail, but it does give "a very full picture of the period" (55). Jardine's book was well known to Laurence, and she draws on it heavily in "The Poem and the Spear," though she distances herself from the British position that he defends.

The British often referred to the Sayyid as the Mad Mullah, but it was in fact the Somalis in Berbera who first gave him the derogatory title. In 1895 Mahammed 'Abdille Hasan returned to Berbera after a visit to Mecca and Aden. While abroad he had listened to the teaching of Mahammed Saalih, and he determined to win converts in Somaliland for the new Saalihiya religious order, which was strict in its observance of Muslim law. This brought him into conflict with the elders of the less stringent Qadariyah order, who controlled religious affairs in Berbera, and it was they who first called him mad, because of what they considered his fanatic condemnation of the luxuries of life.

Failing to make headway in Berbera, Mahammed 'Abdille Hasan withdrew to the interior and made many converts among the Dolbahanta, his mother's people, who gave him the title of Sayyid and who were to provide the core of his support when he embarked on his holy war against the Christian enemy. From the outbreak of open hostilities in 1899 until his death, he kept the British in Somaliland under constant pressure and took hold of their imaginations like a nightmare. The Sayyid's victory at Dul Madoba on 9 August 1913 was his greatest moment of triumph and the blackest day for the British during the twenty years of conflict. On that occasion the reckless but gallant Richard Corfield who had trained the Somali Camel Constabulary died, a bullet from a Dervish rifle bringing him down.

Laurence wrote to contest what she saw as the British portrayal of the Sayyid or, as she expressed it, to answer the question: "How far did the British attitude to Mahammed 'Abdille Hasan correspond to reality?" (70). Her essay attempts to clear the air both concerning the man and the myth; what she does in fact is to cloud the issues even further. Her account of the Sayyid's life was well researched, but it is now out of date because of new information that has become available since 1964. Recently many transcriptions of the Sayyid's poems have been made, and the public archives in Britain and Italy have been quarried for new information. Samatar's *Oral Poetry and Somali Nationalism*, published in 1982, contains a detailed and full version of the Sayyid's life, the most accurate and balanced now available.

Yet Samatar finds it difficult to verify even basic facts, the date of the Sayyid's birth, for example. The Sayyid was born sometime in the middle of the nineteenth century, when the foreign imprints of Burton's footsteps were still fresh, but the exact date is uncertain. Jardine is vague in his book and speaks of "the early seventies" (36), but in an article published in *Blackwood's Magazine* in 1920, in which he gives a short account of the Sayyid's life, based on material he was collecting for his full biography, he suggests the late 1860s. Laurence, using *Somali Poetry* by Andrzejewski and Lewis as her reference book, goes even further back in time and gives 1864 as the Sayyid's birth date (45; Andrzejewski and Lewis 53). Samatar's research has shown that Mahammed 'Abdille Hasan may have been born as early as 1856. In a note he explains that the difficulty facing a biographer has arisen because ". . . students of the Dervish Movement almost to a man place the birth date of the Sayyid at 1864, a date which seems to have a single source: 'Abdirahmaan Sayyid, the notably erudite son whose records give this date." On the other hand those Dervishes who still survive "unanimously reject this date and insist on the 1856 one" (211–12). By 1985 Andrzejewski has also accepted the earlier date (393), and so the legendary precocity of the young Mahammed, which is detailed by Laurence, is in doubt. "He began," Laurence believed, "studying the Qoran at the age of seven and could read The Book by the time he was ten. He left the life of a camel herder when he was fifteen and became a teacher of religion" (46). Samatar believes Mahammed was indeed as young as eight when he began his study of the Qoran, but that his development thereafter was less spectacular (102).

There is also some confusion over the year, the place, and the cause of the Sayyid's death. He had "no known tomb," a fact (or non-fact) that only adds to the mythical aura surrounding him, as Nuruddin Farah has shown in his novel *Close Sesame*, in which the Sayyid's life and poetry is remembered (143). The Sayyid's death occurred in either 1920 or 1921. Most authorities think he died in December 1920 of malaria (or perhaps influenza).[1] Laurence opts for 1920, but is not prepared to make a decision on a physical cause of death, choosing to see the Sayyid as a broken man who died "because there was no longer any reason for him to go on living" (70). News of his death certainly did not reach British ears until 1921, and Perham claims to have been the first European to hear it. She went to Somaliland in 1921, "soon after the defeat of the so-called Mad Mullah." "No European," she writes, "ever set eyes upon this so long successful rebel. He finally died in his bed of malaria and it was while on trek [along the Ethiopian frontier] with my brother-in-law that we were the first to hear the news from some passing Somalis" (*Major Dane's Garden* [ix]). The London newspaper, *The Times*, on 19 March 1921, publishing the news with some natural reservations, reported that "news had been received from East Africa of the death of the 'Mad' Mullah of Somaliland. Reports of the Mullah's death have been circulated from time to time during the past 20 years. The last authentic news of him dates from February, 1920, when, after the rout of his forces by the British, he left his wives behind and fled into Italian Somaliland" ("Imperial and Foreign News Items" 9). Incidentally, the way the myth can be slanted is shown by a comparison of the Sayyid's less than chivalrous behaviour as it is detailed in *The Times* [London] with the way he behaves according to Laurence, who writes that, after the British bombed his fort at Taleh in February 1920, he "is said to have shared his pony with his favourite wife as he slipped through the British lines and got away to the south" (66).

Laurence found it difficult to remain unbiased when discussing the Sayyid, but her account is no different in this respect from many others; such is the power of the man and his myth. Everyone has difficulty depicting someone who has remained an enigmatic figure because ". . . in the end we cannot separate the man from the myth" (*Heart* 76). Laurence was attracted to the legend because she equated the Sayyid's brave fight with that of Louis Riel, the Métis leader who challenged the imperial power on the Prairies of her homeland, but her attempt to establish the parallel and to overthrow what she saw as the British attitude to the Sayyid led her into an interpretation of his story that must be questioned.

To begin with she misinterpreted the British attitude, even though she was using Jardine's book. In her essay, Laurence maintains that the British exaggerated the Sayyid's cruelty, but she fails herself to come to terms with this element of the Sayyid's behaviour. She accepts that the Sayyid had moments of sudden rage that led him to torture his prisoners, but she considers his behaviour as natural "within his cultural framework" (71). She does not dwell on the toll of pain and suffering exacted on the clans who opposed the Sayyid, nor does she mention the dishonourable episode in his early career when he is said to have ordered the assassination of his rival, 'Ali Mahamuud, the nominal head of the Dolbahantas.[2] Her argument is that the British wanted to believe that the Sayyid was mindlessly cruel and depraved, because only this image could "justify their policies" and "perhaps also in some way . . . tame their own fears of him" (72). She maintains that Jardine's portrayal of the Sayyid is "strongly tinged with fantasy" (70). "The British," she maintains "appear to have seen the Sayyid as a kind of grossly exaggerated Arabian Nights figure — unvaryingly and diabolically cruel, a profligate of the worst order, a man who spent his days and nights in riotous living, a glutton and a lecher in the grand style" (71). In *The Mad Mullah*, Jardine cites evidence of the cruelty with which the Sayyid treated prisoners and those considered traitors, but he also questions the accuracy of many of the sensational stories that were in circulation. Doubt is expressed in Jardine's book, for example, about rumours of the Sayyid's gluttony — "his supposed gross obesity which it was erroneously believed had rendered him personally immobile" (216). Laurence herself identifies the possible origin of many of the exaggerated stories, explaining that ". . . the reports of the Sayyid which reached the administration were all from Somalis who sided with the British, and it is reasonable to assume that they would say things which they felt the administration would want to hear" (72). Laurence unjustly suggests that Jardine believed all that he heard and implies that he considered the Sayyid to be no more than a dissolute madman.

To understand the viewpoint of the British administration, which was the only one Jardine could convey, it is important to remember that there were Somalis who opposed the Sayyid. The Sayyid always regarded the Isaaq people as allies of the British. Many of them lived in the north near the coast and were known to the British as "friendlies" because they fought on the side of the colonial power. Laurence knew of a number of such Somali links with the British. Abdi had served with the Camel Corps and Galaal's father had been

74

an interpreter for the British. However, the most famous Somali to fight with the British was Risaldar-Major Haji Musa Farah of the Habr Yunis, a clan of the Isaaq family. Musa Farah served for many years as "Chief Native Adviser to His Majesty's representative" (Jardine 311). Laurence in fact was well acquainted with a nephew of Musa Farah, no one less important to her than Hersi. Hersi thought of his uncle with reverence. Musa Farah's "exploits had become legends. Hersi spoke of him with reverence" (*Prophet's* 155).

Nevertheless the Sayyid's fame was greater than that of Hersi's uncle, and Jardine, who knew Musa Farah well, was honest enough to acknowledge this even in the hour of the Mad Mullah's defeat. Though he would have preferred it to be otherwise, Jardine recognizes that "from the Somali standpoint Musa Farah's prestige is as naught compared with that of Mohammed bin Abdulla Hassan" (312). While strongly criticizing the Sayyid's methods and suggesting that he was motivated as much by personal ambition as religious fervour, Jardine admits that ". . . there can be no question of the greatness of his personal achievements" (314). In Jardine's biography, there is considerable admiration for the man who had proved himself so formidable an enemy. "Give the devil his due," writes Jardine, and this means acknowledging the ingenuity with which the Mad Mullah slipped through the British lines, the loyalty and courage he inspired in his troops, and the effectiveness of his military and religious leadership (180).

Stories circulated among the Somali "friendlies" about the Sayyid's miraculous powers. "There was, indeed," Jardine remarks, "a growing belief in our ranks that the Mullah was immortal" (85). His myth flourished because he remained out of sight; ". . . since his rise in 1899, no Englishman ever set eyes on him" (15). Jardine virtually admits defeat when he writes that ". . . the capture of the Mullah's person was an objective which it was unreasonable to set any military commander" (153). Jardine was among the first to forecast the future significance of the Sayyid. In his article, "The Mad Mullah," published in 1920 before the Sayyid's death, Jardine describes the Dervish Movement as a "nationalist movement" and its leader as a patriot who had succeeded in "eradicating the tribal feeling, which is normally one of the chief characteristics of the Somalis, and substituting his own authority for that of the elders of the tribes" (109–10). In his book, Jardine sums it all up by admitting that though many "Somalis feared and loathed the man whose followers had looted their stock, robbed them of their all, raped their wives, and murdered their children, they could not but admire and respect one who, being the embodiment of their idea of Freedom and Liberty, never admitted allegiance to any man, Moslem or infidel" (313).

Jardine, however, does not ignore the suffering caused by both sides during the war. The price the Somali people paid is made clear in his chapter on the controversial decision by the British to withdraw from the interior to their coastal strongholds, a policy that was adopted after the first four expeditions against the Sayyid had proved inconclusive. Drake-Brockman, writing in 1910 when the withdrawal was complete, indicates the British feelings of disbelief and shock that attended this move. "We might well ask," Drake-Brockman ponders, "what were the peculiar qualities possessed by this leader to enable him, after ten years' struggle, to compel Great Britain to roll up the map of British Somaliland in the face of the friendly tribes, and abandon a vast region, which for a decade had been painted crimson on the map of Africa" (178). When the British withdrew from the interior, leaving their Somali supporters armed, the result was disastrous. Angus Hamilton was one of those who foresaw the inevitable. He recognized that there were economic reasons for the move because the Sayyid held "it in his power to prolong the operations indefinitely, and by so doing to pile up the burden of expenditure," but ". . . it is permissible to urge that the policy of evacuation has been carried, perhaps, a little too far where it countenances the withdrawal of the posts from which it was possible to protect Wells belonging to tribes friendly to us" (xiv).[3]

The fighting during the early campaigns had created many losses that needed to be made good, and, with arms supplied by the British, the Somalis fought each other. The clans also used their weapons to settle old feuds, and a holocaust followed during which, according to the Colonial Office *Report*, ". . . one-third of the male population was done to death" (35). The difficult decision to withdraw from the interior and its terrible consequences greatly distressed many of the British who had to look on, and one passage in Jardine's book is worth quoting in full because it indicates something of his feelings. He tells how the 6th King's African Rifles, British Officers, and Somali troops made their way from up country to the coast during a dramatic storm. The heavy rain that fell was, as it were, a portent of the blood that was soon to flow (Laurence might have described it as another of Nature's cruel ironies). Jardine writes:

76

In the parched desert that stretches from the foot-hills to the sea, the burning sand, bestrewn with the camel dung of a thousand caravans and the bones of many a luckless wayfarer, is for ever appealing to a pitiless sky for moisture. Usually its thirst must find contentment, if it can, with a gentle shower in April. But the last march of the 6th King's African Rifles was attended by a thunderstorm of such violence that its like has never been known, before or since, in the annals of Somaliland. It was a savage and a mocking trick of Nature thus to endanger the lives of man and beast as, whipped by the blinding rain, they struggled through the roaring torrents that swirled and eddied through the thirsty river-beds. To the small band of British officers, it was but another example of the well-worn saw that it is the unexpected that always happens in Africa; but to their Somali comrades-in-arms it was a portent representing the tears of Allah as he gazed down upon the melancholy scene. (196)

Laurence invents her own ending for the Sayyid's story, but it is a disappointing one. She chose finally to see him as a martyr whom she compares to the Canadian Métis leader Louis Riel. The comparison is not an obvious one, and her argument is forced. She closes the article with the words of St. Paul, but her conclusion is not convincing. The essay "peters out in Paulistic platitudes," as Doug Beardsley remarks in a review of *Heart of a Stranger* (164). Laurence suggests that in his final hours the Sayyid may indeed have lost his sanity — "Did his mind break, though, at the very end? It seems to have done" (68) — thus associating the idea of madness with the Sayyid in a way that the British never did, since for them the Sayyid's madness was not that of the feeble-minded but of the fanatic. Laurence interprets the Sayyid's last letters to the British as those of a man "truly broken" who had "fought for twenty years" and "could fight no longer" (69). She rejects the possibility that these letters are proof rather of the Sayyid's cunning attempt, as after previous setbacks, to gain time before renewing his holy war.

It is difficult to accept that Laurence believed in her own conclusion to the Sayyid's story. She wrote "The Poem and the Spear" only a year after completing *The Prophet's Camel Bell*, in which she still saw the Sayyid not only with Hersi's eyes but also with those of Colonel Lewis, who in Hargeisa had often told her stories of British and Somali valour during the campaigns. He used to speak of the Mullah campaigns "almost as though he had been there," fighting in spirit on the British side. It was the Colonel who told her of Musa Farah's great achievement when he "trekked across the Haud with five thousand tribesmen, to attack the Mullah's forts," and, the Colonel added, "The Mullah was holed up with all the water he needed" (217). Laurence, it is true, describes this exploit in "The Poem and the Spear," but her use of the adjective "small" for Musa Farah's achievement might have upset the Risaldar-Major's nephew, though he would have agreed with her description of his uncle as remarkable. Laurence writes, ". . . a remarkable Somali, Risaldar-Major Haji Musa Farah, led a detached Somali levy of 450 rifles a hundred miles across the waterless Haud, picking up some five thousand local tribesmen on his way, attacking the Dervish camps and capturing several thousand camels and sheep. This small triumph was a blow to the Sayyid" (52).

In "The Poem and the Spear," Laurence unashamedly aligns herself on the Sayyid's side, and this is a move from her position in *The Prophet's Camel Bell*. There she left open the question of "[w]hether Mohamed Abdullah Hassan was a madman and a religious fanatic, as the British claimed, or an early nationalist and divinely inspired leader, as the Somalis claimed . . . ." It was not she thought then "a matter that could ever be settled. Perhaps he was both." When in her essay she gave the Sayyid's story her full attention, she came down firmly on the Somali side, but at the same time she did the British, in particular fair-minded people like Jardine and the Colonel, an injustice. For them the Sayyid was never just a mad fanatic. The Colonel told Laurence that " 'The Mullah was a courageous man. . . . Insane at times, no doubt,' " the Colonel added, " 'But he would never admit defeat, and that is something one has to admire, always' " (218). Laurence argues that in the end he did admit defeat, and this is a view that neither the British nor the Somalis share. Samatar's historical reading of the Sayyid's story is convincing. He argues that the cause of the Sayyid's defeat in 1920 was the result of his decision to construct fortified residences that gave the British "a fixed target to attack." This was, Samatar writes, "the greatest strategic error of his twenty-year resistance struggle." When the British, after the First World War, were able to attack his forts from the air, the Sayyid was unable to fight back and he was forced to flee once more into the Ogaden. But Samatar dismisses any idea of the

Sayyid as a broken man, seeing him instead as undefeated in body and spirit. "Once in the Ogaadeen," Samatar writes, "the Sayyid, unbroken by his staggering losses in Nugaal, employed his old talents of charisma, oratory and knowledge of his countrymen to rebuild his battered forces" (135). This view of the Sayyid is shared by Deeriye, the courageous resistance fighter in Nuruddin Farah's novel *Close Sesame*. Deeriye "was reared to revere Sayyid Mohamed Abdulle Hassan as the most important figure the Somali nation had ever produced" (32). Deeriye, like the Sayyid, never gave up the fight; he had "fought for the nationalist cause all his life and would continue fighting till his ending days" (58). The British and the Somalis agree on this point at least, that the Sayyid never gave up the fight. At the end of her essay, Laurence chose to depict a man broken mentally and physically.

However, Laurence's assessment of the Sayyid as a poet is more successful. She has problems with the warrior but far fewer with the poet. There are extensive quotations throughout the essay from the Sayyid's compositions. For the text of his challenging letters, addressed to the British Administration, Laurence uses Jardine. He had had access to the originals, written in Arabic, and to the translations made when they were received. Most of the examples given of the Sayyid's poetry are drawn from Andrzejewski and Lewis's book, *Somali Poetry*, the notable exception being the *gabei* she translated, "To a Friend Going on a Journey."

The special knowledge Laurence acquired while working on *A Tree for Poverty* enabled her to discuss the Sayyid's poetry with confidence and authority. In *Heart of a Stranger*, she summarizes once more the nature of *gabei* poetry and describes Mahammed 'Abdille Hasan as the most talented of all *gabei*-makers. She stresses that the poetry composed and used in his campaigns was not "trite propaganda" but work of a very high standard with all the expected "intricacies of Somali literary style" (50). Laurence quotes at length from the Sayyid's best-known poems, which she lists as "Hiin Finiin, the Poet's Favourite Horse" (which was composed in praise of the swift Somali pony the Sayyid reluctantly parted with to win the alliance of an uncommitted clan), "The Path of Righteousness" (which describes the life of a true Muslim), "The Road to Damnation" (which condemns the Somali who opposed the Sayyid), and Deeriye's favourite poem, "The Death of Corfield" (which is marked as Laurence observes by a magnificent "exultant rage") (62).

In *Oral Poetry and Somali Nationalism*, Samatar places the Sayyid's political poetry within the traditional framework of Somali public debate, while demonstrating how exceptional an artist he was. Samatar explains that the Sayyid, after a defeat, would dip into "his reservoir of rhymes at once to boost the morale of his broken army and to reduce his enemies to confusion." After a success, on the other hand, he would use his poetry with equal effect "to celebrate the victory, and more important, to solemnize it so that it became history" (181).

Writing "The Poem and the Spear" almost twenty years before Samatar, Laurence too admires the Sayyid, "a master of mass communication" (50), whose "passionate beliefs give a strength and carrying power to the lines even in translation" (50–51).

However, the Sayyid's poetry, which Laurence describes as "strong, bloody, and uncompromising" (80), is not always to her taste. The fervour with which the warrior-leader pursued his religious and political ends was a feature Laurence was uneasy with, and, though she admires his poetry, she has reservations about its militant nature. The last example of the Sayyid's poetry that she uses is her favourite one, her own translation of "To a Friend Going on a Journey" from *A Tree for Poverty*. She quotes in full her fine rendering of the passage that shows the Sayyid in a rare, gentle mood, expressing "concern over the departure of a friend on a hazardous journey" (75). This is how she chooses to remember the Sayyid. Like many another mythical figure, he can represent different ideals for different people.

Untangling the Sayyid's myth had proved impossible. It was far easier to tell the story of Elmii Bonderii, the poet who died of love. He was the ideal subject because, Laurence explains, he "remained true to the classic plot of his own story" (84). While the outline of the plot, which has the classic values of simplicity and symmetry, has changed little over the years, it has been worked over and elaborated on by many different story-tellers. In Nuruddin Farah's early work *From a Crooked Rib*, Ebla refers to the story and asks herself about Hodan's feelings. Ebla has often heard accounts of the love story that "occurred somewhere near Barbara between Hodan and Elmi Bowderi." Ebla knows that Elmi died of love, but she wonders if love could possibly be worth such a sacrifice, and what effect, she asks herself, did the affair have on Hodan (83)? The story is known wherever Somali is spoken, and every Somali Laurence talked to about the matter believed "implicitly that Bonderii really did die of love" (*Tree* 43).

He started life as an undistinguished man herding camels near the Ethiopian border, and his story can be briefly told. According to Laurence, he came to Berbera to work in a teashop. One day he saw a girl called Hodan and fell desperately in love. Her family would not consider his offer of marriage because he could not pay the bride-price, and so he left for Djibouti where he could earn more money. When he returned with sufficient funds, he found Hodan already married, and he fell ill. Then this man, who had never shown any previous signs of genius, began in his sickness to compose marvellous poetry honouring his love in the classical *gabei* tradition. His fame spread quickly and far. Many young girls came to offer themselves in place of Hodan, but he turned them all down. Then, just before he died, his beloved came to see him. At the time he lay sleeping after a fever, and, when he woke up, she had gone.

In 1967, which was after Laurence had published her version, Mohamed Farah Abdillahi and Andrzejewski wrote an account of "The Life of 'Ilmi Bowndheri, a Somali Oral Poet Who Is Said To Have Died of Love," with the intention of establishing some basic facts. They maintain that there "is hardly a more popular story in the northern region of the Somali Republic" (191). Abdillahi and Andrzejewski's version of the love story is more factual than Laurence's, though they are not always able to be precise. They suggest dates — "about 1908" for the poet's birth and 1938 or 1941 for his death. They believe that Elmii Bonderii worked first in a restaurant in Berbera but then moved to a bakery, which he eventually managed. When he was head of the bakery, he saw Hodan and fell in love. With love came the gift of poetry, but also sickness — there was no journey to Djibouti to earn a bride-price at this point. In their version only four girls in Berbera attempted to console and cure the lovesick poet, and, while he was sleeping at the house to which they had invited him, Hodan arrived not knowing he was there. She refused to see him, and when the girls told him of the visit he grew worse. His despair increased when Hodan married, and it was then he went to Djibouti, where he died in 1938 (according to his friend Musa Farah he ended his days in Berbera, dying in 1941).

Laurence prefers to follow what Abdillahi and Andrzejewski call the more exaggerated version of the story. They noted down some of the colourful details that were in circulation, for example the account given by a young man of about twenty-five, living in Hargeisa, who maintained that a very large number of girls came to Elmii Bondherii, offering to marry him. According to this source there might have been as many as a hundred of them, coming even from other towns such as Djibouti, Harar, Dire Dawa, and from the nomadic interior (203). Laurence had heard a similar account, and she dwells on it in a lyrical paragraph that plays on the sounds of place names and conjures up a parade of beauties. Among them were some like stately Egyptian queens, some had "the eyes of gazelles," and some "skins as dark and soft as the night sky" (84).

In the same way, Laurence chooses to see Hodan as a fairy-tale heroine, and not as the unconcerned and practical woman described by Abdillahi and Andrzejewski. In Laurence's version Hodan, married to Mohamed the Leopard, whom she loves, is troubled to find herself a public figure and seeks her husband's permission to visit the dying poet, and "[s]he waited by his bedside as long as she dared . . ." (84). Laurence gave a brief account of the story in *A Tree for Poverty*, and there she records yet another version of this bedside scene, one she owed to Hersi. Not surprisingly, Hersi's version is a particularly dramatic one. His vivid interpretation of the scene is that ". . . when Bonderii was on his death-bed, he sent word to Hodan, and asked if she would come to see him. She did come, and stood beside his bed, weeping. As he looked up and saw her, the story goes, he cried aloud and sank back, dead" (43).

Laurence illustrates Elmii Bonderii's story, as she did the Sayyid's, with passages of poetry. She draws on her knowledge of oral traditions to explain Elmii Bonderii's unusual *gabei* poems. He composed a great number, and all of them developed the theme of love. Her quotations are either taken from Andrzejewski's translations or from the poem "Qaraami" (Passion) that she included in *A Tree for Poverty*.[4] In "Qaraami" the poet expounds on the beauty of the woman he loves and goes on to say

> But comeliness is not her only gift —
> Her strong hands weave the mats and tend the fire;
> Swiftly she works, with every task well done.
> She is the one who gives her parents pride,
> She is dear to them — ah, yes and expensive, too! (*Tree* 41)

Laurence obviously enjoys telling the sad story of "The Epic Love of Elmii Bonderii," which "has undoubtedly become changed over the years and been given a kind of dramatic splendour missing from the original events" (77), and her version makes the most of the drama and the splendour.

The study of Somali oral literature had been a worthwhile exercise, but it could not satisfy Margaret Laurence's need to write her own stories. It proved, however, very difficult to get started. Possibly the strangeness of her surroundings added to the problems that naturally face any novice writer. Finding the right fictional voice and theme may have seemed especially difficult when a whole range of new and strange voices and ideas suggested themselves. While in Somaliland she discarded at least one attempt at a novel, and the only fictional work she completed was a short story that she called "Uncertain Flowering." It was published in 1953, by which time she had moved to the Gold Coast. If two short stories that appeared in the 1940s in *Vox*, her college magazine, are discounted, "Uncertain Flowering" has the distinction of being her first published fictional work.

It was not therefore a Canadian but an American anthology that published her first African short story. Whit and Hallie Burnett chose "Uncertain Flowering" to open volume four of their New York series *Story*, in which short stories are collected in book form. In a recent article, Donez Xiques has happily brought to light the series of letters, now in Princeton University archives, written by Laurence and Whit Burnett, which preceded the publication of "Uncertain Flowering." In her first letter to Burnett, which accompanied the manuscript of the story and which was dated 2 November 1951, Laurence comments that " 'the plot and characters are entirely fictitious, whereas the East African setting is not' " (qtd. in Xiques 15). Xiques has shown that Burnett was always ready to encourage young writers, and his response in this case was enthusiastic. He must be numbered among the first to recognize Laurence's " 'fine fictional and character sense' " (17). Xiques raises the question of Laurence's own later feelings about "Uncertain Flowering," which she left out of all accounts of her writing career. This may have resulted from a lapse of memory, but it is difficult to believe that Laurence could have forgotten what was surely the satisfaction of having her work published in an anthology with the fine reputation enjoyed by *Story* and its editors, who discovered, for example, the talent of Richard Wright. Laurence was always her own sternest critic, and it maybe that in comparison to her achievement in *The Tomorrow-Tamer* stories, she could see little of value in this early work, and she chose, therefore, to forget it. Burnett, however, published it with confidence in its merit, and regretfully, Laurence had no word of gratitude for his warm and early encouragement of her work.

Whatever its literary merits, and in assessing them Burnett's enthusiasm for the story should carry some weight, "Uncertain Flowering" is of interest. Written during the years that are recalled in *The Prophet's Camel Bell*, it provides a valuable fictional interpretation of her Somali experiences. Laurence chose her title as a description of her protagonist, Karen Aynsley, an insecure sixteen-year-old English girl who goes to boarding school and spends her holidays with her parents in Somaliland, but it can now be seen as a fitting comment on the story itself, which undoubtedly lacks the sureness of authorial voice later heard in that magnificent flowering of her genius, *The Tomorrow-Tamer*. In this early work the depiction of the Somalis and their country is evocative, but the principal characters, who are English, are not wholly convincing.

When Laurence arrived in Somaliland, she noticed that many of the English, the "sahib-types" as she called them, cut themselves off from the Somalis, and she despised them for this reason. In her fiction she was to satirize, to great effect, the people she called imperialists, but in this early story she allowed caricature to destroy credibility. It took time before she achieved a perceptive understanding of the imperialists and the complexity of their situation. This process was not completed until after she had left Africa, and while she lived among them she allowed her dislike of the imperialists to express itself in an anger that damages her credibility. While in Somaliland she felt that the imperialists as a whole should be avoided. She found their condescending attitudes unjustified, and she kept her distance. Laurence writes with some understanding of and sympathy for Karen, but she cannot relate to the other British characters. She is unable to integrate them into her story, with the result that there is an uneasy divide between the setting and the action of her plot. So, while the sense of place is strong in "Uncertain Flowering," it does little to inject life into the subject matter. As W.J. Keith points out in "'Uncertain Flowering': An Overlooked Short Story by Margaret Laurence," this Somali story, in marked contrast to her West African stories, does not grow from and flourish within its setting. In fact it suffers from a "split between theme and setting," and the crisis that occurs in Karen's life could have happened anywhere (205).

Nevertheless, Laurence's description of the Somali background in the story is of interest. The desert landscape is outlined with a few careful brush strokes. The Somalis are described briefly but sympathetically, and the narrator's viewpoint of them is one of admiration and respect, in marked contrast to the perspective taken of the imperialists. The nomads live on the fringes of the imperialist enclave; "the proud impoverished Somalis" move along the horizon, "across the country herding their camels in all weathers, their brass-bound spears slung across one shoulder" (22). There is no mention in this story of any harsh aspects of the desert landscape, but a tendency instead to romanticize the scenery with the poetic language she was to use from time to time in *The Prophet's Camel Bell*. "Beyond the trees," she writes, "the long ribs of the mountains stretched out, until the black hills faded into blue, and the blue into gray. And past these ghosts of mountains, the flat plain shimmered" (18). When Laurence describes Karen's visit with the old Somali servant Yusuf to a hidden valley in a high mountain pass, she is thinking of a place she discovered with her husband when they lived at Sheikh. Around Karen the "trees grew thickly," their "branches filled with shadows." Vines were threaded "around the trees, like lace around the heavy candelabra." In one corner of the valley, Karen notices an incongruous "small brushwood circle, a long-abandoned zareba, which seemed out of place here, as though a nomad's little shelter had found itself by mistake in the garden of a sultan" (18). In *The Prophet's Camel Bell*, Laurence remembers her own discovery of this same valley, and, since it is recalled with many of the same words and images, it is reasonable to suppose that in both her travel memoir and her story she drew directly on her diary entry for both descriptions:

> The trees were curiously filled with shadows. Vines had threaded themselves through the stalks and hung down like lace around the heavy candelabra. . . . That Somalis had been here was proven by the little brushwood *zareba*, which seemed out of place, as though a nomad's hut had found itself by mistake in the garden of a sultan. (49)

There are other indications that Laurence has incorporated her own experiences into Karen's story. Keith points out that Yusuf appears to be modelled on Abdi. Abdi, who had served in the legendary Camel Corps as a young marksman, "was a warrior, trained as a fighter both with the spear and with the rifle, and his heritage was that of a warrior" (*Prophet's* 189). Yusuf also "had been a marksman in the Camel Corps, in the wild days of the later Mullah Campaigns, and he still cherished a passion for anything that smacked of military tactics and secret plans" ("'Uncertain'" 16). Yusuf, who can guess Karen's feelings as he looks at her with "soft and thoughtful" eyes (18), is Abdi simplified and idealized.

The part played by Somaliland and its people in Karen's story is entirely positive. Yusuf is the only person she comes close to confiding in, and her happiest hours are spent in his company, riding her beloved Somali pony Spice. With Yusuf she is relaxed and happy, able to speak to him in his language, answering with a Somali proverb to make her point. This is not the relationship that might be expected between a young English schoolgirl and a proud Somali warrior, but the moments when they are together are the most moving and, somewhat unexpectedly, the most natural in the story.

The story suggests strongly that the Somalis are at one with their environment, while the imperialists live in an artificial cocoon. This is made clear when the narrator describes the clubhouse on the night of the Gymkhana dance. Promiscuous, self-centred and spoilt, the imperialists dance beneath the artificial fairy lights. They prefer not to see by the light of the sky, and they regard as alien everything that lies beyond their clubhouse verandah. Laurence clearly has the British Hargeisa Club in mind, and her dislike of this institution, so important to the imperialists, is made clear in *The Prophet's Camel Bell*. There she admits that she "did not much like the Hargeisa Club" (145), where she had to watch the *sahib* and *memsahib* insult the Somali servants (206). Some attempt at disguising the locale is made in "Uncertain Flowering," ostensibly set in a town called Bor Mado, but there can be little doubt that Bor Mado is Hargeisa. Hargeisa was the only town in the Protectorate where a sufficiently large British population made possible the club activities that Laurence describes in "Uncertain Flowering."

She captures well the gossipy, complaining voices she must have heard in Hargeisa. Irritable, brash, superior, the imperialists do not appear in a good light. Philip and Jo Aynsley, Karen's parents, are only redeemed by their shared concern for their daughter. They have a far from happy marriage. Philip drinks too much, and Jo is having an affair with a British army officer, Captain Harrison. There are other military types hovering in the background, including young Lieutenant Howard (Howie) Tavershaw, who befuddled with drink takes Karen home from the dance. Jo is dark and vivacious; the other woman in the story, Bess Newton, Philip's lover, is blonde and placid. Bess's husband, John, is interesting, but not because he is any less of a stereotype. He has a blue-veined red face, like the typical fictional English colonial, and was born in British India. He embarrasses Karen with his overbearing manner and clipped speech. "When I was at school," he tells her, "never saw my wretched family, you know. They were in Delhi. Went to Simla for the summers, the lucky blighters. I couldn't go out. Much too far. No planes in those days. You're jolly fortunate" (20). In the nineteenth century, the British presence on the Somali coast had been controlled by the Government of Bombay, and, even when the Colonial Office took over responsibility for the area, links between the Raj and northern Somaliland remained. British army officers serving in India were not infrequently transferred to the Protectorate, and others liked to spend their leave hunting big game across the Guban and Haud deserts. The Raj way of life left its mark in the British Protectorate in an attitude that offended a liberal and open-minded person like Laurence. She may have heard many references to the Raj, and she was left with an aversion to its mentality that she returned to in her last novel, *The Diviners*. There, Brook Skelton, who attempts to reduce his wife Morag to colonial status, was born in India in the days of the Raj.

The narrator's position in "Uncertain Flowering" is that of an eavesdropper, one who looks over Karen's shoulder. The other characters are created from what the young girl overhears and does not fully comprehend. The result is sometimes effective, and the brittle and bitter voices echoing in the Hargeisa Club are evoked with precision. Yet because Laurence watched the *habitués* of the Hargeisa Club with curious as well as critical eyes, there are signs even in this early story of the greater understanding of the British that she would finally achieve in her West African fiction. Her understanding began with the recognition of their isolation and their vulnerability, made especially evident when they gather together in the clubhouse. When discussing Rudyard Kipling, Alan Sandison in *The Wheel of Empire* focuses on the same scene to describe the loneliness of imperial aliens, in this case those that served in British India:

These men are lonely, imperial aliens, whose personal identity and that of their group is in daily peril. In their awareness of their alien nature and of the great darkness beyond the circle of light from the club-room window, the supernatural becomes a sublimination of their fear, heavily on the side of the forces of persecution; an acknowledgement of their alien-ness and of the power of India. (82)

This describes a situation more desperate than that faced by the members of the Hargeisa Club, but Laurence's recognition of the sense of alienation in this less dramatic setting is commendable. She comes to recognize that fear can be the cause of arrogance. The imperialists are afraid to admit that they have never belonged where they are, but they have nowhere else to go: "They themselves were not the aliens; that would have meant the end of too much" (23).

Laurence arrived in Somaliland prejudiced in advance against the English who lived and worked in the colonies. She came across little to alter her attitude, but she realized in later years that her first attempt at portraying the imperialists had not been much different from the "distortions [which] have been presented in detail often enough, both fictionally and journalistically, in almost every tale of colonial life" (*Prophet's* 207). "Uncertain Flowering" is spoilt by its distortions, but it remains of interest, if only as a foil to the fiction that was to follow, where a more subtle and balanced portrayal of the imperialists was achieved.

The Gold Coast gave impetus to Laurence's fiction. While she lived in Somaliland, the excitement of discovery was always intense, and this strange and unknown land had story enough of its own to attract her. Her Somali experience, with the exception of "Uncertain Flowering," is recorded in nonfictional forms. This short story that focuses on the East African desert world was a beginning, but the full flowering of Laurence's fiction was nourished by a West African climate.

Part II

The West African Fiction

4

In Search of a Cast of Characters

Margaret Laurence never regretted the years she spent in Africa, and she considered the opportunity to live first in Somaliland and then in the Gold Coast "a stroke of *enormous* good fortune" (Interview with Sullivan 62). East and West Africa are very different, and Laurence went from the Haud desert to a large city close to humid rain forests. She and her husband settled in Accra, moving later to Tema, a small fishing village that Jack Laurence was helping to transform into a large port. The unchanging sandy landscape of Somaliland had attracted Margaret Laurence because it made no compromise with time and because its people had faithfully preserved their own traditions and language. Accra's teeming city streets also fascinated her, but they signalled change, the effects of which had already spread along the forest roads to the villages. When she arrived there in 1952, Laurence discovered that white culture already had a strong foothold — Christianity as well as the western educational system were well established in the Gold Coast, which had been a British colony for many years, and she found that the English language had become an important factor in uniting a diversity of ethnic groups.

Laurence believed that independence would alter life for the Somalis — she had recognized that Hersi was the victim of a changing society — but she had seen little evidence while she was there of a new order. The people of the Gold Coast, which in 1957 was to be the first sub-Saharan nation to win independence, were in an excited mood and eager for change as the streets of Accra indicated. "Vivid, noisy, chaotic, the life of the street flowed on" (*This Side* 45). The richness and vibrancy of the capital, its tangle of people of many races, and, most important, a shared language encouraged Laurence to involve herself in the life that flowed around her to an extent that had been impossible in Somaliland. Her fiction was to grow from that involvement.

When discussing her Canadian novels, she remarked that ". . . the people were more important than the place" ("Sources" 16) and that her "fate in writing" had been to deal with "individual dilemmas" ("Gadgetry" 89). In her African fiction, too, the people were her main concern even though the place exercised a powerful influence. The novel and short stories that she set in the Gold Coast examine a number of human predicaments, and her ability to create unique and distinct individuals means that her fiction is on the whole free of stereotypical characters.

Graham Greene set two of his novels in Africa, *The Heart of the Matter*, published in 1948, and *A Burnt-Out Case*, published in 1960. In 1961 he put together the two African journals that explain the genesis of both novels, calling the volume *In Search of a Character*. His journals record how he journeyed to Africa looking not only for details to give his characters identity, but also for the eyes and voice that would control the narration of his novels. "Through whose eyes shall I tell my story?" he asks as he considers the possibilities for his character X, who was to become Querry of *A Burnt-Out Case*. Since the story requires that Querry, a stranger and outsider in Africa, should remain a mystery, Greene rejects first-person narration and also decides not to tell the story from the point of view of a close observer. He chooses instead third-person narration, what he calls the "author's 'I.'" He adds, however, that X's story must be told "only in action and dialogue," and the narrator must remain neutral and "not penetrate into the thoughts of any character," in order that the mood of mystery prevail (22). The same questions of voice concerned Laurence but, since her aim was to open up her characters and not, except with Mr. Archipelago and Doree of "The Perfume Sea," to surround them with mystery, she was prepared to use the first-person voice, and, when she chose the author's "I/eye" (the words are virtually interchangeable in this context), it was an all-seeing one with the power to penetrate the thoughts of people of both sexes and of different races.

G.D. Killam in his introduction to *This Side Jordan* maintains that in the attempt to find an African voice "no other expatriate writer has attempted and achieved as much as Margaret Laurence" (xi). This opinion is shared by the Kenyan critic Micere Githae-Mugo, who holds that Laurence's "interpretation of the African setting is that of an empathetic participator and she gets closer to the genuine African personality than any other Western writer has done to date" (*Visions* 146). In her West African novel and stories, Laurence identified with a wide range of different characters, using what Phyllis Gotlieb calls the artist's "third eye, the one with the vision." Gotlieb commends Laurence for venturing into unfamiliar territory (44).

Writing in 1969 about the form and voice of her novels, Laurence, referring to the African male protagonist of *This Side Jordan*, marvels at her temerity as an apprentice writer of fiction and asks herself how she "ever had the nerve to attempt to go into the mind of an African man . . . " ("Gadgetry" 82). Her first novel, she accepts, is "cast in a traditional mould" ("Gadgetry" 81). It is set in Accra during the run-up to independence, and she anchors the narrative on two opposed and male protagonists, the African Nathaniel Amegbe and the Irish Londoner Johnnie Kestoe; but she does not hesitate as all-seeing author to explain the feelings and motives of a large cast of accompanying characters, who are concerned with the changes that independence will bring. Nathaniel and his compatriots were followed by others. In her short stories, she continued to identify with Africans, often using the third-person voice of an omniscient story-teller, which had been her chosen narrative form for *This Side Jordan*.

W.H. New in a 1983 essay entitled "The Other and I: Laurence's African Stories" discusses the narrative voices used in the short stories collected in *The Tomorrow-Tamer*. He opens his essay with some general principles rising from a comparison of African oral and European written traditions. The first, he maintains, interprets history in cyclical terms, while the written tradition prefers a linear development. The distinction is also one of saying (oral) and seeing (written). African oral traditions were often defamed by the colonizers, and, New holds, they can only be reconstructed by those who are able to identify with the neglected oral voice. New's argument is that Laurence, belonging as she does to the European written tradition, is unable to make that restoration. Even though she is an "*un*characteristic Westerner in Africa," she cannot write on behalf of Africa but only about it. She can sympathize but not identify with "the other" (115).

New holds that when Laurence tells her stories from her own perspective or that of an outside observer like herself, as she does in

"The Merchant of Heaven" and "The Rain Child," then she is successful. Both these stories use a first-person and English narrator. "The Merchant of Heaven," a story about an American missionary called Brother Lemon who arrives in the Gold Coast eager to win African souls, is told by a young architect, Will Kettridge, and "The Rain Child," set in an African girls' boarding school, is told by Violet Nedden, an elderly spinster who has taught there for twenty-two years. Laurence's success with Violet Nedden's narrative voice may, indeed, have influenced her choice of form for *The Stone Angel*. Violet Nedden who is elderly, ungainly, and not known for her humility — "Pride," she says, "has so often been my demon" (125) — prefigures Hagar Shipley in a number of ways as Patricia Morley outlines in "The Long Trek Home: Margaret Laurence's Stories." Certainly, as New points out in "The Other and I," "The Rain Child" displays a masterly control of voice effects.

However, New goes on to argue that those stories that presume an African story-teller identifying with African characters — "stories which contrive to appear as folktale" (121), and New particularly has in mind "The Tomorrow-Tamer" and "A Gourdful of Glory" — are flawed because Laurence has no genuine connections with the oral past, and so she cannot bring it to life in a written medium. Because she does not have the "power to invoke and so re-enact the wisdom of the ancestors," New feels that Laurence's narrative is strained when she attempts to speak with their accents (115). While New finds evidence in the stories that Laurence is aware of the incompatibility of African and European traditions, he sees her persisting from time to time in an attempt to combine them, and in this, he argues, she is bound to fail. In 1989 New repeated his reservations in "A Shaping of Connections," advising readers of *The Tomorrow-Tamer* to "read this book cautiously" (157). His is a critical judgement that goes against the general view that "The Tomorrow-Tamer" and "A Gourdful of Glory" along with "God-man's Master" are the most successful of her African stories. Though New does not mention *This Side Jordan* in this connection, he would presumably be unable to accept Laurence's portrayal of Nathaniel, whose inner monologues deliberately attempt to recall the voices of his ancestors.

It is clear that Laurence was alert to the effect of using different narrative voices. *The Tomorrow-Tamer* was put together with care and English and African narrating voices alternate in this perfectly balanced volume. Matthew, the son of English missionaries, tells the opening story, "The Drummer of All the World," and it is followed by "The Perfume Sea," a fairy-tale told by a neutral story-teller. Then Will Kettridge gives his account of Brother Lemon's adventures in "The Merchant of Heaven" before an African story-teller recites the tale of Kofi's death in "The Tomorrow-Tamer." Following that it is Violet Nedden's turn, and after "The Rain Child" comes "Godman's Master," another of Laurence's so-called "contrived folk-tales." The last four stories, which are all third-person narratives, express a variety of viewpoints. "A Fetish for Love" is told from the perspective of an English outsider, Constance, and "The Pure Diamond Man" is told by an African Daniel. The last two stories, "The Voices of Adamo" and "A Gourdful of Glory," bring back the narrator who speaks on behalf of Africans. Laurence thus contrasts the two perspectives and attempts in her use of the African setting to present both an African and non-African vision.

New would be the first to recognize Laurence's skill as an observer of the other, but he maintains that her "illuminations come from outside the community rather than inside" ("Other" 122). This is obviously true in the literal sense, and she herself recognized her position as an outsider, but it can be argued that she penetrated deeply into the society she wrote about and illuminated it from within. She only used traditional material after careful research, and she made a conscious effort to understand African history and traditions from the African perspective. Certainly as an outsider she is exceptional, and she sheds considerable insight in areas that many expatriates have found unclear. She is, indeed, an "*un*characteristic Westerner in Africa," occupying a pre-eminent position among those expatriate writers who have chosen Africa as the setting for their fiction. It is a position that can be demonstrated from just a few comparisons.

For purposes of comparison, the field can be narrowed to the fiction of those English-speaking non-Africans who lived in the British colonies in West Africa that were to become the nations of Sierra Leone, Ghana, and Nigeria. The terms of the comparison will rest on the narrative viewpoint chosen by the writer. Does the narration reflect an African viewpoint? And, if so, how successful is the attempt to identify with another culture?

Killam in *Africa in English Fiction* discusses many of the expatriate writers who visited and wrote about Africa in the colonial era. (He includes an extensive bibliography of expatriate writing.) Only a few produced novels of any quality, and Killam concludes that most authors simply find in Africa a confirmation of preconceived ideas, and that "the sensitivity of [their] writing is limited, its presentation of reality frequently distorted and its intention openly propagandist and inadequate to a full utilisation of the setting" (xi). There are, however, two writers who are clearly exceptions to this generality: Joyce Cary, whom Killam discusses in depth, and Graham Greene. It is with them that Laurence should be compared.

The African novels of Joyce Cary and Graham Greene are based on experience gained living and working in Africa. Cary joined the Nigerian political service in 1913, but returned to England because of ill health in 1919. Between 1932 and 1939 he published four novels set in the Niger river forest interior, which he had known well. These novels have a third-person omniscient narrator, who moves easily among a great variety of characters and who is quite prepared to suggest what may be passing through the mind of a crazed African girl like Aissa or a semi-literate African clerk like Mister Johnson. Though Cary's African characters are remarkable individuals, they are flawed. They are not, as in much colonial fiction, stereotypes, but they are overstated and come close to being caricatures. In the preface to *The African Witch*, Cary comments on the impact of Africa on his imagination and the effect it had on his fiction. "The African setting," he writes, "just because it is dramatic, demands a certain kind of story, a certain violence and coarseness of detail, almost a fabulous treatment, to keep it in its place" (11). Aissa and Mister Johnson are characters suited to that kind of story, but Africa is no more and no less violent than anywhere else and does not require such special treatment.

An American Visitor stands out from Cary's other novels because it captures the forest world in quiet moods. The story is violent enough, but Cary also conveys other qualities: the stillness and grandeur of river and forest, the peaceful everyday family life of the Birri people. Here Cary's unobtrusive and impersonal narrator proves that the author was capable of a sensitive understanding of a different culture, a fact that is more obvious in his nonfictional writing on Africa. In a scene not directly relevant to the plot of *An American Visitor*, the Birri people are observed during the quiet time of the year, before the planting season. The children are playing along the river bank watched by the men who are free to smoke and gossip.

One of the men, Obai, who has lost his first wife, watches the child who is betrothed to him, six-year-old Bobbin, as she plays with the other children in the river. Obai is smoking a large brass pipe shaped like an elephant, and Bobbin runs to him when she feels in need of protection. She stays beside him while the men talk of marriage and children, and the relationship between Obai and his bride-to-be is finely caught. "Obai," Cary writes, "had laid the stem of his pipe across his knee so that the little girl could put down her lips and take a pull at it. As she did so she laid her fingers on the back of his hand to steady the pipe" (161). The special relationship between Obai and Bobbin would not be acceptable within a European context, but it is seen as quite natural in Cary's novel. Infant betrothal was traditionally common in West Africa as R.S. Rattray explains in *Religion and Art in Ashanti* when discussing the practice among the Ashanti people. It was quite usual for a husband and wife to promise an infant daughter "to a friend as his future bride" (76), and the little girl would "address her future husband as *me 'kunu* ('my husband')." Rattray adds that when she could walk and was old enough to carry a small bundle for her husband-to-be, she would "accompany him on short expeditions, but on her return [would] always go home to sleep with her parents" (77). Cary can be a perceptive recorder of the ordinary as in this scene by the Niger river, but too often he allows his fascination with the extraordinary to get the upper hand.

Graham Greene, on the other hand, does not attempt to identify with the African viewpoint, preferring instead to observe the African setting through an outsider. He chose a neutral but undoubtedly European third-person narrator for *A Burnt-Out Case*, and in *The Heart of the Matter* he also narrated his story in the third person, but this time looking closely over the shoulders of Major Scobie, a character for whom he himself was the prototype. Greene, employed by the British Secret Service, served in Sierra Leone during the Second World War doing "government work of rather an ill-defined nature" as he notes in *In Search of a Character* (8). When he created Major Scobie, Deputy Commissioner of Police in Freetown in the 1940s, Greene drew on his own memories and shows Scobie coping with intelligence problems caused by the fighting in Europe. *The Heart of the Matter* is not an autobiographical novel, but it is based on personal experience that allows Greene to speak powerfully on Scobie's behalf. Scobie's fragile hold on a country to which he is powerfully attracted reflects Greene's own position and feelings. "The magic of this place," Scobie thinks to himself, "never failed him: here he kept his foothold on the very edge of a strange continent" (37). Freetown, like Laurence's Accra, is a tangle of people; "the original Tower of Babel," one character calls it, made up of "West Indians, Africans, real Indians, Syrians, Englishmen, Scotsmen in the Office of Works, Irish priests, French priests, Alsatian priests" (14). For the most part, however, this babble of voices is interpreted for the reader by Scobie, a stranger in a strange land.

Most of the expatriate writers who have drawn on their experiences of Africa in their fiction are like Greene and find it easier to narrate their stories as if from their own viewpoint. This is certainly true of the Canadian writers who followed Laurence to West Africa and lived there during the first years of independence. Dave Godfrey taught in Ghana at Adisadel College from 1963 to 1965. In *The New Ancestors* he gives his reading of the eventful years that followed independence. Black and white characters in his novel join in marriage and in conspiracy but the focus centres on the Englishman, Michael Burdener, teacher at Bishop Adisa school, who is the first-person narrator of the opening section of the story. The succeeding sections of the novel retell the events through African eyes, with considerable effect, but the continuing narrative cannot be dissociated from that first perspective. In an interview with Graeme Gibson, Godfrey has conceded that he structured the novel around Burdener who "is simply an English me" (162).

The novel Audrey Thomas set in Ghana is clearly autobiographical. *Mrs. Blood*, published in 1970, the same year as *The New Ancestors*, painfully and brilliantly details the fragmented thoughts of a woman suffering, as Thomas did, a miscarriage in a Ghanaian hospital. The novel's epigraph is taken from *Alice's Adventures in Wonderland*, and for the disorientated narrator the African setting is disturbing, since it strikes her as totally unpredictable and surreal: " 'How do you know I'm mad?' said Alice. 'You must be,' said the Cat, 'or you wouldn't have come here' " (qtd. in Thomas [7]). Evelyn Waugh had much the same feelings about the time he spent in Abyssinia when he attended the coronation of the Emperor Haile Selassie, a "preposterous *Alice in Wonderland* fortnight," which he turned into fiction as *Black Mischief*. Waugh considered that the only "parallel for life in Addis Ababa" was to be found in the "peculiar flavour of galvanised and translated reality" that marks *Alice in*

Wonderland (90). Africa fascinated Thomas's Mrs. Blood because it mirrored in charged and subverted images the problematic, even demented, nature of the world she had left and to which her thoughts compulsively return. Laurence's interpretation of Africa is never in these terms.

Laurence avoided putting herself into her characters. The nearest she came to doing so was in the creation of Miranda in *This Side Jordan* and Constance in "A Fetish for Love," both young white liberals, recently married and starting a family. Miranda and Constance, however, are English and so firmly removed on this count from Laurence's perspective. As a Canadian she belonged neither to African nor European society, and, because there were few Canadians in Africa when she was there, she perhaps saw no place for herself in the world she was describing.[1] Yet her writing has throughout demonstrated a reluctance to come to terms with her own experience, which is partly the result of her unusual interest in others but may also indicate the strength of the personal emotions bound up in her early years, which made them difficult to handle. While other writers are more likely to start with their portrait of the artist as a young person and move away from the autobiographical, Laurence has done the opposite. Even when she began the Manawaka novels she turned first to her grandparents' generation, and it was only with Stacey, a young mother in Vancouver, that she first clearly put her own experience into her fiction. The process was completed when she drew on her childhood in *A Bird in the House* and her adult life in her last novel, *The Diviners*. In her African fiction, the viewpoints she presents are of people — black and white, men and women — with backgrounds far removed from her own. The result is a remarkable richness of characterization and one that is especially successful in its presentation of the African position. Like Cary, she was curious about and attracted by African voices, but in her use of them she demonstrated more integrity than he did. Her African characters lack the extravagant vitality of his, but she creates individuals who are convincing and complex and who live ordinary but rounded lives.

In her interview with Laurence, Rosemary Sullivan suggested that what was remarkable in Laurence's West African fiction was "the degree to which you penetrated the cultures, the degree to which you reached inside, as it were." In response, Laurence explained that any insight she had came from having African friends and from reading extensively about the history and traditions of the Gold Coast. ". . . I not only had," she told Sullivan, "a number of Ghanaian friends, but I had read enormously widely, books of anthropology and books written by Ghanaians too about their own culture" (64). The writers who were of most importance to her are acknowledged at the beginning of *This Side Jordan*. They are four in number. Three of them were contemporaries of Laurence's, but the well-known anthropologist Robert Sutherland Rattray, who lived from 1881 to 1938, belonged to an earlier era. He was a Provincial Commissioner in the Gold Coast for many years, and his position gave him the opportunity to follow his anthropological interests to advantage. His work on Ashanti traditions and folk-tales is still highly regarded. Joseph Buakye Danquah (popularly known as "J.B."), who was born in 1895, was living in the Gold Coast when Laurence was there. In 1921 he went to University College, London, and later completed his law training at the Inner Temple. On his return to the Gold Coast, he studied Akan religious beliefs and published *The Akan Doctrine of God* in 1944. He was, however, to become better known as a politician who opposed Nkrumah. He died in detention in 1965. Eva Lewin-Richter Meyerowitz, also born in 1895, carried on Danquah's work. Her book, *The Sacred State of the Akan* was published in 1951. Finally, Laurence acknowledges the work of J.H. Nketia, who made a detailed study of the music and words of Akan funeral dirges, and his book, *Funeral Dirges of the Akan People*, was published in 1955. Her research allowed her to extend her fiction into areas that she did not know from first-hand experience. She was able to connect her African characters with their past while they lived in a contemporary world and planned for the future. It is her interpretation of this material, however, that New questions. He dislikes her use of an omniscient story-teller who presumes to speak for Africa, a voice that claims familiarity with African customs. It is a voice representing more than an individual viewpoint as, with the authority of a village elder, it tells modern folk-tales and fables from the point of view of Africans. It describes places presumably closed to Laurence: the room in "Godman's Master" where the fetish priest Faru keeps his oracle and the village home where Kofi grew up. This is a world, New maintains, that Laurence cannot reclaim. "Her omniscient-author stories never know enough to convince us of the Africa they tell us about," he argues, "whereas her limited-perspective narrators convince us ably of themselves" ("Other" 127).

New's opinion must be challenged. Laurence's omniscient "African" voice can be trusted to tell us a great deal. New underestimates her knowledge of the history and traditions of the peoples of the Gold Coast, which she incorporates into her fiction with remarkable success. Her evocation of Kofi's family life in "The Tomorrow-Tamer" is not unconvincing, built as it is on direct observation and on wide reading, to which is added her own powers of imagination. Clearly Laurence's African fiction does not aim at cultural homogeneity since it uses western and African reference simultaneously. Many would see this cross-cultural patterning as a virtue, and Wilson Harris in "The Fabric of the Imagination" would advise the creation of "a new space or interrelationship in which to transform a threat that may overwhelm us if we adhere to block, institutional habit" (179). At times Laurence recalls the African past using western and Christian terms, evoking an African Garden of Eden, with "palms and the dark river and red earth" where an African Adamo had his origin (*Tomorrow* 207). Kofi's village will be changed dramatically by the new bridge, but outside influences had effected life there long before the construction crew moved in. The local store is known as the "Hail Mary Chop-Bar," and it is perhaps no surprise that when the city workers do arrive their leader is called Emmanuel. But this combination of traditions is also marked in the fiction of African writers, that of Chinua Achebe and Ngugi Wa Thiong'o to name but two. It does not indicate a denial of the values of either culture, but a recognition that they exist side by side.

New recognizes Achebe's achievement in restoring the past, adding that Laurence "cannot claim such a reclamation" ("Other" 117). She does not, indeed, attempt historical recreations on the scale that Achebe does. However, when she writes of contemporary Africans, her assessment of the interplay of traditional customs with imported ideas both in the villages of the interior and the cities on the coast is shrewd. She knows what concerns trouble the present generation and how they feel about their past. When Achebe recreated his grandfather's world, he could do so because the voices of the ancestors spoke to him in accents familiar from his childhood. Yet even he needed more than memory to achieve restoration; he too had to rely on records made by others and above all on imaginative effort. It must also be remembered that Achebe's recreation of the traditional past through the written word is done in a new language.

Neither Laurence nor Achebe use the exact voice of the ancestors. Neither writer can reproduce the oral voice on the printed page; it is inevitable that the saying be expressed as seeing. Achebe as much as Laurence is working within western literary traditions. Achebe, of course, found the way back with less difficulty, but that does not render Laurence's effort invalid.

Both Achebe and Laurence recognize that it is not the exact reproduction of the oral voice that is of paramount importance, but the attempt to rescue its message for succeeding and less oral generations. Each new story-teller should give a new performance, and it is his or her right to decide how to present the story, how to honour the past and suggest continuity, making whatever changes seem necessary. The shift to a written text is only another stage in the continuous process of preservation.

Until recently, African oral literature was largely known outside Africa through the work done by non-Africans. The discussion of the subject by missionaries, linguists, and anthropologists, along with the material they chose as evidence, inevitably reflected specialized interests. When Rattray made his collection of Ashanti folk-tales, *Akan-Ashanti Folk-Tales,* he was concerned to make "the English translation as nearly literal as possible."[2] He values the stories as literature, but they are of more importance to him as a way back into the past. He is interested in the source of the stories, and so he goes to "remoter villages," where the "old folk" tell the tales under the stars (vi). Rattray considers as less valuable, from an "anthropological standpoint," transcriptions made by what he calls "Europeanized African helpers," who have been mission-educated and have a good knowledge of English. Rattray maintains that such ". . . transcribers are prone to ignore the African idiom, and to omit just those apparently trivial details which stamp these tales with individuality and make them of value to students of language and customs" (v). Rattray's collection is a testimony to the richness of African oral traditions, but his concern to preserve them in an unchanged and "pure" form marks him as European. Africans are more likely to feel that unless the traditions can survive change, they have little value. The Ashanti stories Rattray has recorded have become museum artefacts, because their oral life was inevitably lost once they were frozen in print, and he was not prepared to breathe new life into them so that they could live in their changed environment.

There are those who think the old "time-free" stories, unlike the "time-bound" poetry, should reflect change. If the stories are to live on, it is essential that an artistic contribution should be made by succeeding story-tellers, who should be judged not on their ability to reproduce their predecessors' performance, but on their own originality and capacity to make the old tales comprehensible to a new audience, be it as spoken, or as is more common today written, texts. Ruth Finnegan in her book, *Oral Literature in Africa*, hopes to correct some of the misconceptions that have arisen from the work done by anthropologists. Finnegan believes that initially too much interest was focused on the stories at the expense of poetry, partly because the stories were regarded primarily as folklore, with archetypal and mythopoeic patterns reaching back into primitive beginnings, partly because ". . . this field of study has been particularly subject to the vicissitudes of anthropological theories and has reflected only too faithfully the rise and fall of fashions in interpretations of African (and 'primitive') cultures" (317). Too little interest, Finnegan claims, has been paid to the contemporary relevance of story-telling. Individual presentation and originality, she believes, have been played down in order to emphasize the " 'survival' " aspect of story, its links with "an earlier and even more primitive state" (318). Finnegan has drawn a further important conclusion from her extensive study of oral literature: ". . . the distinction between oral and written forms," she believes, "may not be so rigid and so profound as is often implied" (20).

While she objects to some of the misconceptions that have resulted, Finnegan does not question the value of collecting and translating African stories. She, however, is interested in the latest rather than the earliest version of a tale, and what delights her is the way the story-teller brings the material up to date for the audience. She bases her arguments on her knowledge of Limba story-telling. The Limba are rice farmers who live in the hills of northern Sierra Leone. Finnegan carried out her research there between 1961 and 1964. Her method when collecting stories for *Limba Stories and Story-Telling* was as careful as Rattray's and as respectful to the original. The stories were all recorded in Limba — on tape, by dictation or written down by a Limba assistant — and then translated by Finnegan who preserved as far as possible the syntax and word order of the individual performance (107). Her notes also add where, when, and by whom the story was told, focusing not on its earlier history but its present relevance.

Laurence did not have Finnegan's or Rattray's linguistic capabilities, but her respect for oral literature equalled theirs. Her renderings of the Somali stories were literary rather than literal, but she anticipated Finnegan's work in many ways, especially in her recognition of the importance of individual composition and performance. In the introduction to *A Tree for Poverty*, Laurence examined the contemporary social background to her chosen translations, and she did so not as an anthropologist nor, indeed, as a literary critic, but as a writer herself. The Somali stories she translates are not museum artefacts; they live as a result of Hersi's artistic efforts overlaid by her own literary skills. When she invented her own African stories, her deep knowledge of the nature of oral story-telling was an advantage that did not hinder the writing process.

When Laurence was in the Gold Coast, the Africans she knew best were those who had been "Europeanized" by western education, often referred to as "been-tos" because they had finished their education abroad. They were used to speaking and writing in English. Their attitudes were in part shaped by western thought, which inevitably altered but certainly did not destroy their relationship with and understanding of their own culture and traditions. A certain western condescension towards the educated African can be seen lingering on when New classes these people — "the 'been-to's' and emigrés, or the uprooted, orphaned, dwarfed, or middleclass villagers" ("Other" 118) — as outsiders. It is these "outsiders" who have been able to reclaim the past and speak with authority of their homeland. They may no longer wish to live as their ancestors did, but they recognize their debt to the past and acknowledge it as they prepare to play their part in the present. If they are outsiders in Africa, it follows that Laurence, too, had become an outsider when, with her outlook changed and with a new and penetrating understanding of her homeland, she returned to the country of her birth. She understood why young aspiring Africans objected to the "anthropological zeal" with which Europe has interpreted Africa while ignoring the changed world in which "the African continues to live, as man and as artist" (Healy 24). Kwabena in "The Drummer of All the World" argues with Matthew because he senses in the Englishman the unwillingness to allow that the African might not wish " 'to stand still' " (17).

Laurence aligns herself with Africans rather than Europeans in that she recognizes that the Africans look forward to change, and her stories explore the subject. She uses her fiction as the vehicle of change, showing how the oral voice can be adapted for a written English text. Admittedly she does so on a small scale compared to Achebe's magnificent achievement in his historical novels, but nevertheless she belongs to the circle of African story-tellers who see themselves, not as part of folklore, but as writers of today who give due honour to yesterday but look with concern to the future. These story-tellers see the advantage of using a means of communication and western literary traditions that international audiences understand.

Laurence saw no reason why her African story-teller should not perform within a western literary framework, and African writers were adopting the same attitude. Her narrative voice is designed for the printed page; she relies on complex syntactical structures and rich descriptive imagery, both more natural in a written than in a spoken text. When she wants to suggest an oral voice, she knows how to do so with accepted artifices. She can, for example, address a presumed listening audience directly, as she does at the end of "The Tomorrow-Tamer," where the invocation " 'oh, my children, my sons' " (104) suggests that a village story-teller has given an account of Kofi's story. However, her methods of invoking the oral voice are usually more subtle and remain an integral part of her written texts. The "repetitive rhythms" that in "The Rhythms of Ritual in Margaret Laurence's *The Tomorrow-Tamer*" James Harrison sees as characteristic of *The Tomorrow-Tamer* stories, and which he feels are appropriate to her African work, are worked into her written texts with literary crafting. It should be noted, however, as Cecil Abrahams points out in "Margaret Laurence and Chinua Achebe: Commonwealth Storytellers," that Laurence's use of oral techniques is most marked not in her African writing, but in *The Diviners*.

The omniscient narrator who seems to speak as an African in some of her stories is, in fact, taking on a more ambitious task than an attempt to reproduce an oral voice. In stories like "The Tomorrow-Tamer" and "Godman's Master," Laurence intends to conceal her own ethnocentric position and write as someone who could be an African. Some would say she succeeds. Craig Tapping can commend Laurence's brilliant act of "ventriloquism" in "The Tomorrow-Tamer" because he can find in this "magnificent tale," even after several readings, no indication that ". . . its author is not one of the new generation of African writers whom she praises and brings to our attention through her studies of their fictions in *Long Drums and Cannons*" (76). This is to beg the question as to whether Laurence's style is not distinctively her own, but Tapping's premise could be disproved only with difficulty if it is applied to the story's content.

As she set out in search of character and voice for her fiction, she set herself no limits, but she did not undertake the task without serious thought and study. Men and women, old and young, from within and without Africa, living in the city and the village, are portrayed in her fiction for the most part with insight and detail, and her right to speak for them should not be denied on grounds of her nationality. She should only be disqualified as an African story-teller if she can be shown to be guilty of either ignorance or prejudice.

5

White Players

The few traces of prejudice in her portrayal of character manifest themselves mainly in her depiction of Europeans. In 1969 Margaret Laurence re-read *This Side Jordan* and found to her surprise that ". . . it was actually not the African chapters (which I had liked best when I wrote it) which stood up best at this distance, but the European ones. In the end, I was able to understand the Europeans best, I think, even though my sympathy with colonial Europeans was certainly minimal or even non-existent" ("Gadgetry" 82). Her satisfaction on this score was the result of considerable revision after realizing that her original interpretation had been prejudiced. ". . . I decided," she writes, "after leaving Africa and getting a fresh perspective on colonial society, that I'd been unfair to the European characters" ("Ten Years'" 17). In her memoir *Dance on the Earth*, she acknowledges her stepmother's invaluable help in this process of adjustment. Her stepmother read the second draft of *This Side Jordan* shortly before her death. The older woman, her step-daughter writes, analyzed the novel with "perception" and "fairness" and "hard, reliable honesty." What she had to say about *This Side Jordan* was sound and wise. "She understood," Laurence reports, "I was against colonialism and she didn't take issue with that. She just felt I had put my heart and soul into a portrayal of the African characters and had, unconsciously or deliberately, made stereotypes of the whites. For a novel, that was not good enough" (117). Laurence acted on this good advice, and the European chapters were rewritten.

Nevertheless, she is not always the best judge of her own work, and in *This Side Jordan* her white characters are pale figures indeed beside her Africans. She tended to underestimate her achievement in the portrayal of, for example, Nathaniel, knowing as she did how often Africans had been misrepresented by outsiders. But her stepmother had recognized that her heart and soul had gone into the creation of her black characters with the result, so clearly put by Clara Thomas in *The Manawaka World of Margaret Laurence*, that "[t]he Africans are more believable than the English characters because Margaret Laurence's sympathies were primarily engaged in their portrayals" (53).

Nevertheless, the Europeans in *This Side Jordan* are on the whole convincing enough. The process of understanding that had started in Somaliland led finally to a fair portrayal of the imperialists. This does not mean that she forgave them their faults. Her Europeans are for the most part embittered, unhappy, and antipathetic to Africa, but they are carefully differentiated, and the reasons for their bitterness are made clear.

The European parts of the novel are concerned with the affairs of the Textile Branch of Allkirk, Moore & Bright, a company that imports the dress fabrics often referred to as mammy-cloths. Specially designed for the African market, these fabrics are noted for their striking colours and original designs. James Thayer, Bedford Cunningham, and Johnnie Kestoe all work for the company. The product marketed by Laurence's Europeans is exploited brilliantly in metaphorical terms, illustrating how imaginatively she used the African setting. As other visitors to West Africa have done, Laurence noticed the variety and colour of the patterns on the clothes worn by Africans. She was fascinated by their bold and unusual designs and was quick to see their potential for her fiction. For example, Nathaniel's mother-in-law, Adua, wears a cloth which is "black and red, patterned in hands outspread" (70), hands that remind Nathaniel of the demands made on him. His uncle Adjei's shirt is made of a cloth "dark purple and green, patterned with long-legged cranes as lean of shank as himself" (97), and his wife, Aya, buys a new cloth for the church parade, and it is "deep blue, with a pattern of drift-tailed fishes and unnamed sea-creatures in swirling lines of yellow and orange" (108). The symbolic use of mammy-cloths is even more pronounced in the short stories. In "The Perfume Sea" Mr. Archipelago's landlord wears "a new royal blue cloth infuriatingly patterned with golden coins" (*Tomorrow* 40), and the enigmatic child-wife Love has two cloths, an old one, "a shabby salmon-pink, faded and hideously patterned in what appeared to be the keys for some giant prison door" (166) and a new one "of a blue delicate as sky, printed with yellowing green leaves like ripe limes" (162).

It is significantly the responsibility of James Thayer, in *This Side Jordan*, manager of the "all-important Textile Branch" of Allkirk, Moore & Bright (7), to choose such patterns. Surely Laurence is recollecting a scene she had witnessed when she describes the warehouse, where the women traders who have come to choose their cloth patter "up and down the narrow aisles, their bare or sandalled feet slapping softly on the grey splintered wood" (33). She builds James Thayer into this known environment, and, when she leaves him fingering the sample bolts, tracing the patterns of "the black giraffe, the orange palm, the sea-monster and the serpent" (35–36), the reader knows without being told that his job has become his obsession. James Thayer clings desperately to the idea that his knowledge makes him indispensable. " 'I've been studying pattern trends in tradecloth for many years,' " he says, and " 'I fancy I know what these people want better than they know themselves' " (239). James, however, cannot ignore the fact that his reign must end, and people will choose their own patterns from now on. He feels rejected by a country that he has loved, at least to the extent of collecting "the ebony heads and the brass figurines" (130), and to salve his pride he predicts that independence will lead to chaos.

His wife on the other hand hates all things African, as Johnnie realizes when he visits the Thayer house where Cora has made sure " 'Africa shan't enter' " (126). She is obsessed like her husband with cloth, but she collects remnants of expensive brocade. The difference between Cora and James is evident in their house. " 'I sent to Harrods for the curtain material,' " says Cora. " 'James wanted mammy-cloth, but I said no' " (126).

Cora is typical of Laurence's white women, skeletal and jaundiced: "Face, hair, dress — all were the same colour, the faint yellow of age" (10). But life has not been easy for Cora, and, when Laurence has filled in her background, the reasons for her attitude to Africa become clear. When the Thayers lived up country, the only Europeans for miles in jungle that was hot and dank, Cora had malaria, and James caught typhoid. Then they moved to a mine in Ashanti, and James had to face alone a violent mob of strikers. Finally, Cora lost the baby she was carrying during another bout of malaria.

There are reasons, too, for the way the Cunninghams behave. Bedford Cunningham has dreamed of earning enough to send his son to his old public school, Walhampton, but he lacks the drive to succeed. His descent into alcoholism is hastened when his position with Allkirk, Moore & Bright becomes uncertain. Not without cause, his wife is driven frantic with worry. She is afraid of Africa, and added to her concern for her husband are her neurotic fears for the health of her children, who, she feels, have been put further at risk because the childless Thayers have pulled rank to obtain the only decent bungalow available, leaving her to care for the family in a " 'ghastly old wreck,' " with " 'scorpions underneath the stoep' " (95). Helen's neurotic fears for her children, Brian and Kathie, are astutely conveyed because they are fears that Laurence understood only too well. In 1982 she told an audience of students graduating from Emmanuel College in Toronto that she could "remember as though it were yesterday — and it was in fact nearly thirty years ago — [her] own sense of helplessness and anguish" when her two children had malaria in the Gold Coast ("Statement" 59). Understandably, Helen Cunningham frets about scorpions and puff-adders and worries ceaselessly about " 'malaria, dysentery, the sudden high fevers' " (120).

Laurence recognizes that other aspects of colonial life in West Africa encourage depression: the inevitable Sunday curry lunch, "heat-sodden afternoons" (128), dull evenings of gossip and complaint at the club. Her evocation of the last days of British imperialism elicits more pity than scorn, and, as Mary Renault writes in her review of *This Side Jordan*, her "sad, sun-dried English men and women" are "consistently believable" (104). Laurence's description is not an unfair portrayal, and the fact that it calls to mind E.M. Forster and Graham Greene at their best is further proof of its validity. More than one reviewer of *This Side Jordan* is reminded of Forster. In the *New Statesman*, Gerda Charles agrees that the book has "an almost Forsterian quality of understanding," her only reservation being the "suspiciously sunny conclusion" (802). F.W. Watt, who also confesses in his 1960 review to "uncertainty as to the mood of this conclusion," admires the portrayal of the white community in which Laurence portrays "all the varieties of moral and racial obtuseness familiar from Forster's India, the death throes of the imperial class" (407).

Greene in *The Heart of the Matter*, in which there is little respite from depression, conveys the same picture of the English, especially the women. Louise Scobie, her "skin a little yellow with atabrine" and her "eyes bloodshot with tears" (59), is permanently unhappy. Her daughter, an only child, died at the age of nine at boarding school in England. The club is her one escape from the house, and there is little to console her in either place because Scobie "had been out-manoeuvred in the interminable war over housing," and his repeated failure to win promotion leaves her open to the malicious pity of others (21).

Laurence's English community is viewed through the eyes of Johnnie Kestoe who is part of it and yet a loner. He is the white counterbalance to Nathaniel, and the entire action of the novel takes place in the presence of one or both of them. As Clara Thomas has pointed out in *Manawaka World*, there is "an insistence on symme-try and balance in plot" that results in an overstructured framework (50). Johnnie, newly arrived from England, becomes the confidant of his colleagues and their wives, and in turn James and Cora, Bedford and Helen divulge their hopes and fears to him. Johnnie's role as sympathetic listener has to be contrived, and the trust placed in him by others is not readily understandable, since he is a far from pleasant person. Laurence must further invent a background for him that will show why he is prepared to betray all the confidential secrets entrusted to him as he concentrates selfishly on making his own way upwards.

His past, which is one of violence and superstition, explains, too conveniently, much of his behaviour in the novel, and the impression that it has been invented for just this purpose undermines its credi-bility. Johnnie is keen to leave his past behind and carve out a new life, but he cannot escape his memories. Because of them he is strongly prejudiced against black people while being secretly fascinated by miscegenation. The son of a slow-witted Irishman, who worked as a lavatory cleaner on a London underground station, Johnnie devel-oped a hatred for blacks, which crystallized when a Jamaican took his father's job. Johnnie took his revenge on the Jamaican's son with a knife. In her description of the scene, Laurence attempts to suggest the vocabulary that Johnnie himself would use, but she creates an effect that is over-theatrical and borders on the ludicrous:

The Irishman's son was ten, and small, but he had his blade-friend. The buttocks of the Jamaican's son bled profusely like life turned to mere meat, and the nigger, who was thirteen and a head taller, bawled like a raped nun, each huge tremulous tear setting off an orgasm of laughter in the bitter Irish bellies of young bystanders. (5)

Johnnie's sexual obsessions, which lead him to treat his pregnant wife Miranda with little sympathy and to hanker after black girls, are attributed to the experience of watching his Roman Catholic mother die without absolution from a self-induced abortion in a squalid attic room in Kilburn High Road, another scene described in dramatic and lurid detail. Johnnie's "gutterstreet" childhood in London (4), with its poverty and despair, is hastily described and lacks conviction. In "Muddling into Maturity," the reviewer for the *Times Literary Supplement* considers Johnnie the "least satisfying character" in the novel (101) and can see no merit in the "rather cursory flashback to his childhood in an English slum where there were coloured immigrants . . . ." The depiction of this childhood in a novel centred on black and white confrontation in Africa is, as the reviewer goes on to note, laboured, a piling of "Pelion upon Ossa as far as race relations are concerned" (102). Before leaving for Africa, Laurence lived in the unfashionable part of London known as Finchley and worked at an employment agency. She may well have witnessed the suffering and discrimination that could have created someone like Johnnie, but she fails to assimilate this material believably into her novel.

An understanding of Johnnie's conduct towards his wife and towards young African girls, in particular the child-prostitute Emerald, is essential if he is to have any share of the reader's sympathy and if he is to sustain his half of the novel. As well as carrying his own guilt, Laurence also holds him responsible, at any rate symbolically, for the evils done in the name of imperialism. His rape of Emerald is seen as more than the offensive behaviour of one individual; it symbolizes the exploitation of Africa by the European powers.

Laurence used the rape scene as a vehicle to carry her anger, and it functions as much more than an incident in the narrative. It is in symbolic terms a condemnation of the repressive years of Africa's history when the slave trade flourished. There can be no doubt of the significance of the action or the players. Emerald is sold into a life of slavery for Johnnie's pleasure. He tears off the green cloth that fails to protect her as the forest had failed her to protect her people. Historical patterns are repeated because it is an African, Lamptey, tempted by gain, who betrays Emerald, and Nathaniel is too weak and too much in need to prevent him. The squalid and ugly room above the nightclub "Weekend in Wyoming," where the rape takes place, represents the colony despoiled by the colonizers for their own

ends. "Many people had used the room, but none had lived in it."
The conquerors have left their marks there, "a basin half full of
swampy-looking water" for "conscientious sons of Islam," who
must perform a ritual washing after they have taken their pleasure,
and a "stout black Gideon Bible," as a reminder of the Christian
missionaries (228). Laurence suggests to her readers that nations
supposedly guided by Islamic and Christian principles benefited
from the slave trade. Johnnie has the grace to regret his action, but
he is required to carry a heavy burden in the novel, and it is a weight
he is unable to sustain without damage to his credibility.

There is one imperialist who lacks any sign of grace: Cameron
Sheppard, easily the most offensive person in the novel. It should be
noted that Miranda dislikes him on sight. Cameron represents a new
colonial breed whose motives are entirely selfish because ". . . he
knew exactly what he wanted and he was going after it, methodically,
scientifically, and without the slightest scruple." In condemning him,
Laurence condemns the selfish and cynical attitude adopted by those
who have recognized that independence is inevitable and intend to
exploit the new nation in new ways. Cameron, who views Africans
with cold disinterest — " '. . . I neither like nor dislike the Africans' "
(169) — believes that the Gold Coast is not ready for independence,
and he tells Johnnie that Britain must cut her losses and salvage what
is possible from the coming maelstrom (170–71). When compared
to Cameron, the old-style imperialists are easy to forgive.

The European treated with the most sympathy in the novel is the
significantly named Miranda, though her naïve wonder and enthusiasm as Prospero's daughter is at times held against her. Yet Miranda
as much as anyone sees with Laurence's eyes, and she has been
created in part out of Laurence's personal experience. Miranda has
more in common with the Europeans featured in *The Tomorrow-
Tamer* stories, most of whom do not belong to the old class of
imperialists and have come to Africa in a different spirit. Laurence
learnt to give unqualified credit to those who came "to do what work
they could, not as crusaders in a desperate darkness and not as
godlings in a solitary Eden, but as people in a world of people both
different and similar to themselves" (*Prophet's* 229). Such Europeans
stand as bridges between black and white, and Laurence uses them
as narrators and observers. Violet Nedden and Will Kettridge, along
with Dr. Philip Thrane, from the short story "Mask of Beaten Gold,"
who is married to an African, have connections linking them to the

Gold Coast, and there is never any question of the integrity of their motives or the warmth of their attachment to their part of Africa. Yet they are beset with fears. As a result of their insight, they know themselves to be strangers who must one day leave the land they love so well. Laurence, who was always conscious of being a stranger, used this insight in her portrayal of Miranda.

Miranda is very aware of the ways in which she differs from the African women, who puzzle her with their inscrutable and poised manner. She is especially made to feel the difference when she goes into hospital in Accra to have her baby. Miranda's daughter is born about the same time and in the same hospital as Nathaniel's son and Miranda tries without success to make friends with Nathaniel's wife Aya. In spite of her efforts, Miranda also fails to make friends with Nathaniel. When they meet, Miranda chatters enthusiastically to him about African culture. Laurence can describe Miranda's feelings with sympathy because they were suggested by her own experiences. Laurence has recalled how she would seek to impress her African friends with her "keen appreciation of various branches of African culture — African sculpture, African literature, African traditions and proverbs" (*Heart* 35). Miranda, who is taking drumming lessons, reads and studies local history and culture with much of the fervour that Laurence did. Miranda foolishly persuades Nathaniel to take her to the Accra market just as Laurence insisted on exploring Hargeisa market with the unwilling Mohamed (*Prophet's* 23–25). As Miranda attempts to make friends with Africans, with Nathaniel when they meet at the British Council, or with Aya when they are together in the hospital, she is often puzzled and hurt by the lack of response, something that Laurence is able to suggest with understanding.

Constance, in "A Fetish for Love," is another version of Miranda. Laurence probably found her own household servants as bewildering as Constance finds Sunday and Love, but Constance is an extreme example of the naïve westerner who tramples, albeit with good intentions, on the sensibilities of others through lack of understanding. The story of Love, a young child married to an old and impotent man, is told entirely from Constance's bewildered viewpoint. What Love feels must remain an unsolved mystery, and her story is compelling because the white narrating voice is puzzled to the end. In this story, Laurence returns to the riddle of Hawa, the child-wife she encountered in Somaliland. She touched on the subject in *This*

Side Jordan but, in "A Fetish for Love," she explores the theme in more detail. In the novel the Kestoes' cook Whiskey, who is childless, takes a second wife, aged fourteen but "ripe and developed as necessary" (133). Johnnie secretly desires the young girl who is "the wife of a man old enough to be her grandfather" (135).

That Laurence was never as naïve as Constance is obvious. She is more closely related to Violet Nedden in "The Rain Child." Violet Nedden is a tactful and understanding observer, who has become familiar with the customs of the people she lives amongst. Laurence's concern for the problems African women have to face is expressed in Violet Nedden's troubled thoughts about the three African rain children in her story: Ayesha, Kwaale, and Ruth. Ayesha the child-prostitute disturbs Violet as Asha had disturbed Laurence in Somaliland. The child-prostitute, like the child-wife, appears more than once in her fiction, as a haunting and lost figure. Ayesha was stolen as a child and taken to Lagos, and nobody knows where she was born. It should be remembered that Emerald, whom Johnnie rapes in *This Side Jordan*, comes from somewhere in the north of the Gold Coast. " 'I don't know where the hell she comes from,' " says Lamptey uncaringly, " 'somewhere up past Tamale, some place nobody ever heard of, I guess' " (220). Ayesha has been rescued, but the damage done her spirit can never be repaired, and Emerald in all likelihood is condemned to a life of prostitution.

The future for the other two rain children seems equally grim, and their antithetical predicaments illustrate what happens when cross-cultural communications are closed. Kwaale, the daughter of a village elder, will go straight from school to marriage and childbearing, unable to capitalize on the education she has been given. She knows the traditions of her people and will never be able to escape them. Ruth, the daughter of a doctor and born while he was training in England, has lost contact with her people and will live, as her name implies, forever a stranger in the land. Their stories are told with perception and sympathy. Using an Akan tradition known to her from her reading, Laurence through Violet Nedden demonstrates her understanding of the contrasting predicaments that face Kwaale and Ruth. Laurence almost certainly drew on Eva Meyerowitz's book, *The Sacred State of the Akan*, for her description of the Odwira festival where the differences between Kwaale and Ruth come to a head. During the parade, Kwaale enacts an old custom, one that is not obsolete, though those who keep it alive today may not appreciate its meaning. Violet Nedden has already remarked that Kwaale must pay for the sense of security and belonging that she enjoys. The price will be "bearing too many children in too short a span of years, mourning the inevitable deaths of some of them, working bent double at the planting and hoeing until her slim straightness was warped" (113). But at the festival it is important that Kwaale should be almost overpoweringly beautiful as Laurence makes her. Kwaale "was all sun-coloured cloth and whirling brown arms," Violet Nedden remembers. "I had never seen anyone with such a violence of beauty as she possessed, like surf or volcano, a spendthrift splendour." A young man in the crowd approaches Kwaale and shouts " 'Fire a gun at me,' " and Kwaale's "hands flicked at her cloth and for an instant she stood there naked except for the white beads around her hips, and her *amoanse*, the red cloth between her legs" (127). Ruth is shocked but Violet Nedden, who has been told the reason for the custom, is not. Laurence knew the details of this tradition from Meyerowitz, and the following passage from Meyerowitz reveals just how much Laurence owes her:

> This concept of the transmission of life by Nyame's arrows is expressed or enacted during any Akan festival where there is merry-making and a type of carnival freedom. Any young man may then walk up to a girl and ask: *"Bo me tuo"* — "fire a gun at me" — (in olden times 'Shoot an arrow at me") and the girl will then throw off her cloth and stand naked before him, except for a belt of precious beads around her hips and her *amoanse*, the red cloth between her legs. What the young man has asked for is the sight of something that he knows will overwhelm him, for the female body is regarded as the incarnation of all beauty and is admired and venerated on this account. (70–71)

As New has pointed out in "The Other and I," this story is convincingly told by an outside observer, but it is one who knows a great deal about the land she has lived in and who will feel most a stranger when she returns to "the island of grey rain" that was her birthplace (*Tomorrow* 133).

The last story Laurence wrote out of her African experience was "Mask of Beaten Gold," and in it she considers for the only time a mixed marriage. This tragic story of a young couple and the death of their only child was not included in *The Tomorrow-Tamer*, and it is often overlooked as a result (see Laurence, "Letter to Bob Sorfleet"). Laurence tackles the sensitive question of a mixed marriage delicately but honestly as she suggests the complex emotions that trouble Candace and her English husband, Philip Thrane. Candace and Philip have a five-year-old son, Jeremy. They are very much in love, but still over-sensitive about the differences between them. The narration of the story is arranged so that the reader can watch them watching each other, while Jeremy, who has a disturbing habit of disappearing from view, is studied with the anxious eyes of both his parents. Candace is Laurence's only female "been-to"; she trained as a nurse in a London hospital where she met her husband. Candace has learnt to value the protection that western medical skill can provide, and she will not let her son play with the children of their steward-boy " 'because,' " she says, " 'you have no idea what he would pick up' " (9). Philip is the one who enthuses about African traditions, and he tries to interest Jeremy in the stories of the Ashanti people who were his mother's ancestors. Once again Laurence turns to Meyerowitz. Philip takes his son to the beach, and there he reads while the child builds sand castles. The book Philip is reading in this story is almost certainly Meyerowitz's *The Sacred State of the Akan*, and he has come to the chapter entitled "The Queenmother, owner of the State," which describes "the role of the queen mother in the matriarchal Akan society" (15). Jeremy is fascinated by one of the photographs in his father's book. It is of the death mask of King Kofi Kakari (plate 64 in *The Sacred State of the Akan*) described by Meyerowitz as a "gold mask from the treasure of the Asantehene Nana Kofi Kakari." It has, Jeremy notices, no eyes. Candace with her western training and Philip with his interest in anthropology should be learning to see each other more clearly, but ironically as husband and wife in good faith accept each other's traditions, the unease between them and their chameleon child grows.

Candace is a complex person, who in contrast with her quiet husband and son is energetic and bright, her darkness all the more dramatic when she is seen in her canary yellow bathing suit (dressed in gold as an Ashanti should be). But she lives with some unease in a world where the colour of one's skin, one's identity, becomes a problem when it stands out against its background or when, as in Jeremy's case, it merges with it. A chameleon is brought into the story to make exactly this point. Laurence considered "Mask of Beaten Gold" to be "attenuated and strained" ("Letter to Bob Sorfleet" 52), and perhaps the symbolism is forced — she adds an albino child to her eyeless mask and colourless chameleon — but it is a reflective and honest story with a bleak message. *The Tomorrow-Tamer* stories are never over-optimistic, and they deal with defeat and death, despair and loneliness, but they usually end suggesting the possibility of hope or promise or grace. The end of "Mask of Beaten Gold" predicts only disintegration for the couple whose child disappears in death the way he so often eluded them in life, while they are left in the isolation they chose for themselves, cut off from others by "the splintered glass on their castle walls" (21). It is a sombre story, strained because of its difficult subject matter, but it would have been worthy of inclusion in the collection because of its unusual and moving picture of a mixed marriage and the problems it brings.

There is a considerable range in the cast of white characters. From the closely related group of imperialists in *This Side Jordan*, Laurence turned in the short stories to Englishmen and women whose associations with the Gold Coast were close and complex. Though her sympathies lay primarily with the Africans, her overall picture of the Gold Coast is not one-sided, and her fiction helps towards an understanding of both the problems and rewards that result when different races come together.

6

Black Players

That Margaret Laurence put her heart and soul into the portrayal of her African characters is self evident. Such commitment could itself have resulted in distortion, in an interpretation no less biased than her initial portrayal of the imperialists, but the individuals she created developed from a realistic and not an idealistic conception. They exist in a specifically rendered time and place, namely the last years of colonial rule in the Gold Coast, and like her Europeans they must accept responsibility for their faults and failures. They may be motivated by greed, ambition, and vanity as well as by love and an honest desire for a better life and for freedom. Hardship has made some bitter so that they hurt those they love, and poverty has led others to care only for themselves.

Laurence is particularly successful at portraying the "been-to," the young African who returns to his or her country after studying abroad, a figure that other expatriate writers have often treated unsympathetically. Killam has shown that once the university-educated African is back in the homeland he/she receives little sympathy from the very people who should understand this predicament best. Westerners who consider themselves enlightened because they admire the traditional cultures of Africa often choose to honour the old and "unspoilt" villager at the expense of the young African who has acquired an education as good if not better than their own. This gives rise to what in *Hopes and Impediments: Selected Essays 1965–1987* Achebe calls the European phenomenon of the "authentic African," that is one "as yet unspoilt by Western knowledge" (17–18).

In *Africa in English Fiction*, Killam particularly singles out Cary in this respect when discussing *The African Witch*. Louis Aladai, an Oxford graduate, is the archetypal educated African of English fiction, and the novel, writes Killam, "verges on total failure because of Cary's shoddy treatment of Aladai" (155). Laurence has considerable sympathy for the "been-tos" because such people were her friends. She has given a fascinating account of one such friendship in an article, "The Very Best Intentions," first published in 1964 and then included in *Heart of a Stranger*. She describes an African whom she calls Mensah, but whose true identity she does not disclose. He was "one of the first well-educated Africans" she met after arriving in the Gold Coast (34), and she was anxious to impress him with her "sympathetic, humanitarian, enlightened" attitude and her keen appreciation of African culture (37). His mocking reaction was offputting, and she was taken aback when he declared that Africa had no history or culture of its own. "History is too complicated a concept for us," Mensah told her sarcastically (36). Mensah resented westerners who enthused with nostalgia about traditional Africa while lamenting the changes education had brought. "[T]ense as strained wire" (34) and speaking with "a soft vehemence" when angered, he seemed to Laurence like a snake coiled taut and ready to strike. She eventually realized that Mensah's irony, "which was partly a kind of self-torture" (36), did not indicate a denial of the past but anxiety for the present and the future. Laurence and Mensah learnt to understand each other better and eventually enjoyed the frank interchange of ideas that is only possible between people who trust each other. Laurence made friends with Mensah's wife Honour, and the two women found themselves in hospital together when both gave birth to a son. Clearly her friendship with this couple influenced *This Side Jordan* and *The Tomorrow-Tamer* in a number of ways.

The portrait given of Mensah emphasizes his sardonic humour, and, as Morley demonstrates in "Canada, Africa, Canada: Laurence's Unbroken Journey," he is clearly the model for a number of Laurence's fictional characters (84). Her young intellectuals, often "been-tos," reject the customs and beliefs of their parents, as the young often do, but they also question the legacy of imperialism, the changes brought about in the name of progress. As a result they often feel isolated from their less-educated contemporaries who adapt happily to change without questioning its nature.

Victor Edusei is a forceful presence in *This Side Jordan* though his part in the plot is small. He spent six years in England, where he obtained a degree from the London School of Economics, and then studied accountancy and journalism. Back in Accra he works for a "small, vituperative" newspaper (51). Like Mensah, Victor hides his anger beneath a cultivated languor, a languor that is "dropped like a snake's sloughed-off skin" when he is angered (39). Victor's sardonic bitterness can even be heard when he makes fun of his friend Nathaniel, who teaches African history. Victor teases the idealistic Nathaniel by "claiming there were no African civilizations of the past worth mentioning" (22).

But Victor's anger is kept barely under control, and, when he visits Johnnie Kestoe's office, he wears his scruffiest clothes as an intentional insult. He arrives dressed in "Crumpled khaki trousers, torn at one knee . . ." and "[h]is yellow cotton jersey was splattered with food and grime. He wore canvas tennis shoes with no socks, and his heavy-jawed face bore a day's dark wiry growth" (38). This kind of behaviour is, as Laurence makes clear, a form of self-torture. Victor is intelligent and proud and determined to make no concessions to anyone. By far the most cynical person in the novel, Victor faces reality while others dream. He can foresee the problems that will follow independence and he expresses his fears with asperity. " 'The city,' " he predicts, " 'will be piled six feet deep with the backwash from the sewers. The spitting cobra and the spider will be happily nesting in the Assembly buildings, and we will be there gabbling about Ghana the Great' " (52). Yet his bitterness hides concern, and it is fitting that he is finally united with Charity, named after a virtue that he has only seemed to lack.

Victor has his counterparts in the *The Tomorrow-Tamer* stories. In "The Merchant of Heaven," Danso is metaphorically clothed in a cloak of mockery (63), but once again there is the association of snake imagery since he is literally dressed in a mammy-cloth shirt with "vivid viper markings." He becomes the personification of venom when angered by Brother Lemon; "Danso, slit-eyed and lethal, coiled himself up like a spitting cobra" (62). Danso's life has been changed by "a scholarship to an English university and an interest in painting" (53). His words often echo Victor's and, maybe, Mensah's. " 'My people . . . drink dreams like palm wine' " (67), Danso complains to Will, which brings to mind Victor's despairing cry: " 'We're a race of dreamers' " (52).

"The Drummer of All the World" contains Kwabena, who has not had the benefit of foreign education. He is a medical orderly but is hoping to get a scholarship to England to study medicine. Yet he is already subject to deep anger, which he turns on Matthew who laments the loss of the old traditions. Laurence understands Kwabena's anger, and so ultimately does Matthew, who finally admits that it was only "I who could afford to love the old Africa. Its enchantment had touched me, its suffering — never" (18).

As well as Victor and Danso and Kwabena, there is Moses in "Godman's Master." Four years at an English university have made him into a pharmacist, and he is seen as one of those trained to deliver the people from their bondage of poverty and disease. There is also Dr. Quansah in "The Rain Child," somewhat older and a specialist in tropical medicine after many years of study in Britain, who finds it difficult to readjust to life in the Gold Coast. There is a cameo portrait of a "been-to" in "The Pure Diamond Man" where Daniel, educated at an English college and now a journalist, returns to the Gold Coast where he runs into his childhood friend Tetteh. The two were together at school, where Tetteh was a resourceful if not a conscientious pupil. "Tetteh had not changed in the five years since they last met. If anything, he seemed younger now to Daniel, who had changed so much" (182).

The concern of people like Daniel and Mensah, those who have been trained as lawyers, journalists, doctors, and teachers, is primarily for the health, the education, the government (since independence is coming) of their country, and, though they value the old traditional customs, they cannot afford to dwell on the past when the present makes so many demands. Such people are vividly presented in Wole Soyinka's novel *The Interpreters*, which Laurence discusses in *Long Drums and Cannons*. She warmly commends the "picture Soyinka draws of the interpreters themselves," who are all intellectuals who went to England or America to study, because for Laurence "[e]ach man steps from the printed page with all the paradox and conflict and warmth of a living man" (74). It would not be unrealistic to compare her "interpreters" with Soyinka's. The Africans Laurence could sympathize with best were doctors, lawyers, and teachers, artists and writers — the young "interpreters" of their day, as Soyinka would call them. They are restless and no longer at ease, but feel they are back where they belong and where they must make their future.

Nathaniel, Laurence's most important African character, is also an interpreter, not always a confident one, but certainly one who struggles with the doubts and fears shared by many. In their discussions of *This Side Jordan*, Killam (Introd., *This Side Jordan* xi–xii) and Clara Thomas ("Morning Yet on Creation Day") have compared Nathaniel with Obi Okonkwo, the protagonist of Achebe's novel *No Longer at Ease*, published in 1960, the same year as *This Side Jordan*. Thomas remarks that Obi's story is like Nathaniel's in its basic elements, though not in its final dénouement. Both men, who initially anticipate the coming of independence with hope and idealism, lack the strength needed to succeed in a changing society, and both are driven to accept bribes, encouraging albeit on a minor scale the corrupt practices they have themselves castigated as evil. For Killam, the similarities indicate how useful Laurence's work is for an understanding of a particular period of African history. Nathaniel is, as it were, the page on which that history is written, and for most readers the success of the novel lies in their acceptance of his portrayal. Though Laurence herself came to doubt her achievement, Killam and Thomas believe firmly in Nathaniel's credibility.

Nathaniel is not a "been-to." It had been his ambition to win a scholarship to study abroad, but he failed to do himself justice in the final exams. He lacks the armour of confidence and scepticism that protects Victor Edusei, but he believes that time cannot be made to stand still and that, if the choice has to be made, then it is important to look forwards not backwards. Nathaniel, estranged from the past of his ancestors as a result of his mission schooling, feels he exists in a terrifying vacuum. " 'I belong between yesterday and today,' " says Nathaniel, and that, as his uncle recognizes, " 'is nowhere' " (106–07). However, he clings grimly to his hopes for the future.

Laurence sent the third draft of her novel, with the European chapters rewritten, to an American publisher, and it came back with a reader's report criticizing Nathaniel's interior monologues. Regretfully, she agreed "to cut some of the more emotive prose" from these monologues ("Ten Years' " 17), since what remains of Nathaniel's inner thoughts contains some of the most interesting material in the novel. As narrator she gave Nathaniel, and only Nathaniel, an inner voice, used for soliloquizing and dreaming. Hovering between first- and third-person articulation, this voice is usually introduced by a dash, a technique that Laurence developed fully for a later novel as she acknowledges when discussing *The Fire-Dwellers* in "Gadgetry or Growing: Form and Voice in the Novel." When she came to write Stacey's story, she felt she "had moved a long way . . . from the ornate and rather oratorical quality of Nathaniel's inner thoughts in *This Side Jordan*." Yet she still needed the same artificial means to convey "dreams, memories, inner running commentary," which in a brief and fragmented way would "convey the jangled quality of Stacey's life" (86).

Laurence thought that she had not entirely succeeded with Nathaniel's inner voice, perhaps feeling that the intensive research that had been required to produce it rendered it unnatural. It does, however, convey very forcefully the jangled quality of Nathaniel's life, and it is not unconvincing. Nathaniel has his ancestry in perhaps the best known of the Gold Coast civilizations, one that Laurence had read about in the work of Rattray, that of the Ashanti people who used their gold to build kingdoms of material and spiritual richness. They fought bravely to defend their way of life. Frederick Myatt notes that in 1824 they had defeated the British Governor, Sir Charles McCarthy, and made his skull into a royal drinking cup (17–18). Nathaniel, worried, short, and "a little stooped despite his youth" (17), is an unlikely descendant of his warrior ancestors. Yet Laurence succeeds with him as protagonist largely because he is weak and something of a failure, but buried within him lies memories of and an attachment to his splendid historical past. Nathaniel as a child suffered from fears and dreams, particularly those aroused by the terrible mysteries of the Akan religion, and he carried these hauntings into adulthood. Nathaniel's father, who had been a *kyerema* or drummer at the court of an Ashanti chief, worshipped the Akan gods and, indeed, had an important part to play in their religious ceremonies, but he sent his son, at the age of seven, to a mission school. The child was converted to Christianity so that "The stamp of the mission was deep on him" (28). Nathaniel turned away from the ways of his ancestors, but the splendid and terrifying — many of the British colonialists would have said barbaric and not entirely in a derogatory sense — customs of the Ashanti people are buried in his mind, like ashes in an urn that are "relics of another self, a dead world" (29). His ancestral past is still important to him, and the only time he holds his pupils' interest is when he teaches them about African civilizations. Then "his own fire" overcomes his usual hesitancy (22).

Nathaniel's inner monologues are not unsuccessful. In spite or some might consider because of them, Nathaniel is a far more credible character than Johnnie. Nathaniel's inner voice keeps up a constant commentary, but it breaks into lengthy and dramatic declamation when he has to meet the demands made on him by others, by his wife Aya or his mother-in-law Adua, by his maternal uncle Adjei or the European couple, Johnnie and Miranda Kestoe. But Nathaniel's first inner monologue comes when he recalls the recent funeral of his father, which was conducted with elaborate traditional ritual. The occasion is conjured up with considerable effect, the mourners singing the dirge, the drums beating in homage to a dead drummer and palm-wine clouding the mind. During the funeral, Nathaniel is swayed again by the old faith and in his thoughts turns against the Christian God who would condemn his father as an unbeliever. Laurence drew on *Funeral Dirges of the Akan People* by Nketia to describe the funeral. Nketia is an outstanding and imaginative scholar, and it is not surprising that his work should have captivated her. He prefaces his collection of dirges with a general introduction about funerals that clearly provided Laurence with important details. Nketia writes that the ". . . celebration of a funeral is regarded as a duty" (5). He describes how the body is prepared for the lying in state, and he remarks that the singing of the beautiful funeral dirges is the function of the women because ". . . wailing does not become a man" (8). Nketia adds that ". . . singers of the dirge rarely sit down: they pace up and down the place of the funeral, flanked on all sides by members of the lineage" (9). Among the dirges Nketia gives is one suitable for the funeral of a drummer (179). Drummers are known as sons of the crocodile because the crocodile is said to drum in the river with his great tail. "Hence all members of the drummers' group . . . are associated with it in much the same way as other groups are associated with other creatures" (178n2).

Nathaniel's recollection of his father's funeral accords with all this. He remembers his sister pacing the room "like a she-leopard caged" as she sings her mourning (29). Laurence chooses from Nketia's book, as appropriate for the funeral of a great drummer, an extract from the dirge that belongs to the drummers' group: " '*I am the drum of the Crocodile, / I can drum my own names and praises —* ' " (30).

Early in the novel Laurence takes the reader into one of Nathaniel's tormented dreams, one which has resulted from a bitter disagreement with his wife. They quarrel because Nathaniel wants his child to be born in the new city hospital, and he resists her pleas, seconded by her mother, that the new baby be born in her family village. He sees change as progress when it means that the village fetish priests and their insanitary charms will be replaced by qualified doctors and scientific medical care.

The argument leaves him disturbed by the polarity of village and city, and that night he dreams of wrestling with the forest monster Sasabonsam, who has changed into a city pimp, dressed in a pink nylon shirt, and dancing a highlife. Laurence probably intends the reader to recall her description of Nathaniel's colleague Lamptey when he "snaked into Nathaniel's classroom, his shoulders jiggling to the tune he whistled under his breath. He was elegantly outfitted in a lavender silk shirt and fawn draped trousers" (18). This is significant in light of the part later played by Lamptey in the rape of Emerald. Nathaniel, who has always associated Sasabonsam, the ogre of his childhood, with "the forest, old as the shadows" (74), is horrified to find the monster loose on the streets of the city where he planned a bright future for the son Aya would give him.

Sasabonsam is a powerful figure in Akan mythology, as Laurence's description of the monster indicates: "His fur was black and his fur was red and his face was a grinning mask of rage. . . . He jumped up and down like the great mad gorilla, and he drummed on his chest" (74). She was almost certainly indebted for this visual conception to Rattray, who describes Sasabonsam in his chapter on "Fairies, Forest Monsters and Witches" in *Religion and Art in Ashanti*. There he maintains that "The *Sasabonsam* of the Gold Coast and Ashanti is a monster which is said to inhabit parts of the dense virgin forests. It is covered with long hair, has large blood-shot eyes, long legs, and feet pointing both ways. It sits on high branches of an *odum* or *onyina* tree and dangles its legs. . . . I cannot help thinking that the original *Sasabonsam* may possibly have been the gorilla" (28). Sasabonsam also comes into Laurence's short stories. Matthew ("The Drummer of All the World") lies awake as a child dreaming of "the red-furred Great Devil, perched on his *odum* tree" (3), and in "The Tomorrow-Tamer" he is described as "red-eyed Sasabonsam, huge and hairy" (78).

Nathaniel liked to think of the city as modern and progressive and of himself as fortunate to have escaped from the backward ways of the village. His confidence, however, is precarious, and he is disturbed when his uncle arrives to ask him to return to the village. Adjei, who addresses Nathaniel as " 'my sister's son, and my heir' " (98), has a special authority because, as Rattray explains in *Religion and Art in Ashanti*, ". . . the dominant person in the family is the maternal uncle" (320). Summoning all his courage, Nathaniel refuses to comply, but the strain causes memories of the "rank, hot and terrible" jungle (105) that had surrounded his village home to invade his mind, bringing images that suggest the stranglehold exerted by things old and decayed. "The trees are hairy with strangler vines, beautiful green-haired death" (104). Hoping for a better future, Nathaniel had escaped along the great road excavated by whites, which cut through the forest and led to the city. He has no desire to return even though the promise of the road remains unfulfilled, and the city has proved no less a place of monsters than the forest.

Nathaniel's monologues are often rhetorical, with extensive use of repetition to convey the disturbance within: "— Oh, Nathaniel, how can a man forget? A man cannot forget. Deep, deep, there lies the image of what the eye has lost and the brain has lost to ready command" (104). They become even more dramatic after encounters with Europeans. He accompanies Miranda reluctantly to the market and, once there, is angered by her obsessive interest in the fetish stall. "What was it," he asks himself bitterly, "that made some Europeans behave this way when they came in contact with these piles of rotten bones? What was it made them want to touch, touch, touch, and stare — as though to remember a past that was for them so comfortingly long ago?" (158). This anger is followed by a long powerful monologue on the mixed nature of his heritage. "— My heritage," Nathaniel claims, "was the heritage of gold, the heritage of kings, of women splendid as silver, and the brave message of the drums." But there was another side to the coin, and Nathaniel also recalls the many useless fetishes in which the people trusted. Such things, and there are numerous illustrations of them in Rattray's books, could still be bought in the market where they excited the interest of curious Europeans like Miranda. With Nathaniel beside her she saw "reeking bones, dried leaves, stones, sea-shells curiously curved, small jingling bells, medicine yam like dead brown phalli, rock sulphur, bluestone, gourds that rattle when you shake them" (159). Nathaniel remembers with shame and horror how his two-year-old sister died while a fetish priest performed frightening and useless rites. This theme recurs in the short stories of *The Tomorrow-Tamer* where other "interpreters" react as Nathaniel does. Kwabena, for example, is bitter because his mother died after buying "bush medicine and charms instead of going to a doctor" (16).

Nathaniel recalls a different aspect of the past after his humiliating interview with Johnnie. As Nathaniel walks home, "a short stolid figure, his wide face expressionless" (208), he rages internally with hatred for all whites. He cries out against the years of exploitation, lamenting first the arrival of the slavers who "stirred the fires of tribal hate" (209) so that black sold black into bondage. Then Nathaniel describes the old fort that symbolizes the slave trade, Elmina Castle near Accra, built by the Portuguese in 1482.

The American Richard Wright, in search of his roots, visited Elmina Castle, "the great slave headquarters of the Gold Coast," and described it in his book *Black Power*: "I reached Elmina just as the sun was setting and its long red rays lit the awe-inspiring battlements of the castle with a somber but resplendent majesty. . . . I saw the dungeons where the slaves had been kept — huge, bare rooms with stone floors" (340–41). Wright's lament for the slaves, whom he thought of as his ancestors, is passionate. He conjures up a dramatic scene in which a "black woman torn away from her children" is "led toward those narrow, dank steps that guided her to the tunnel that directed her feet to the waiting ship that would bear her across the heaving, mist-shrouded Atlantic . . ." (341–42). Nathaniel's lament for the slaves is equally powerful. He imagines the conditions in the underground cells of the great stone-walled castle where the "sea-captains bid" for his ancestors and then led them along "the underground passage, out to the sea and the waiting ships" (210). Once again a theme that concerns Laurence in her novel is taken up in her short stories. In "Godman's Master," Moses remembers "hearing once about the fetish grove at Elmina, where a crucifix and baptismal bowl were said to be used in the rites of the god Nana Ntona, who had centuries before been Saint Anthony when the Portuguese built a chapel there. Moses had found a sour amusement in that transformation — history's barb, however slight, against the slavers" (141).

Nathaniel passes from the wrongs done by the slavers to the those committed by the British soldiers who fought and finally defeated his people in the Ashanti Wars. Nathaniel is versed in the details of the campaigns, how the British soldiers destroyed the Ashanti palaces and temples but did not succeed in capturing the sacred Golden Stool. Nathaniel makes only a brief reference to the Golden Stool, but it is sufficient to make a very important point. Laurence knew the history of the Golden Stool, which has been dramatically told by Rattray in *Ashanti*. He describes how the Asantehene Osai Tutu, the king who founded the great Ashanti empire, became the first guardian of the

Golden Stool. The priest Anotchi in front of Osai Tutu and his subjects "brought down from the sky, in a black cloud, and amid rumblings, and in air thick with white dust, a wooden stool with three supports and partly covered with gold" (289). Anotchi told the people that this stool, which must never be sat upon, "contained the *sunsum* (soul or spirit) of the Ashanti nation, and that their power, their health, their bravery, their welfare were in this stool" (290). Rattray writes,

> In 1896 during the Ashanti Wars the Asantehene Prempeh I was defeated and sent into exile but the Golden Stool was spirited away and hidden. In 1900 the British Governor precipitated the final phase of the Ashanti Wars by demanding that the Stool be produced so that he, as Queen Victoria's representative, might sit on it. However, the whereabouts of the Stool remained a secret until 1921 when its hiding place was nearly uncovered during the building of a new road. The custodians removed it secretly but robbers discovered its new hiding place and stripped it of its gold ornaments. This sacrilegious crime was only detected when an old woman recognized one of the stolen ornaments. The robbers were arrested and the whole of Ashanti went into mourning, but the Stool itself was undamaged. (9)

Myatt writes that Prempeh I returned from exile in 1923 and was reinstated not as Asantehene but as Kumasihene. He was succeeded by his son Otumfo Osei Agyeman "who in 1935 was appointed Asantehene on the re-establishment of the Ashanti federation; on this great occasion the Golden Stool was paraded in public for the first time" (183). When driven into a corner by his uncle, Nathaniel cries out against his ancestral past, indicating his knowledge of it. " 'Our souls are sick,' " he says in his anger, " 'with the names of our ancestors. Osei Tutu, he who made the nation, and Okomfo Anoye [Anotchi] the priest, he who gave the nation its soul, and Nana Prempeh exiled by the English' " (103).

After his interview with Johnnie, however, Nathaniel recalls with pride how the soul of the Ashanti nation was saved, but he laments that his people found it hard to hide their own souls from the missionaries. When the whites tried to steal the people's souls, they were often successful as Nathaniel knows from his own experience, but when "[t]hey tried to steal the Great Golden Stool, wherein lay the soul of Asante," they failed. "But we were as fire then," Nathaniel recalls. "It was enough. We said NO. We hid the nation's soul. But many men could not hide their own souls so well" (211). Nathaniel moves into his last monologue when he is reminded of how his own soul was lost. He is sitting with Aya in her church, listening to an African preacher who is saving souls in the name of Jesus. Laurence captures the mounting fervour well, just as she was later to convey the hypnotic effect of a similar chapel service in *A Jest of God*. The preacher's words, brilliantly caught, run as a counterpoint to Nathaniel's memories as he remembers how he acquired a new name and how "[t]he new name took hold, and the new roots began to grow. But the old roots never quite died, and the two became intertwined" (243).

Throughout the novel Nathaniel has come close to hysteria, feeling himself to be the battleground where the Akan and Christian gods fight for his soul. During the conflict, the two religions merge. They do after all have much in common. They both rely on powerful fetishes — "Nyame's Tree or the Nazarene's Cross" (32). They both unscrupulously use the splendour and drama of ritual, and they both have their devils of the night, Sasabonsam and Lucifer. However, Nathaniel also dreams of a triumphant integration of the two godheads when King Jesus, adorned all in gold, bracelets, anklets, shoulder chains, rings and headband, "arrayed like a King of Ashanti," with "the brown skin of His body . . . afire with the dust of gold," crosses the river of Jordan (77). This opens the way for the resolution at the end of the novel that sees Nathaniel as the ferryman who will take the soul of the future across Jordan where a new land awaits a new generation. The ground has been well prepared for this symbolic interpretation, which is expressed, perhaps a shade heavily, by Jacob Abraham Mensah, headmaster of Futura Academy, who says to Nathaniel,

> "You will be Futura's 'kra,' eh? How is that?"
> He laughed uproariously at his joke.
> Nathaniel tried to laugh, too, but the laughter stuck in his throat. He was to be its "kra," then, its soul, seeking perfection? Its guide in a new land, its ferryman across Jordan. All that, when he did not know the way himself?" (273)

Nathaniel's final vision is an intertwining of faiths that promises a new inheritance across Jordan and the possibility of hope.

Nathaniel's monologues have left some critics unconvinced of their effectiveness, even when they are persuaded of his credibility by his outward behaviour. In *Visions of Africa: The Fiction of Chinua Achebe, Margaret Laurence, Elspeth Huxley and Ngugi wa Thiong'o*, Micere Githae-Mugo admires the realistic picture Laurence gives of a weak and insecure man. Githae-Mugo, who considers Nathaniel's fantasizing confused and his behaviour unheroic, would be happier with Victor Edusei, "a man of principles and firm decisions," as hero of the novel. Githae-Mugo sees Nathaniel as a victim and an unsuitable protagonist, but yet ". . . his character is so well realised that I cannot agree with critics who find him unsatisfactorily drawn — Margaret Laurence herself among them" (142–51). Nathaniel is, indeed, carefully portrayed as a victim, caught between yesterday and today, but he is perhaps more coherent about his predicament than Githae-Mugo allows, and he is not without heroism in his make-up.

Nathaniel no less than Hagar is "rampant with memory" (*Stone Angel* 5), but his memories are not of an individual's so much as a nation's past. His inner voice takes on an oratorical richness that suggests the magnificent and terrible power of the Ashanti kings and priests. Throughout the novel, the reader is reminded of Nathaniel's apparent insignificance — a worried man with a perpetual frown and heavy horn-rimmed glasses. "He did not have the gift of spoken words — only of imagined words, when he made silent speeches to himself" (22). Insignificant as he may seem outwardly, it is not incredible that as a teacher of history and as the son of one of Ashanti's great drummers, he should rage inwardly and on a grand scale.

Laurence may have chosen a male protagonist because, as had been the case in Somaliland, she felt her own foreignness most when she watched the women. There are many memorable African women in her fiction, but they are usually seen through the eyes of their menfolk or of Europeans, to both of whom they are something of an enigma. They have a puzzling ability to accept change easily and adapt gracefully to a new environment. Nathaniel's wife Aya may be illiterate, but she has a wisdom he lacks and has become a Christian without losing her faith in the old traditions. In advance of the publication of *This Side Jordan*, an extract from the novel appeared in *Prism* where it reads like a short story. The extract focuses on the relationship between Nathaniel and Aya as they discuss superstition and faith with reference to the imminent birth of their child, for which they have waited eight years. Nathaniel is trusting in modern medicine for the safe delivery of the baby but Aya, after two miscarriages and a difficult pregnancy, wants the birth to take place in her village where her mother can care for her. The isolation of this scene in *Prism* draws attention to Laurence's sensitive portrayal of Aya's character, which is overshadowed in what is a crowded novel. Aya, as the *Prism* extract emphasizes, is more discerning and capable than her husband seems to realize. Nathaniel is often puzzled by his wife, and never more so than when he finds her in the dreaded hospital after giving birth to her son, wearing her new nightdress, calm and happy, and, though she cannot read, "looking at a magazine as though she had been used all her life to such things" (257).

In spite of a certain hesitancy in her interpretation of women and their role in society, Laurence fortunately found the nerve to develop in as much depth as the form of the short story allowed the viewpoint of Mammii Ama, market woman and seller of gourds, and to do so without the mediation of an outside observer. Mammii Ama is realized as an individual who becomes known and familiar, but she also grows larger than life in order to carry the weight of a nation's dreams and disillusions. Her story, "A Gourdful of Glory," includes a description of the coming of freedom, and it was chosen appropriately to close *The Tomorrow-Tamer* collection.

Mammii Ama, like so many of Laurence's characters, does not at first sight seem to be of much significance. She is a "petty trader" (225), not apparently one of the great queen mammies of the market place. She lives with her daughter Marcella and cares for Comfort, Marcella's illegitimate child. Marcella, who is a call girl at the Weekend in Wyoming (the night club featured in *This Side Jordan*), works by night and sleeps by day. So every morning Comfort goes to the market with her grandmother and helps with the calabash and pot stall that makes barely enough money to keep this small family fed. In more ways than one, Mammii Ama brings comfort to the market where her fellow stallholders, who are mostly poor and ailing, have come to rely on her warm good nature.

"A Gourdful of Glory" was first published in 1960, the same year as *This Side Jordan*, and it is set in a market similar to the one Miranda visits in the novel. However in the story, unlike the novel, the curious white woman and the embarrassed African guide — the Miranda/Nathaniel configuration — are described as they appear to the stall-holders. This time the scene is not viewed from the western perspective. The white woman — she does not need a name — has come to the market with Ampadu, a clerk who works in her husband's office. With "very little flesh on her, just yellow hide over bones" (233), she is another of Laurence's typically skeletal and jaundiced European women, very different from Mammii Ama with her well-fleshed hips and plump shoulders. Though the two women can only communicate with difficulty, they discuss the coming of freedom, and the white woman predicts with scorn that independence will not usher in the golden era Mammii Ama dreams of, a time when Africans will be given free bus rides and the means to buy fine white china dishes. Independence comes and is celebrated with a day of festivities, but next morning Mammii Ama finds nothing has changed. She makes her way to market, paying her bus fare as usual, and one of her first customers is the white woman, returning for amusement at Mammii Ama's expense. Mammii Ama refuses to be patronized and declares with bravado that her bus ride that morning had been free — " 'I no pay bus dis time' " — and she defiantly asserts her new freedom by refusing to sell the white woman one of her gourds, and it is a brave gesture since the white woman had agreed to pay far more than the going rate. When Mammii Ama snatches back her gourd and lifts it overhead, she feels as though she were holding "the world in her strong and comforting hands" (242), and for a moment she is earthbound no longer as her gourd is filled with golden sunshine. The story ends as the other stallholders gather round the comforting figure of Mammii Ama while she proclaims herself a "queen mammy." Indeed, Moki, the old firewood seller, has always thought of Mammii Ama "as though she were a queen mother" (228), and it should be remembered that at the courts of the Asantehenes the queen mothers had exercised great power. Like them Mammii Ama is a maternal and royal figure on whom others can rely.

This is one of the stories with which New quarrels in "The Other and I." He dislikes the rhetoric of the "closing flourish" (116), and he distrusts Laurence's use of traditional references. In his view because she is an outsider, she can only give a unreliable reconstruction of the past. Yet the customs of the Ashanti people have been well documented by Africans and westerners, and they are not so strange as to be incomprehensible to a foreigner. The peoples of the world have more in common than is sometimes recognized. Religion, politics, social conduct, and the arts may all find expression in varying ways, marking the differences between races, but they come into being because of needs and principles shared by all men and women. Hermann Hesse's Joseph Knecht, the Master of the Glass Bead Game, remarks that there are no two persons, let alone people, in the world between whom complete understanding is possible, but we have enough shared experience to make communication in some form always attainable. He concludes that, ". . . though we may speak different languages, if we are men of good will we shall have a great deal to say to each other, and beyond what is precisely communicable we can guess and sense a great deal about each other. At any rate let us try" (275). Fiction is a medium where guessing is permitted, and, since Laurence was certainly a woman of good will, her attempt to communicate with the other is both legitimate and valuable. Mammii Ama the queen mother is as convincing a creation as Mammii Ama the market woman — both are figments of Laurence's imagination, but she had the knowledge needed to make them both credible.

The Ashanti traditions Laurence reconstructs were different from her own, but she honoured them nonetheless and could sense their value. She realized that one way to preserve them in a changing society that still had need of them was to hold on to them as symbols. She deliberately exploits Mammii Ama's symbolic potential throughout the story and can see no problem in structuring it into her realistic narrative. Laurence delights in symbolic reference, but she employs it with a care that keeps her realism intact. Most readers are prepared to accept the two Mammii Amas as one, unworried by the intertwining of realism and symbolism, a partnership that many would accept as natural in a work of fiction.

Yet the story is built on a duality, as Coral Ann Howells has demonstrated in "Free-Dom, Telling, Dignidad." Its two-fold nature, however, does not lie in Mammii Ama's double significance. The narrative is divided neatly and intentionally by the coming of Ghanaian independence. In both parts of the story, that is before and after independence, the colonizer comes face to face with the colonized when the white woman and Mammii Ama meet. They debate the meaning of freedom. For Mammii Ama the word itself is divided into two, and she finds that after independence "Free-Dom" needs to be re-interpreted. The white woman who has always understood the prosaic meaning of freedom is of minor importance in the story since the days of imperialism are passing. She is there as the catalyst that brings about Mammii Ama's realization of what freedom means in real terms for herself and the market people. Once Mammii Ama knows this, she can assert her own freedom from the white woman, as she does with a brave lie, knowing that there is "a truth in her words, more true than reality" (242). Accepting the reality was a painful and humiliating experience, but the miracle of this story is that Mammii Ama wrestles from the wreck of her dreams a vestige of hope, which will give her the courage to continue the daily struggle. As Howells persuasively concludes, ". . . the narrative has its triumph, doublefaced as it is" (39–46).

Laurence chose her central character for this story about freedom with care. It is now widely recognized how necessary the market woman is to Ghana's economic and political well-being, and Mammii Ama succeeds as a symbol because she represents in her small way an important force. Her daily routine is carefully put together with realistic detail. We know how early she gets up every day and the miserable inadequacy of her breakfast of tea and cold yam. We can see her in her fish-patterned cloth holding Comfort's small hand as they clamber together onto the crowded bus to go to market. We honour her position among the market people, admire her zest for life, and are prepared to see her both for what she is and for what she can represent.

The story can sustain complex interpretations because the realistic and the symbolic have been carefully and imaginatively intertwined. The market place represents a nation and the stallholders its mixed population, while Mammii Ama, the royal palm, the "queen-mammy," will endure beyond the hour of disillusion to give comfort to her people. Mammii Ama's role is unashamedly and clearly stated: "When she spoke, it was not to the white woman. It was to the market, to the city, to every village quiet in the heat of the sun. She spread her arms wide, as though she would embrace the whole land" (237). So the reader is prepared for the splendid and surely acceptable finale. "Like a royal palm she stood, rooted in magnificence, spreading her arms like fronds, to shelter the generations" (244). This conclusion is certainly rhetorical, but appropriately so since it represents a defiant flourish by the human will against despair.

Mammii Ama, Nathaniel, Victor Edusei, and Candace, among many others, represent the hopes, fears, dreams, and disillusions of a whole nation as independence is realized. This in no way diminishes their individuality. As individuals they come from a wide spectrum, and they include many memorable people. Laurence signals their importance as she names them. There are those who keep their traditional African names, Aya, Mammii Ama, Kwabena, Kwaale, and Kofi, and they are names of dignity that recall the old ways. There are the new names that appeal to the young who are keen to adopt new ways: Victor, Marcella, and Candace. There are also the mission names, which, as Mammii Ama knows, are "decent" names that have been used for so many years that they seem "to have been African always" (226). Among these are numbered the Old Testament names weighty with associations — Abraham, Moses, Nathaniel, and Ruth — and names that speak of virtues — Mercy and Comfort. When the roll-call is made of Laurence's black players, it becomes clear that she has assembled a cast of characters who together represent a remarkable achievement.

7

An African Consciousness

While she placed more importance on people than on place, it is clear that Africa itself plays a starring role in her work. There is a danger inherent in using the terms Africa and African in a generalized sense, since the continent is one of great diversity and, as Abiole Irele points out in *The African Experience in Literature and Ideology*, there is no African nation as such. To assume that Laurence's observations are valid beyond their particular local reference would be to do her an injustice. However, Irele does think there is "an African sentiment, an African consciousness," that implies "a common African vision unified not only by history but by a fundamental groundwork of values and of cultural life" (48), and, if we seek to understand the nature of this great continent as a whole, then the individual pieces, such as those Laurence provides, have importance. She will not mislead those who want to learn about the continent, and through her writing the special nature of Africa makes itself known.

The narrative voice of "A Gourdful of Glory," which clearly speaks on behalf of Africans, and Mammii Ama in particular, is used with equal authority in "The Tomorrow-Tamer" and "Godman's Master." These three stories are told with elegance and dramatic effect, but beneath the crafted writing a passionate commitment to freedom, and specifically to freedom for the people of the Gold Coast, makes itself heard. The right of the individual to live in freedom and peace was a cause Margaret Laurence supported with passion, a passion that took her in the last years of her life into the political at the expense of the literary arena. In these three short stories, however, her concern for an African cause is evident but carefully controlled. The narration moves easily with the use of dialogue and plain reporting, but it also rises to eloquence when the occasion demands. In "Figments of a Northern Mind," Godfrey had praise for *The Tomorrow-Tamer* because in it Laurence combines an objectivity that "comes from studying a foreign culture" with a subjectivity that arises from an "emotional involvement with it" (92). She achieves the same effect in *The Diviners*, when Christie tells his tales about the Scottish clearances, speaking as Piper Gunn who had *"the voice of drums and the heart of a child, and the gall of a thousand, and the strength of conviction"* (329).

The strong conviction of her African story-teller's voice can be clearly heard if the stories that are told from the African perspective are compared to "The Perfume Sea," which is narrated with very different effect. The story of Mr. Archipelago and Doree has a disturbing fairy-tale quality, and it is told at an unhurried pace, set by the opening description of a small African town sleeping in the mid-day sun. More than any of the other stories, this one extends its reference beyond Africa, to which Mr. Archipelago and Doree have drifted from across the seas. Africa, writes Greene in *A Burnt-Out Case*, encourages drift because ". . . the high tide deposits the flotsam on the edge of the shore and sweeps it away again in its withdrawal" (119). " 'No question of it,' " says Mr. Archipelago, " 'I am flotsam' " (20). He and Doree make no attempt at integration and shut themselves up in an enchanted walled garden on a coastal headland. Though their hairdressing salon has depended for its survival first on European and later on African custom, Mr. Archipelago and Doree live apart from both communities in a dwelling "off by itself" (31). Mr. Archipelago it seems is an Italian, and when creating him Laurence must have had in mind the Italians, permanent exiles, with whom she sympathized in Somaliland, where they "lived apart, in a separate community" (*Prophet's* 145). Mr. Archipelago comes from Italy, from Genoa, the city the Laurences visited on their way to Somaliland. Mr. Archipelago spent many hours of his childhood in the Staglieno cemetery in Genoa where the white marble angels guard the tombs of the rich, a scene remembered with precision in *The Prophet's Camel Bell* and at the beginning of *The Stone Angel*. The narrator's touch needs to be light to tell this fairy-tale and to carry off without sentimentality the apparently happy ending for this strange pair, Beauty and the Beast or perhaps the two lost Babes in the Wood, who are saved by an act of mercy. The ending of their story is muted and ambiguous. Mr. Archipelago and Doree stand holding hands looking out to sea, and the effect is Keatsian, as though his nightingale is once more charming listeners at "magic casements, opening on the foam / Of perilous seas, in faery lands forlorn" ("Ode to a Nightingale" lines 69–70).

"The Tomorrow-Tamer" and "Godman's Master" tell of people who belong to the land, whose past, present, and future lie in Africa; they have not been washed up on its shores like bits of flotsam. Since it gives the collection its title, Kofi's story can be expected to bear an important theme. It is a story firmly rooted in the present, but, like the bridge with which it is concerned, it links the present to both the past and the future. The tale is told not from the viewpoint of the Europeans, whose part in the story is secondary, but from the perspective of those to whom the land belongs and who will be its mythmakers in years to come.

In an interview Sullivan talked to Laurence about the genesis of "The Tomorrow-Tamer" story, described by its author as "one of the most difficult stories [she] ever wrote" (64). Laurence and her husband went one day to visit the construction site of the spectacular bridge across the Volta, and there they met a friend of their cook. A week later she learnt from her cook that his friend had fallen to his death while working on the bridge. The story grew from this seed, and it was a story that lent itself to allegorical amplification without the loss of its hold on contemporary relevance and reality. Even a history book of the period points to the symbolic significance of the new Volta bridge. W.E.F. Ward, when describing development projects in Ghana, explains that ". . . the Volta, hitherto untamed, was bridged for the first time in 1956, but that is only the beginning of its servitude" (413). Laurence knows that the bridge will bring change, destroying the sacred grove in Kofi's village, but opening up the future for the young. Reaction to the bridge depends on whether it is seen as threat or promise. Laurence used her imagination, nourished by her "reading of the different religions," to conceptualize how the bridge could be sanctioned by the village people whose lives it so dramatically alters (Interview with Sullivan 65). She shows how Kofi's death enables the villagers to accept the bridge as their own.

While the narrating voice is unidentified, there is no doubt that it speaks on behalf of the villagers. Their feelings are described. They see the Europeans as outsiders who require the services of an interpreter to make themselves understood. Laurence clearly indicates the racial identity of her narrator. For example, when the whites arrive in the village, their strange complexions, which in the heat turn "red as fresh-bled meat," cause uneasiness, and the narrator is responding as an African: "Red was the favoured colour of witches and priests of witchcraft, as everyone knew . . ." (85). The same African consciousness is evident in "The Voices of Adamo." Adamo's immediate reaction to Captain Fossey is one of repulsion partly because of the Englishman's reddish hair "which seemed to Adamo a particularly offensive colour, for he associated it with forest demons who were said to be covered with red hair" (218).

All the images and references in Kofi's story were chosen to confirm the African identity of the narrator. This is a village like Nathaniel's childhood home, where the children dream at night of "red-eyed Sasabonsam, huge and hairy, older than time and always hungry" (78). To describe the excited children, the narrator likens them to "a pot of soup boiling over" (79) and Kofi's "brittle and small and fleshless" grandmother is compared to "the empty shell of a tortoise" (83). When the Volta bridge is painted with aluminum the story-teller reminds his audience of the Ashanti silver stool, which was always the property of the queen mother. "The bridge was being covered with silver," we are told, as though it were a great queen's chair, which would be covered with "thin-beaten silver leaf" because "Silver was the colour of queen mothers, the moon's daughters, the king-makers" (100). When Kofi stands on the top of one of the towers of the bridge, he sees other villages, their "huts like small calabashes in the sun," and the new road, stringing "both village and bridge as a single bead on its giant thread" (102). Finally when he falls to his death it is in a great arch "like a thrown spear" (103).

All the details of village life are sharply drawn. Laurence surely went inside a village store similar to Danquah's where "two fly-specked pink paper roses" stand in a jam jar on the counter along with an assortment of bottles: "gin, a powerful red liquid known as Steel wine, the beer with their gleaming tops, and several sweet purple Doko-Doko which the villagers could afford only when the cocoa crop was sold" (84). The narrator also describes the meeting of village elders and preparations for the evening meal in Kofi's hut. Laurence may not herself have witnessed such scenes, but she knew enough to make them convincing for most of her readers. Finally, as Laurence told Sullivan, she created Kofi's songs herself, but she did so by modelling them on those collected by Rattray and Nketia (64).

It may seem overweening and foolhardy for a foreigner to seek such a close identification with the dreams and hopes of a different race, but it was not done unthinkingly or carelessly in this case. Laurence's keen powers of observation backed up by extensive reading and her considerable talent as a writer equipped her for the task. The authorial voice of confidence with which she speaks in "The Tomorrow-Tamer" has been legitimately acquired, and it is controlled with integrity and artistic skill.

"The Tomorrow-Tamer," a thoroughly successful story on both an allegorical and a realistic level, is equalled in the collection only by "Godman's Master," a tale in which Europeans have no part. The narration follows Moses on a personal level, but the story also contains a parable, which refers to the nature of freedom and the difficulties attendant on winning it. The parable has a personal and a universal relevance and also, appropriately, a particular national one since it was written with the independence movement in the Gold Coast in mind. Laurence agreed that "The story is allegorical to a very large extent. But it's a personal story of the little dwarf as well" (Interview with Sullivan 65).

Laurence found the idea for Godman in Rattray's work. When he travelled through the Ashanti regions of the Gold Coast, he notes in *Religion and Art in Ashanti*, he met "persons of both sexes, of very diminutive stature . . . called in Ashanti *pirafo* or dwarfs" (26). Most memorable of these "little folk" was "Kojo Pira — the wise little man," less than three feet in height, who "had been court-jester to many Ashanti kings" (26, 27). Rattray has a photograph of Kojo Pira standing next to an average-sized man, which gives some idea of the effect Moses and Godman would have created when together. Godman complains to Moses about his size and the difficulty of achieving independence now that his traditional profession is lost to him. 'Some of the *pirafo*," Godman says, "used to be court jesters to the kings of Ashanti. But not any more. No one wants to laugh any more, perhaps" (145).

Moses takes Godman from the forest to the city, and both locations are graphically created with their noise and colour. The village is seen in a torrential downpour, and Moses takes refuge with the villagers in the one chop-bar, very like Danquah's store, for on the counter "stood an old marmalade jar full of pink and dusty paper roses" (137). Godman finds a temporary home with Moses in his rented rooms in Accra, and their days together, the domestic activities they share, are realistically described to include all the ordinary details of an ordinary life.

However, the story has clear allegorical implications. Godman is delivered from bondage by Moses from Faru's house in a scene with biblical and colonial associations. Moses and Godman leave the forest in a downpour along the red muddy road, as the children of Israel crossed the Red Sea between the tall banks of water. Faru is seen as an African Pharaoh, his cheekbones "high and prominent" (140), and Godman once safe from his tyranny must start the long journey which will end without Moses in the promised land across Jordan. The story is rich in symbolic imagery, but it is incorporated carefully and is not obtrusive. As in *This Side Jordan*, the colonial history of the Gold Coast is suggested by a collection of ornaments. In the novel they were found in the sordid bedroom above the Weekend in Wyoming nightclub; in "Godman's Master" the same "conglomeration of symbols" appear in the sinister room in Faru's village hut where the oracle Godman is kept imprisoned. In Faru's room there is "a string of Muslim prayer beads," "an ebony cross," and two African "figures male and female, crudely carved in a pale wood." The room makes Moses feel "queasy and apprehensive" and fills the villagers with "nervous reverence" (141).

The allegorical beginning to the story allows Laurence to close it with a simple image that has wide reference. When Godman, the individual, takes "his place with the other performers on the broad and grimy stage" (160), it is to demonstrate the freedom he has won, in spite of its insecure and limited nature. In this way Laurence can acknowledge the emergence of a young and independent nation, proud to take its place in the world, however imperfect that world may be. The political background behind "Godman's Master" and also "The Tomorrow-Tamer" may seem out-dated now, but the voice of conviction responsible for their narration retains its strength today and acts as a persuasive reminder of the values of freedom and justice.

Laurence's careful constructions of African scenes are alive with movement and colour, but they would have been nothing more than museum pieces if she had not brought to them the literary gifts of fine writing and imaginative interpretation. Rattray, whose work she used so extensively, knew that his anthropological texts could not convey fully the reality of the Ashanti culture he admired, so he turned to fiction in an attempt to give life to his research. The result was the novel *The Leopard Priestess*, published in 1934. It tells of the forbidden love of Opoku for the priestess Amalagane in a world where whites exist only as rumour. The attempt defeats itself because Rattray had little talent for fiction and because he was consciously writing for an ignorant European public to whom he must explain much of his subject matter. Laurence does not make such concessions. Her story-teller expects to be understood without the aid of comment or explanation. It must be added that since she never sees her characters with the eyes of an anthropologist — even when she is indebted to so fine an anthropologist as Rattray — the need for explanatory footnotes is seldom felt.

Fiction, Laurence writes in "Ivory Tower or Grassroots?: The Novelist as Socio-Political Being," is "primarily a matter of portraying individual characters," but people "do not live in a vacuum" (15). She makes this point when discussing the work of Achebe. Like him, she maintains that individual characters must be seen to move through their history. "Fiction has many facets," she explains. "For myself, it encompasses both history and belief, both social and spiritual themes. It speaks first and foremost of individual characters, and through them it speaks of our dilemmas and our aspirations, which are always in some way or other those both of politics and of faith" (25). Laurence fills in the local African scene comprehensively. She examines in detail social and spiritual themes as she takes account of politics and faith. In this area she comes closest to contemporary African writers, and her interpretation of the issues she considered important is shared in many instances by Africans themselves.

Religious issues can be especially complex; they play a part in her novel and in three of her stories: "The Drummer of All the World," "The Merchant of Heaven," and "The Pure Diamond Man." Laurence takes a stand shared by many Africans towards the work of missionaries. Any attempt, past or present, by bigoted missionaries to destroy traditional religion is to be deplored. Laurence believed that salvation was not something that could be imposed from outside; ". . . one man cannot find it for another man, and one land cannot bring it to another" (18). Fanatics such as Matthew's father or Brother Lemon may initially win disciples, but in Laurence's fiction their initial success is never sustained, usually because the Africans in the congregation have interpreted the new message from the pulpit in their own way. This is something Brother Lemon finds difficult to accept since his eyes are closed to any viewpoint but his own.

Yet Christianity, like Islam, has been successful in West Africa and altered the lives of many people. In the Gold Coast the Christian God did win true converts, and there are many churches, like the one Aya goes to, that have large congregations. They are African churches where God has proved adaptable and where those who mourn the displacement of the old faith can be consoled, as Nathaniel finally is, because their traditional beliefs can continue alongside the new religion. The conclusion of *This Side Jordan* contains the affirmation of this possibility.

In Laurence's novel, Christianity and the Akan faith are constantly compared, and the comparisons continue in the stories. She recognizes that the first missionaries opposed any integration of the two faiths. Indeed they condemned the Akan faith as pagan. It is perhaps natural for a priest to protect the power of his god and to oppose the intrusion of any other god. Compromise would indicate diminished faith. In the land of Egypt, the Children of Israel grew lax in their adherence to Jehovah and began to worship the old gods so that Moses had to break "the idols of his own people" (5). In Faru's house, where Godman is imprisoned, an African Moses is distressed by the assimilation of faiths evident in the decadent images that hang on the walls. He found that the "presence of the crucifix bothered him" in what seemed to him a heathen room where he was aware above all of the one eye of Faru the priest "winking goldenly" (141). Matthew's father broke "idols literally as well as symbolically" in defence of his jealous god, but the "idols" he was breaking were the true gods of the place (4–5).

All religions have their mysterious sides, which is why Danso can equate Brother Lemon with the superstitious fetish priests he came across in his childhood. However, tolerance on both sides can lead to an understanding that there is also a common and ethical denominator, as Laurence demonstrates in "The Pure Diamond Man," where the Reverend Timothy Quarshie of Saint Sebastian Mission, after fourteen years of friendly overtures, finally persuades Bonsu, the fetish priest in Tetteh's village, to come to the Christian church. In *Things Fall Apart*, Achebe draws the same parallels. In his novel the missionary Mr. Brown, his name indicative of his willingness to compromise, spends long hours with the village elder, Akunna, discussing their two faiths. Akunna and Mr. Brown recognize that the point where their two religions can harmonize is in the conception of a Supreme Being. Mr. Brown is replaced by the dogmatic

Reverend James Smith who thinks in terms of "black and white" and, of course, of black as evil (130).

Most African religions recognize a Supreme Being. The Igbos call him Chukwu; the Ashantis call him Nyame. Rattray argues passionately that the Supreme Being is an innate African conception. In this he goes against the belief, current at the time, that the Africans borrowed the idea from Christianity or Islam. Rattray holds it as natural for an all-powerful god to sanction the existence of lesser deities, as, indeed, the Christian God immortalized his saints. Nyame in his full glory was unapproachable, so he delegated his responsibilities to lesser gods, spirits of rivers and lakes, who were more accessible and became for all practical purposes more important. Rattray writes of these lesser gods that ". . . their power emanates from various sources, the chief of which is from the great spirit of the one God, graciously delegated by Him, that the affairs of mankind may have attention given to them" (*Ashanti* 144).

Rattray recognized that belief in a Supreme Being could act as a unifying force between people of different faiths since "In a sense . . . it is true that this great Supreme Being, the conception of whom has been innate in the minds of the Ashanti, is the Jehovah of the Israelites" (*Ashanti* 141).

Danquah explores more fully the nature of Nyame. He writes that ". . . the Akan designate the Supreme Being by three distinctive names, Onyame, Onyankopon and Odomankoma," and that the "most used name of God in Akanland is Onyame, often pronounced Nyame" (30). The "O" in front of the name is a vocative prefix. Danquah conjectures that the name means "bright" or "shining," whereas Rattray always associated Nyame with sky. "The Nature of Nyame," Danquah concludes, "is that he is the Shining Power," but he is also seen as Creator, Inventor, Carver, and Architect (40). His different names reflect this multiplicity. Onyame according to Danquah is the general name, Onyankopon is the more "knowable" aspect of the god, often closely associated with the sun, and Odomankoma is the god as creator or carver. These names are carefully used by Laurence.

Danquah was able to reconcile the Christian and Akan faiths through the Supreme Being, and he believed that "God is not of several kinds, but he can be known under several degrees or colours, for each people has a name for God, and in the name is to be found that quality or colour in God which most appeals to their racial minds" (1). Rattray had already taken the idea this far, but Danquah would take it even further. While both of them equate Nyame and the God of the Old Testament, only Danquah identifies the Ashanti equivalent of Christ the mediator. He believes that enshrined in the Golden Stool of Ashanti is the spirit of a Nana, once a king or elder, who acted as "a bridge over the gulf" between people and god. Danquah praises the Englishman's insight into the Akan religion, which went far but not far enough. Danquah, always an eloquent writer, concludes that ". . . great as Rattray's discoveries make him in our estimation for the immensity of thought he brought to his quest, his conclusions, however, confirm the view that while he saw shafts of light here and there in the Akan religious dawn, he just missed seeing the whole sunshine" (7).

Laurence was attracted by Danquah's argument, and she was to return to it in *Long Drums and Cannons* where she calls for "[t]he respect which Dr Danquah advocated towards one another's gods . . ." (15). She found his and Rattray's discussions of the Supreme Being enlightening, and the result is that her references to the Akan faith are numerous. Matthew recalls that in his childhood he was interested in Nyame, something he kept secret from his missionary parents, and when alone he used to recite "some of the other names of Nyame — the Shining One, Giver of Rain, Giver of Sun. Once for a whole year [he] called God by the name of Nyame in [his] silent prayers" (10).

In *Long Drums and Cannons*, Laurence notes that Danquah, pleading for a spirit of understanding and tolerance between people of different faiths, felt a start could be made if the gods were called by their proper names. Nyame should be called Nyame and not " 'the Sky God,' " which was a "patronising" name (15). The names for the Supreme Being — God, Allah, Nyame — should always be used. Laurence took this suggestion seriously. In *A Tree for Poverty*, she always referred to Allah as "God," which seemed right at the time, but after reading Danquah she saw it as disrespectful. So when she chose extracts from *A Tree for Poverty* for inclusion in *The Prophet's Camel Bell*, she made a few revisions, the most important of which was to change "God" in every instance to "Allah," honouring him, as appropriate, with his Islamic name. Nyame is carefully evoked by his proper names throughout *This Side Jordan*. The magnificent opening to chapter four suggests his power as Nyankopon the sun god. "The sun sucked everything into itself. The circle of gold,

Nyankopon's image, which shot its arrows of life into man and leaf, now shrivelled the life it had made" (61).

Laurence believed that the attempt by missionaries, be they Matthew's parents or Brother Lemon, to force their image of god on others was bound to fail, but she saw that Christianity had succeeded when the people had been able to interpret the new faith in their own way. In *This Side Jordan* the congregation at Aya's evangelical church, which is strongly supported by women, sings and rejoices in the name of Jesus, but Aya calls God "Nyame" and interprets his teaching "in terms of the faith of her people" (108). The need to achieve this synthesis is indicated in "The Merchant of Heaven." Brother Lemon is a false prophet and he represents intolerance, prejudice, and superstition. When Will and Danso attend his church, they are reminded of the old superstitious and cruel rites practised by unscrupulous fetish priests. They watch Brother Lemon perform in "the flickering flarelight of torches and tapers," surrounded by acolytes and dressed in a "resplendent peacock-blue" gown; he preaches of hell and damnation, and, as a fetish priest might, he tempts his congregation with the promise of a cure for their ills. For Danso the comparison becomes a cruel mockery when his mother, who has a malignant growth and " 'will not see a doctor,' " falls down in front of Brother Lemon in the vain hope that he will cure her (66–67).

In order to open Brother Lemon's eyes, Danso paints Christ as an African, but he knows that in truth God is neither black nor white, and it will only be possible to portray Him correctly if humankind can " 'invent new colours' " (76). It seems there is no cure for Brother Lemon, who remains blind to any conception of God that does not match his own. He is as much a cripple as the "damaged creatures" who cluster round the Son of Man in Danso's picture, so it can be presumed he will find forgiveness even if he never perceives the extent of his own blindness (77). Danso's picture does, however, enable Will "to see through black and white, until they merge and cease to be separate or apart" (77). Dorothy Livesay, another Canadian whose rapport with Africa was close, learnt like Laurence to see God in a new light. During the early 1960s she lived in Northern Rhodesia, shortly to become Zambia. One of the poems written out of this experience, "Before Independence (Zambia)," published in 1964 in a slim volume called *The Colour of God's Face*, tells of a visit to a cathedral in Africa. The poet, noticing the presence of black people in the paintings and statues, realizes that "Christ was a black man too" (*Collected Poems* 256).

Such illuminations led to the need for revision; the changing of "God" to "Allah" is an example. Laurence always took revision seriously and, as her daughter has confirmed in her preface to *Dance on the Earth*, she "would normally write at least three drafts of a manuscript, and sometimes as many as five" (xii). By choice she allowed only her final draft to appear publicly. However, a comparison of the texts of the short stories as they first appeared and after they had been revised for *The Tomorrow-Tamer* provides a rare opportunity to watch her scrutinizing her own work. Many of the changes are questions of stylistic detail, toning down a purple passage, for example, but some have larger implications and show her arguing out questions of politics and faith. The theme of "The Merchant of Heaven" is obviously one to which Laurence attached great importance, and writing the story seems to have given her some problems. It was the second of her stories to be published, appearing in the September 1959 edition of *Prism*. Laurence made a considerable number of changes to the story before including it in *The Tomorrow-Tamer*. One of these concerns the bitter and somewhat confused argument between Danso and Brother Lemon about the Akan Supreme Being. While Danso had come to distrust the fetish priests who traded on his people's superstitions, he still valued the underlying moral principles of the Akan faith. When "The Merchant of Heaven" first appeared it contained this passage:

> "You are thinking of fetish," [Danso] said curtly. "But that is not all. *There may be a lot of gods, Mr. Lemon, but the most important aren't worshipped through images. How about that?* Invisible, intangible — real proper gods. *And above all others is Nyame the Creator. In time* if we'd been left alone, our gods would have grown, as yours did, into One. It was happening already — we needed only a prophet. But now our prophet will never come. Sad, eh?" (62; emphasis added)

Danso's explanation in the heat of the argument is confused. When Laurence came to look over the story, she saw the confusion and decided the easiest but somewhat unsatisfactory correction was to cut part of the passage without rewriting it (she took out the italicised parts). The scissors were also used to take out Danso's confession that he first thought of painting Jesus as a " 'caricature' " behind a fetish mask in order to " 'really shock' " Brother Lemon (74). She took out a further exchange between Danso and Brother Lemon that accounts for the title of the story. Brother Lemon questions Danso's right to paint " 'the throne of heaven.' " In reply Danso quotes from *The Merchant of Venice*, " 'Hath not a Jew eyes?' " a reference that is lost on Brother Lemon, itself an ironic comment on the cultural backgrounds of the two men. In another long passage, which she also later cut, she explains Danso's thinking at length. "To Danso, the word 'pagan' meant only the fear-producing aspects of any religion. Fetish and witchcraft came under that heading; so, also, did the evangel's hell. But the old Akan devoutly washing his soul at the proper times, to keep it from harm or hate, and seeing above all lesser gods a mother-father of Creation — that was a different matter entirely" (63). The final version of her story makes this statement forcefully enough, and she may have felt that she initially made her point with too heavy a hand. However, the number of changes indicates her interest in this religious question.

Laurence would have found particularly attractive the idea of a Supreme Being who, though more often than not referred to as He, was sufficiently undefined to represent "a mother-father of Creation." She has explained in *Dance on the Earth*, her memoir, that as she grew older it became important for her "to recognize the female principle as part of the Holy Spirit" (13). She was undoubtedly thinking back to the Ashanti faith when she added that ". . . those very religions that early Christian missionaries believed so evil had and still have the concept of a god unseen and above all other gods, a god both male and female, mother and father, earth and sky" (15).

Political issues are also important in Laurence's fiction, but it is her perspective of them that dates her work. Her novel and her short stories, as she herself has said in "Ten Years' Sentences," "were written out of the milieu of a rapidly ending colonialism and the emerging independence of African countries." She added that "[t]hey are not entirely hopeful books, nor do they, I think, ignore some of the inevitable casualties of social change, both African and European, but they do reflect the predominantly optimistic outlook of many Africans and many western liberals in the late 1950s and early 1960s" (18). In fact, her record of an actual time and place is of lasting value because of its testimony to a moment in history. In Ghana by 1963, when *The Tomorrow-Tamer* was published, many of the promises made to Mammii Ama and her compatriots had been broken, and Nkrumah, the nation's *Osagyefo* or Redeemer, whom Mensah in *Heart of a Stranger* described as the "African king-figure, the greatest of all paramount chiefs" (40), had lost the trust of his people. When revising "The Drummer of All the World" for *The Tomorrow-Tamer*, she was able to erase one passage that had become a mockery. In the original version published in *Queen's Quarterly*, Nkrumah was seen as his people's saviour, as "a leader with thoughtful, anxious eyes, trying to untangle the Ananse-like web of conflicting tribes and beliefs, a man who had impulsively cried — 'If I refuse to lead them, they will kill me!' " (499). Laurence predicted to some extent the disillusion that would follow independence. Any note of optimism is usually dampened by a voice of caution — Victor Edusei's, for example — and so her political comments are not based on complacent euphoria. Yet, in the days before neo-colonialism became a danger, it was natural to welcome the end of the colonial era and look forward to a better future, as many of her characters do.

"Mask of Beaten Gold" is a personal story, but it is able to make some political points from a later perspective. It was the last of her African stories to be written. The action is not tied to a specific date, but Philip and Candace seem to be living in independent Ghana. There is a reference to the wealthy Ghanaians who live in dwellings that stand out "in unabashed opulence beside the yapping and rakish shanties of the poor" (10). Philip seems unworried about the future in Ghana but, as he looks south to Angola and the Congo and beyond, he is shaken with "unreasonable fear" at the thought that Candace might have been born there. Philip tries to ignore such fears, just as he avoids endless discussions about South Africa where revolution seems inevitable (11).

It is, however, with the last days of colonialism and not the birth of neo-colonialism that Laurence is mostly concerned, and she passes judgement on the people who came to Africa as conquerors and lived there as rulers. When Emerald is raped, colonialism is condemned by means of a metaphor, one that Jane Leney considers to lack "subtlety" (69),[1] but which nevertheless makes its point forcefully and within the framework of realism. Laurence makes her case against imperialism most effectively through individuals who, in the clear light she sheds on them, can be seen to provide all the evidence she needs, making any strident political comment unnecessary. She is able to show in convincing fictional terms how the system has affected people like Victor, Nathaniel, Kwabena, Candace, Mammii Ama, Kofi, Ruth, James and Cora Thayer, the Cunninghams — and the list could go on. She gave some thought to why colonials and colonized behaved the way they did, and she had already discovered in Somaliland that there was no ready explanation. When she came across Mannoni's book in 1960, she felt he provided her with the key to the problem as it applied to West as well as East Africa.

In "Books That Mattered to Me," the talk she gave at Trent University, Laurence described Mannoni's book as "the exact book I needed," adding that she discovered it "at the exact time I needed it" (244). *Prospero and Caliban* had resulted from Mannoni's experiences in Madagascar. In his book Mannoni describes how the young Malagasy soldiers, whom he considered dependent by nature, discovered in the French army "a system of very close-knit and numerous bonds of dependence which replaced the family and social bonds" (137). Laurence was not the only one to find this book "a real, literal revelation" ("Books That Mattered" 244). She would have agreed with Philip Mason, who wrote in the foreword to the English version, that Mannoni's conclusions "set in order what had hovered unformulated on the fringe of consciousness" (9). But striking though the metaphor from *The Tempest* may be, it cannot be used with such ease to explain the causes and results of colonialism. It was not always with happy results that Laurence allowed Mannoni's work to influence her thinking (see Zabus).

The story that was deliberately written in response to Mannoni is "The Voices of Adamo." It tells how Adamo, the only person to survive a smallpox epidemic in his village, comes as a stranger to the city where he understands neither the language nor the manners of the people. He joins the army as a drummer and puts his complete trust in the British bandmaster, Captain Fossey, depending on him as he would have depended on the authority of clan and family in his village. When the time comes for Captain Fossey to return to England, he signs Adamo's discharge papers, wrongly believing that the young African wants to leave the army. Adamo feels himself betrayed, the authority on which he depends again taken from him, and his reaction is violent. The choice of a military setting for the tale was the obvious one, given its debt to Mannoni. Laurence gives his Malagasy prototype a new habitat, but she had little knowledge of army life, and Adamo's story seems contrived, its tragic ending unconvincing.

Mannoni's work has been influential, and his metaphor has been widely applied. For example, Canadian women writers have used it to explain male imperialism, as Diana Brydon argues in "Re-Writing *The Tempest*." She discusses Mannoni's metaphor and applies it to Canadian writing in feminist terms, in particular to Laurence's *The Diviners* and to Audrey Thomas's *Munchmeyer and Prospero on the Island*. There can be no doubt that Laurence regarded Mannoni's book highly but, when his theory is used to interpret all her West African fiction, distortion inevitably results. Leney, who applies Mannoni's theory to *This Side Jordan* and to all *The Tomorrow-Tamer* stories, forces Johnnie and Nathaniel into "a rather tightly structured version of the Prospero-Caliban tension" (73). She sees Brother Lemon and Matthew's father as "white Prosperos in the forms of missionaries" and Moses as "the phenomenon of a black Prospero," whose actions are "regrettable," though there is "a positive outcome" (75).

Mannoni if not his followers recognized the weakness of his argument, which he put forward in humility in face of the colonial problem, "one of the most urgent of those confronting the world to-day" (17). Mannoni knew that his own view of the problem was itself a prejudiced one. "However consciously watchful we are," he writes, "we can never entirely eradicate this assumption of superiority from our unconscious, and it must be included among the data of the problem if we are to avoid all risk of error" (18–19).

Another psychologist trained in the French schools, but born in Martinique, saw the basic fault in Mannoni's theory. In *Black Skin, White Masks*, Fanon acknowledges that Mannoni's ". . . analytic thought is honest," but flawed (83). Fanon argues passionately that Mannoni was wrong to see the dependency complex as an inherent characteristic of the Malagasies. Fanon maintains that any dependency is the result of "the arrival of white colonizers on the island" and that to regard the African as Calibanic by nature is yet one more insult from a "superior" European (108). There is no evidence that Laurence read Fanon's work, but her interpretation of individual Africans, Kwabena, Victor, Tetteh, Mammii Ama, and others, whom she may see as angry or uneasy but never as dependent by nature, would suggest that she might have been persuaded by Fanon's *Black Skins, White Masks* to modify a whole-hearted acceptance of Mannoni's metaphor.

The social environment in which her characters live is seen clearly and without idealism. Her descriptions of poverty, disease, and dirt are specific and unsparing, and they often conceal a political statement. When he returns as a grown man to Africa, Matthew drives to the village where he grew up to visit Afua, whom as a slender young girl he had loved, and he is forced to see the injustice of her lot compared to his. The fact that he owns a car immediately puts a barrier between them, a barrier her pride will keep in place. Four of her six children have survived and have aged her. Standing at the door of her hut, with flies on the eyelids of the sleeping child on her back and with the hot still air "clogged with latrine stench" (*Tomorrow* 14), she is as conscious as Matthew of the gulf that now divides them.

Mammii Ama's market place is the home of the poor and dispossessed, and the unjust gap that exists between the haves and have-nots is made obvious when the rich and curious visit it. It was in the market place of Hargeisa that Laurence was first made aware of the outrageous inequality that exists in the world. The market, "the whirlpool of humanity" that Miranda visits with Nathaniel (155), is alive with gaiety and good humour, of which they feel the edge, but Laurence never ignores the other side of the coin and puts into her picture a child crawling through the mud, "its mother lost, its nose pouring mucus onto its lips" (*This Side* 156). When Ampadu, looking prosperous in "white shirt and grey flannel trousers" (*Tomorrow* 233), goes to Mammii Ama's market, he is seen next to old Moki, the firewood seller, who has continually to wipe his rheumy eyes with the end of his dirty turban (228).

There is a struggle against poverty at Ampadu's level, too, and this is something Laurence conveys well when she describes the compound where Nathaniel lives, in a "decaying suburb in Accra" (44). The compound, "[w]eed-flecked and unkempt" (46), is full of litter, and the house is a "warren of tiny rooms" (47), two of which are rented by Nathaniel and Aya. Laurence clearly understands the pressures such conditions cause, and she identifies the social problems that come with city life. The reasons for Nathaniel's acceptance of a bribe are made abundantly clear, and in dealing as she does with corruption, albeit on the seemingly insignificant level of the gift of two silk shirts and a gilt necklace, Laurence demonstrates an unerring instinct for a topical theme, one that has concerned many African writers. The theme recurs in Nigerian fiction as she was to discover when writing *Long Drums and Cannons*. She also spots one of the social problems that would lead to serious unrest in the years after independence. The presence in the Gold Coast of many immigrant labourers caused tensions in society, and Nathaniel is drawn into the jealous competition for space in the compound between Ankrah, the woodcarver from Asante, and Yiamoo, the immigrant tailor from Togoland.[2]

Laurence was conscious that however shabby and dirty a compound like Nathaniel's might be, there would still be a place in it for beauty to flower. She liked the effect such ironic incongruity could have in her fiction. Outside Nathaniel's door, "[b]eside the open reeking drains a patch of portulaca flaunted a purple-red defiance to the barren earth" (46). In Africa she continually saw such incongruities, and she came to see them as signs of grace that she later transposed to a Canadian setting. In *This Side Jordan*, beside the dirty lavatory in the compound of Nathaniel's school, Futura Academy, "grew a tall frangipani tree whose tender scented blossoms fought a losing battle with the latrine stench" (17); in *The Stone Angel* she allows the sweet-scented lilac, "a seasonal mercy," to grow in the depressing Shipley farmyard that was "puddled with yellow ammonia pools where the horses emptied themselves" (29).

To counterbalance the dirt and smells and decay of poverty, there is in Laurence's West African fiction a celebration of life, evident in the often lyrical and always rich descriptions of the African setting. Vivid movement swirls as she leads her reader into Kofi's pulsating village environment where "[t]he dust rose like clouds of red locusts around the small stampeding hooves of taggle-furred goats and the frantic wings of chickens with all their feathers awry. Behind them the children darted, their bodies velvety with dust, like a flash and tumble of brown butterflies in the sun" (*Tomorrow* 78). Visual clarity and humour mark the market scene as the stallholders lay out their wares: ". . . a Hausa man was hanging up his white and black wool mats and huge pointed hats and long embroidered robes which only men tall as the Hausas could wear. Sabina the cloth-seller snapped at a small boy who pissed beside her stall, complaining that he was spraying her second-best bolts, draped outside to catch the eye" (*Tomorrow* 228).

Sharp images drawn from the African setting are often skilfully handled to illuminate her narrative, as in the passage from *This Side Jordan* where Miranda dreams uneasily under the *niim* tree in her garden. The ritual dance of the mudwasps, like the duellistic pattern that Laurence has given to the conflict between Johnnie and Nathaniel, is played out against a background of red and gold and black imagery that recalls the violence of a London slum as well as that of the magnificent golden kingdom of Ashanti:

> The season had kindled a flame tree into flower. Its blaze of red blossoms covered the top branches, spilling embers down onto the ground. A gold and ebony salamander lay sleek and still in its hunting blind, the bed of marigolds. A pair of mud wasps, trailing hair-thin legs like vines, came out of their dwelling, a tube of clay they had painstakingly built on the stoep wall. Their dance was slow and perfectly measured, the dance of hunting, their delicate poisonous bodies absorbed in the dream-like gyrations of their flight. (137–38)

Recurring images can be traced in Laurence's work that show how powerfully the African setting worked in her imagination. The white egret perched in a tree with folded wings acquires sinister associations. In the moment of tense silence when Johnnie became aware of Whiskey's young wife watching him, ". . . the white egrets were still, wings folded in baobab or niim tree" (*This Side* 134), and as Moses drove into Faru's village, the forest withdrew into itself and in "the grey-green baobab trees, the egrets wrapped their cloakwings around themselves like flocks of sorcerers, white as mist" (*Tomorrow* 134).

There is agreement among critics of her work that Laurence's descriptions of the African setting have an exceptional literary quality. Clara Thomas sums up the general reaction when she states in *The Manawaka World* that "[a]t their best her descriptions realize an all-dimensional world, vibrant with colours and dense with sensual effects" (55). If Laurence portrays her foreignness, it is in the extravagant delight that she takes in what can be called "local colour": food, clothes, transport, the furnishings of a house or hut, the weather, the scenery, the flora and fauna of garden and forest. For her these things have an exotic flavour that their equivalents in Canada did not have. All her work demonstrates a good eye for sensual detail, but the West African fiction is more vibrantly textured than the Manawaka novels. The "abundance of experience, imaginative energy, and resourcefulness" (Watt 406) that Laurence draws on, together with "the magnificence of the land itself and its obsessive appeal for the stranger" (Tracy 119), make her West African fiction exciting reading. This led a few to consider *The Stone Angel* "a disappointment after *This Side Jordan*" (Robertson 124) and "less exciting than *The Tomorrow-Tamer*" (Hicks 115).

The outsider has to avoid the temptation to react like a tourist, a trap that Cary identified in *The Case for African Freedom*. "The tourist mind," he wrote, "is not uncommon among officials; I had it myself, that love of the picturesque which invites the traveller to delight in anything unfamiliar and racy of the soil; in national government, native costume, native dances; national religious ceremony, even national dirt and poverty, so long as it is different from that which he can see at home" (63). Laurence's Matthew, who shares his creator's acute sensitivity, is also aware of the danger. "I had always been the dreamer," he admits, "who knew he could waken at will, the tourist who wanted antique quaintness to remain unchanged" (*Tomorrow* 18). By being on her guard, Laurence avoids the trap, but only just. She is saved by the authenticity, integrity, and perception of her interpretation of the land that was to become Ghana and of that nation's first citizens. Godfrey, who reviewed *The Tomorrow-Tamer* while actually living in Ghana, wrote that he was "properly amazed by the accuracy of her perceptions and conclusions" ("Figments" 92–93).

With "Mask of Beaten Gold" written, Laurence felt she had exhausted her African experiences. In the interview with Sullivan she explained that ". . . I really knew that I didn't want to go on writing about Africa, because otherwise my writing would become that of a tourist. I had written everything I could out of that particular experience, and I very *much* wanted to return home in a kind of spiritual way" (68).

Laurence told Donald Cameron in "Margaret Laurence: The Black Celt Speaks of Freedom" that as she grew older she became more aware of "man's isolation from his fellows and how almost unbearably tragic that is," adding that when she had been "much younger" she had "believed that total communication between two people was possible, but it isn't. At least I don't think it is" (105). Fortunately, before she entirely lost that early faith, she undertook to communicate between two cultures and, though such a task may in the complete sense be impossible, it is one that is worth attempting, for the rewards of even partial success are great.

In 1970 John Metcalf chose "The Tomorrow-Tamer" for his selection of short stories, *Sixteen by Twelve: Short Stories by Cana-*

dian Writers. To accompany it, Laurence wrote a short "Author's Commentary," in which she explains the significance of Kofi's story. When Kofi climbs to the top of his bridge, he discovers that it "links his village with other villages," and for a brief moment he has "a vision of a world which includes his own and yet goes far beyond it" (72). Laurence invented Kofi and his bridge, the myth and the metaphor, and they symbolize the achievement of her African fiction, which, as she says of Kofi in her commentary, should be recognized as a bridge, one that serves as a link "not between better and worse cultures, but simply between different cultures, between people who do not understand one another, and who, at some point, must try" (73).

Part III

The Novelist as Critic

8

A Nigerian Palm Grove

When she was writing *Long Drums and Cannons*, Margaret Laurence did not pretend to be a professional critic. The notes she made when preparing the introduction for her study of Nigerian fiction and drama make two points clear. One, her work, which she describes as a collection of essays, was not meant to be a complete survey of the subject; and, two, she was guided in her choice of material by personal preference. "I do not delude myself," she concedes, "that this is a work of literary criticism. It is a commentary, written from the point of view of a reader and a writer" ("Long Drums and Cannons," ts.). She uses little literary theory in her discussion of her chosen material, but her commentary is sustained by the same strong commitment that underpins her fiction. It was with dedication that Laurence pursued her objective, which was to bring to the attention of a wide audience the extraordinary richness and originality of Nigerian writing between 1952 and 1966.

Another factor that should be clearly appreciated is the point of time at which her book was written, that is just before the outbreak of the Biafran War. That war drew into its vortex many of the foremost Nigerian writers, with the result that both creative activity and critical interpretation of it were considerably interrupted. Laurence's pioneering work was done with few signposts to guide her, and the selective bibliography of *Long Drums and Cannons* indicates the limited extent of secondary reading available when she started her research. This meant — and it was not necessarily a disadvantage — that her dependence on her primary texts was heavy. When the Biafran War ended in 1970, it was inevitable that the Nigerian renaissance of the 1950s and 1960s was viewed from a new perspective, and the writers themselves began to comment on their own early work and that of their compatriots with an understanding born in years of ordeal and pain. David Carroll notes in a review that *Long Drums and Cannons* "has a rather dated air" (360), and its critical judgements disappoint Anthony Boxill since her "method is largely descriptive" (105). When Alastair Niven in his review of 1969 maintained that *Long Drums and Cannons* was "perhaps the best book relating to Nigerian literature in English that has been produced," he had to qualify his praise with the admission that there was little of value with which to compare it (17). Indeed, early critical writing on African literatures was often disappointing and was, not surprisingly, censured by Irele as "an indiscriminate lumping together of significant works with those that really belong to a different order . . ." (50). Laurence's study is also to some extent guilty of this fault, but the value of her work as a pioneering analysis is considerable, and her line by line commentary is not without many well-argued and perceptive judgements, which, more than twenty years later, have lost none of their point and value.

Because Laurence prefers to interpret rather than evaluate, she does not submit her material to comparative criticism, either within the Nigerian context itself or within the broader spectrum of other contemporary literatures. Indeed, even practised academics avoided this approach when faced with the first West African writing in English. Jack Healy has written of the unsatisfactory nature of the early criticism. Referring to an observation by Claude Levi-Strauss, Healy remarks that a new work from Africa was too often welcomed as a museum piece, "as an object to be understood, to be re-constituted in human and historical terms" and then sent for "preservation" either to the Louvre or the Musée de l'Homme, most likely the latter (15). Instead, Healy argues, African writing should have been allowed to explain itself with the emphasis on its relationship with other literary works and not on its possible anthropological significance. Healy suggests that each work should not only be discovered "where it is, recognizing that it has a nomic [*sic*] function to perform in its own place and time," but it should also be seen as the expression of an individual consciousness working along with many others in a symbiotic world (24).

While he does not mention Laurence's work, Healy believes that the kind of approach she adopted was better than most. Her commentary, which for the most part sticks to an interpretation of the text with the addition of some details on the writer's biographical and cultural background, provides the basic information that a critic needs to understand the literature within its national context. She did not carry comparative critical assessment as far as Healy might have wished, but at least she did not view the texts as museum pieces.

Laurence's book has positive virtues because of her ability to respond on two levels, as a reader and as someone who was herself a practised writer. She reads with care, paying close attention to the text and alert to the need to respect the author's intentions. Her book contains a number of finely written passages, especially about Achebe and Soyinka, the two writers whom time has distinguished from the rest. But even as a general guide *Long Drums and Cannons* is still a valuable work and essential reading for those embarking on a study of Nigerian literature since it explains its beginnings with thoroughness and sensitivity.

Though Laurence never visited Nigeria, and so had to work without the sense of immediacy that informs her writing about Somaliland and the Gold Coast, she was able to meet a number of the writers when they came to London. Her conception of Nigeria is largely based on what she learnt from them and from their writing. When Nigeria became independent in 1960, it was as a nation that had been invented by the British for, as Achebe puts it in "English and the African Writer," "their own ends." Yet in 1965, before Biafran secession became a fact, Achebe could see the value of the invention, believing that the "arbitrary creation called Nigeria holds out great prospects" (57). A great number of ethnic groups were brought together within a big political unit, and the colonial power left them "a language with which to talk to one another," which Achebe along with other writers proceeded to do (28). The Gold Coast had accustomed Laurence to a similarly mixed community that used English as a common language. This helped her understand the Nigerian mosaic, but she had to rely on others for the knowledge she needed to explain the complex traditions of the Yoruba, Igbo, and Ijaw societies that inform the writing respectively of Soyinka, Achebe, and John Pepper Clark.

When the British, with the sanction of the Berlin Conference of 1884, set about the invention of Nigeria, they drew an arbitrary frontier that showed little regard for ethnic sensibilities. They enclosed together many races, each with their own language and customs. Among them were the Fulani and Hausa of the Islamic north where city states like Sokoto and Kano had grown as centres of trade. In the southwest, the Yoruba people had established a multiplicity of kingdoms, all originating from the holy city of Ife. To the east the Igbo, mainly living in the forests, had created a multitude of egalitarian village communities, linked by markets, while the Ijaw, along the river deltas, had developed a way of life dependent on the fishing industry. These and many others were required to come together as one nation. If the colonial power takes credit for the formation of so diverse and rich a nation, it must also bear much of the responsibility for the suffering its interference caused. Nigeria won independence in 1960 as a democratic federation of three largely self-governing regions, but this arrangement did not last long, and a series of coups led finally to a military government under General Yakubu Gowon, a Christian from a northern minority group. Gowon sought to restore national unity, but failed to stop the massacre of thousands of Igbo in the north of the country. In response, the Igbo in the east called their people home, and in 1967 under Colonel Odumegwu Ojukwu they declared themselves the independent state of Biafra. The civil war that broke out just as Laurence's book went to press ended when the Igbo were starved into surrender in 1970. Nigeria was again one nation, and, after the bitterness and suffering, the difficult healing process began.

Writing before the Biafran War, Laurence was able to bring together in her book the separate Nigerian traditions, delighting in the diversity they represented. To cover such an extensive historical and cultural area, Laurence had to rely on the work of a number of anthropologists and scholars, most of whom had wisely confined themselves to individual areas of study. Her bibliography indicates the nature and extent of her debt. She turned, for example, to Margaret M. Green for details about the Igbo social order, to Robin Horton for information on the Ijaw culture and to Ulli Beier for an explanation of Yoruba customs.

There were a number of specialized journals and magazines that provided Laurence with useful articles, and they form the core of her bibliography. Some of these journals and magazines have interesting histories, and their editors and contributors have included scholars and writers of importance. *Africa*, which has been appearing since 1928, is the journal of the International African Institute in London. *Nigeria Magazine*, which focuses on the country rather than the continent, was subsidized first by the colonial and then the independent government of Nigeria. *Black Orpheus: A Journal of African* and *Afro-American Literature* was founded by Ulli Beier in 1957 with the help of Gerald Moore and Jahnheinz Jahn. The magazine was very influential in promoting the work of African writers. Beier ran it until 1966, and Laurence used articles from this first series. Clark and Irele launched the second series, *Black Orpheus: A Journal of the Arts from Africa* in 1968. *Black Orpheus* inspired Rajat Neogy to start *Transition* in Kampala in 1961 (Christopher Okigbo was its West African editor). Neogy was arrested in 1968, and he relocated *Transition* to Accra in 1971. Wole Soyinka took over as editor in 1974. The fascinating story of *Black Orpheus* and *Transition* has been told by Peter Benson in *Black Orpheus, Transition, and Modern Cultural Awakening in Africa*, published in 1968 by the University of California at Berkeley.

Two of Achebe's influential essays appeared before Laurence completed her research, and she makes good use of them. In the first, "English and the African Writer," Achebe explains why he writes in English, not Igbo. Laurence comments on his remarks in her epilogue, adding her admiration for his style, which is "admirably suited" to his irony with its "enormous range of expression" (199). The second essay she uses is "The Novelist as Teacher." In this well-known essay Achebe briefly and clearly defines his creed as a writer. His words were designed in the first place for those attending the September 1964 conference at the University of Leeds, but they later received wide-spread exposure, first in the *New Statesman* in January 1965 and then in John Press's *Commonwealth Literature: Unity and Diversity in a Common Culture*, which is the text Laurence used. Achebe never altered his creed, and he included "The Novelist as Teacher" in both his essay collections, *Morning Yet on Creation Day* (1975) and *Hopes and Impediments* (1988).

All this background material was useful but enlightenment was best found in the novels and dramas with which she was concerned, and her study is of value because she discusses their content with thoroughness and care. While Laurence did not live in Nigeria, she can be said to have visited it in the company of its writers. In the Haud, she felt that she had been able to hear the Prophet's camel bell. While working on her study of Nigerian fiction and drama, she felt she had heard through the words of the Nigerian writers the voices of their ancestors sounding in the sacred palm groves. So she chose as title for her work a line from Okigbo's poem "Heavensgate," which she cites as her epigraph:

I have visited, the prodigal . . .
in palm grove,
long drums and cannons:
the spirit in the ascent.

9

An Igbo Story-Teller:
Chinua Achebe

Anyone interested in Igbo traditions will find, as Margaret Laurence did, valuable information in Margaret Green's book, *Ibo Village Affairs*. Green, a good linguist, lived with the Igbos between 1934 and 1937 in the Owerri district, some forty miles from where Achebe, born in 1930, would have been growing up. As with Rattray in the Gold Coast and Andrzejewski in Somaliland, Green's experiences left her with profound respect for the people whose tongue she had learnt. Laurence, who quotes in *Long Drums and Cannons* only once directly from Green's book (103), draws on it heavily for her overall picture of Igbo society, a picture that is substantiated and brought to life in Achebe's historical novels. Before discussing Achebe's novels, Laurence gives an outline of the characteristics of Igbo society, and her debt to Green at this point is considerable.

Green described the Igbo as a "great people" who were "broken up into hundreds of small, more or less independent, social units, the largest being, in many cases, what we may call the village-group" (3). They did not live under any central authority but co-existed, scattered through the forest lands of Eastern Nigeria in isolated independent clusters. When it came to managing their affairs, the Igbo favoured "a dispersal rather than a concentration of authority," and Green admired the involvement of the whole community in all aspects of government (73). Yet she recognized the weaknesses inherent in such a fragmented and democratic society. Although the Igbo had a common language and common traditions, their world all too quickly fell apart when it came under external pressure because it rested on a finely suspended internal balance of power.

Green points out that the Igbo had always been aware of the dangers of fragmentation and had adopted certain unifying measures, such as shared markets and exogamy — the latter required that a man marry outside his village group — but these were not enough to protect their way of life when the colonial power came on the scene. Green criticized, in particular, the British policy of indirect rule, which, since there were no natural hierarchical leaders to whom authority could be given, often upset the precarious but equitable balance of power in the Igbo villages.

Laurence can only agree. The Igbo, she writes in *Long Drums and Cannons*, rejected "any inherited or hierarchical system of authority." She repeats Green's criticism of British policy, the terrible consequences of which were demonstrated for her in Achebe's *Arrow of God*. Laurence states that "the British administration in Nigeria met with considerable opposition for a long time from the Ibo people, whose natural resentment of foreign intrusion was heightened by the fact that the British system of courts and government-appointed chiefs went directly against Ibo social institutions." Having read Green, Laurence moves easily and systematically through *Things Fall Apart* and *Arrow of God*, novels in which Achebe "deals with the traditional society of the Ibo people, the reasons for its breakdown and the ways in which social changes have affected the lives of individual men" (98).

Laurence sometimes ventures beyond her close analysis of character and plot to comment on Igbo customs. She undertakes, for example, with commendable hesitation, to explain the complex nature of *chi*, perhaps the most important characteristic of the Igbo religion. Laurence had to pick her way through an undergrowth of conflicting opinion on, as Achebe notes, "a concept so central in Igbo psychology and yet so elusive and enigmatic" (*Morning Yet* 93), but she wisely uses Achebe's fiction as a guide while evaluating the other available evidence.

Today, anyone discussing the very complex concept of *chi* in Achebe's novels would turn to his essay, published in his *Morning Yet on Creation Day* in 1975, "Chi in Igbo Cosmology." Achebe advises that the best way to "visualise a person's *chi*" is to think of it as one's "other identity in spiritland" (93). He adds that ". . . every person has an individual *chi* who created him," and ". . . a person's fortunes in life are controlled more or less completely by his *chi*" (98). Men and women, however, have been given the right to bargain with their *chi*, since they believe that Chukwu, the Supreme Being or great *Chi*, "will discuss His universe with man" (103). The Igbo fiercely protected the freedom of the individual, and, as Achebe indicates, they took democracy to its limits. Achebe draws attention to the significant title — *The King in Every Man* — of Richard Henderson's study of the Igbo community of Onitsha. In "Ibo and Yoruba Art," Beier calls the Igbo "the super democrats of West Africa" (49). The Igbo believe firmly in the fundamental worth and importance of every individual and impose limitations even on their gods in defence of their egalitarian principles.

Clearly the relationship between Okonkwo and his *chi* is important in *Things Fall Apart*. When Laurence wrote about the novel, she did so without Achebe's essay to guide her. However, Green had defined the *chi* as "the personal spirit which everyone has and which is in the nature both of a creating and a guardian spirit" (163), and Laurence considered this a good starting point (103). She noticed that Green's definition accorded with Achebe's fictional example. Laurence writes well on the reasons for Okonkwo's tragedy. Her arguments are sound and perceptive as she explains his tragic downfall. Okonkwo desired a place of authority and honour in his society because he had been humiliated as a young man by the lack of respect shown to his good-natured but weak-willed father. Okonkwo, who had the freedom of choice to do so, goes against his *chi* in order to convince himself and others of his own strength of character. Laurence, never assertive, suggests that Achebe's intentions were to show "with the character of Okonkwo a man whose inner god prompts a gentleness which is always ignored" (103).

Laurence never adopts an authoritative attitude about an author's meaning, feeling that as an outsider her own knowledge is limited. She therefore avoids the patronizing tone adopted by some critics, among whom might be numbered Austin J. Shelton who wrote a short article for *Transition*, "The Offended *Chi* in Achebe's Novels," in which he discusses Okonkwo at some length. Laurence, and she was not the only one, considered this article presumptuous. In it Shelton claims that "Achebe makes a vainglorious attempt . . . to ascribe all the evils which occurred in Ibo society to the coming of the white men" (37). This is an extraordinary mis-reading of the text since Achebe never idealizes traditional Igbo society and was well aware of its weaknesses. Shelton then ventures to explain on Achebe's behalf how Okonkwo himself was the cause of his own downfall. Shelton is at the receiving end of the only tart remark in Laurence's otherwise courteous book. Shelton, she writes, "suggests that in a way it was Okonkwo himself who made things fall apart — as though Achebe were totally unaware of this interesting possibility" (105). Donatus I. Nwoga, an Igbo, is more scathing in a letter to the editor of *Transition* about Shelton's interpretation of Achebe's novels: Shelton's studies have "confused him thoroughly" when he states that Achebe suffered from a " 'jaundiced attitude toward his own people's religion' " (5). Judith Gleason in her essay on *Arrow of God* has critics like Shelton in mind when she recalls that "Achebe's first novel was criticized by a European scholar and critic in residence in Nigeria for showing a lack of understanding of the religious organization of the Ibo — a rather shattering example of that European expertise and presumption with which Africans in all enterprises still have to deal" (35).

Laurence never makes such a mistake, though this means sometimes going too far in the opposite direction. She is slow to criticize and puts forward any evaluative judgements with hesitation. As Alastair Niven comments in a review of *Long Drums and Cannons*, ". . . her book would have been more stimulating if she had occasionally dared caution to the winds for, although there is nothing outrageously stupid in her criticism, neither is there anything boldly original" (16). Yet this is not altogether a fair assessment of *Long Drums and Cannons*. There is certainly nothing bold in Laurence's method, but there is much that is original, and she provides a great deal of honest, generous, and knowledgeable comment, which remains of value today.

Certainly her book did not displease Achebe, who has not always liked the way western critics have approached African literature. In 1974 at Uganda's Makerere University, Achebe read "Colonialist Criticism," a strongly critical paper, which he later published in his first collection of essays, *Morning Yet on Creation Day* and revised slightly for his second collection, *Hopes and Impediments*. In his essay Achebe vigorously condemns western critics who are "unwilling to accept the validity of sensibilities other than [their] own," as a result inevitably failing to understand the intention of the African writer (*Morning Yet* 17). However, Achebe makes an exception of Laurence's book and quotes directly from *Long Drums and Cannons*. He feels that Laurence assessed the African viewpoint with understanding. He welcomed and seconded her judgement that no

African "writer of any quality has viewed the old Africa in an idealised way, but they have tried to regain what is rightfully theirs — a past composed of real and vulnerable people, their ancestors, not the figments of missionary and colonialist imaginations" (*Long Drums* 200; *Morning Yet* 12).

Armed with this wisdom, Laurence comments on Achebe's *Things Fall Apart* and *Arrow of God*. She expresses her admiration for the latter novel — "unquestionably his best," and "probably one of the best novels written anywhere in the past decade" (111) — with a clear and often lyrical outline of the story. She concludes with a passionate defence of Achebe's position:

> Underneath the restraint of this novel, there is an almost choking sense of rage and sorrow. Not that Achebe would have wanted the old Ibo society to go on unchanged, for he sees plainly the weaknesses within it. But the rage is because it broke the way it did, by the hands of strangers who had convinced themselves that they were bringing light to a dark place, and whose self-knowledge was so slight that they did not recognise the existence of darkness within themselves. (116–17)

Laurence's readings of Achebe's two modern or urban novels, *No Longer at Ease* (1960) and *A Man of the People* (1966), are also sympathetic. The earlier of these novels is still concerned with traditional Igbo customs that continue to have importance in the contemporary setting. In particular, Achebe examines the modern attitude to the *osu*. Laurence again turned to Green for the information she needed on this Igbo tradition. Green wrote at length on the role of the *osu* in Igbo society, explaining the intensity of feeling on the question. The *osu* were by tradition a religious caste of slaves, who had been dedicated to the service of a god. Green gives an example to show how difficult it was for the missionaries to destroy the traditions relating to the *osu*:

> Intermarriage and sexual intercourse with an *osu* is not only *nso* [taboo] for a free-born, but the idea of it fills him with horror. And this is true, though unofficially, of Christians as well as of pagans. I discussed the matter often with a middle-aged man in Owerri who was an earnest and educated Christian of many years standing. He admitted that *osu* status was

incompatible with Christian principles and was not recognised by the Church. But he was emphatic that he would not contemplate a daughter of his marrying an *osu*. (158)

Green explained that the free-born Igbo thought of *osu* as "horrible and holy" (50). Laurence, writing twenty years later, echoes Green. The *osu*, Laurence writes, are still regarded as "holy and horrifying," and, though the caste had been abolished, "the emotional feeling against the *osu* cannot be obliterated so quickly" (109). The nature of this emotional feeling must be understood to appreciate the pressure that is brought on to bear on Obi, the central figure in *No Longer at Ease*. This novel was designed as part of a trilogy, of which *Things Fall Apart* was the opening volume. Obi is Okonkwo's grandson and son of Nwoye, who at the end of *Things Fall Apart* disappointed his father by accepting Christian religion and changing his name to Isaac. Isaac became a catechist of the Church Missionary Society and made it possible for Obi to acquire western education. After his return from England, Obi announces his intention of marrying Clara, an *osu* by descent. His father's opposition is unexpectedly fierce, like that of Green's earnest and educated Christian of Owerri. As Laurence so clearly understands, "Obi's father is shocked and grieved at the thought of his son marrying Clara, even though he knows that the concept of *osu* goes against Christianity . . ." (109).

Laurence had some reservations about Achebe's other modern novel, *A Man of the People*. She finds it disconcerting because it "begins as a comic novel" and ends as "incisive social satire" (122). The novel's dramatic conclusion turned out to be prophetic — the book was written just before the first army coup in Nigeria — but the ending, Laurence argues, is not convincing and "appears slightly contrived. The fact that it actually happened this way in real life does not alter the impression that the novel ends rather too conveniently" (122). Laurence's use of "slightly" and "rather" are indicative of her hesitation to be critical.

Although she considers *A Man of the People* less successful than *Arrow of God*, she gives both novels the same attention and takes trouble to explain Achebe's different purpose in his contemporary novel. She takes as her starting point the essay "The Novelist as Teacher," Achebe's well-known justification of the moral responsibility of his role as a writer. In the essay, Achebe described his task in *Arrow of God* as that of rewriting history in order to teach his people "that their past — with all its imperfections — was not one long night of savagery from which the first Europeans acting on God's behalf delivered them" (*Morning Yet* 45). But Achebe also felt a writer must be involved with his own generation, prepared to "go into rebellion against it if need be" (*Morning Yet* 43). This is what he does in *A Man of the People*. Laurence maintains that Achebe, "in company with most Nigerian writers of today, is definitely not disengaged from the events and questions of his society" (122). Though she obviously prefers his historical recreations of Igbo society, Laurence does justice to Achebe's intentions in his contemporary and satirical work. In both, Achebe's intentions were serious because as he put it in "Colonialist Criticism," "earnestness *is* appropriate to my situation" (*Morning Yet* 14).

"The Novelist as Teacher" is a short article, but it had a lasting effect on Laurence. It clearly influences the argument in her essay "Ivory Tower or Grassroots?" where she maintains that "serious fiction," though it may deal with the individual, "must of necessity include social commentary" (15). Writers, she feels, should concern themselves with political and religious issues, and she gives Achebe as an example. With conviction and feeling she reaffirms the serious purpose of all his writing, as also of her own.

Others beside herself have seen similarities between her work and Achebe's (see C. Thomas, *The Manawaka World* 47; Abrahams). Laurence's Nathaniel has been compared to Achebe's Obi Okonkwo, but she herself sees an even wider affinity. In *Long Drums and Cannons*, Laurence remarks on the historical span of Achebe's work:

Taking into consideration the memories of an older society which must have been passed on to him, Achebe's personal knowledge spans three different eras — the pre-mission and pre-colonial time when the old Ibo society was still firmly fixed, the mission-oriented era of his parents, and the quite different era, emancipated and yet troubled, of his own generation. (97)

Achebe's first novel, *Things Fall Apart*, reaches back into the last years of the nineteenth century. Laurence notes in "Ivory Tower" that she read it after she "had completed the first draft of *The Stone Angel*," in which she creates a life that began in those same years. She continued to read Achebe's writing as it appeared, "feeling about it the kind of kinship that one does feel with another writer who is working within some of the same broad human territories" (22). In the interview entitled "Margaret Laurence: The Black Celt Speaks of Freedom," Donald Cameron commented on the historical flow of the Manawaka cycle. In answer, Laurence explained that its time range "covers four generations: my grandparents' generation, my parents' generation, my own generation, and my children's generation." "Interestingly enough," she adds, "I think you would find in the writing of Chinua Achebe the exact same historical span" (112–13).

But the comparison can be taken further than that. The Okonkwo trilogy Achebe originally planned remains incomplete, with *Things Fall Apart* and *No Longer at Ease* as the opening and closing volumes. Achebe has explained why the middle volume, which would have centred on Isaac, was never written. Achebe sees Isaac as representing his own father's generation. Achebe's father became a Christian in spite of a strongly traditional village upbringing, and to his son he remained an enigmatic figure with whom it was difficult to communicate. "There was something," writes Achebe, "I have not been able to fathom. That was why the middle story in the Okonkwo trilogy as I originally projected it never got written. I had suddenly become aware that in my gallery of ancestral heroes there is an empty place from which an unknown personage seems to have departed" (*Hopes* 22). Laurence experienced a similar difficulty. Like Achebe, she was able to recreate her grandparents' generation with far more immediacy than that of her parents. When writing about *No Longer at Ease* in *Long Drums and Cannons*, Laurence comments that Obi feels "closer to his grandfather than he does to his parents" (107). The same could be said of Vanessa MacLeod as she takes leave of Manawaka in *A Bird in the House*. Fictionally for Laurence there is at best a shadowy enigma but usually an empty place where her father should stand. In *A Bird in the House* Vanessa's father dies, Rachel and Stacey's father is already dead when their novels start, and Morag starts life in *The Diviners* as an orphan.

As she interprets Achebe's work in *Long Drums and Cannons*, Laurence makes many comments that could be applied to her own. For example she holds that "with Achebe's writing, one has a sense of inevitability about the main character's life" (109). "Achebe's method is always the method of the genuine novelist," she can say with authority, because he "never makes his characters speak; he listens to them" (123). Her insight enables her to see that Achebe's passionate concern to reach out to his own people in all his novels is part of his Igbo psyche. He knows of the need to communicate from one individual forest village to the next, "through the thickets of our separateness" (125). She returned to Achebe's work in her essay "Ivory Tower," where she anticipates in a remarkable way the novel *Anthills of the Savannah*, which he would publish after her death. In her afterword to *The Prophet's Camel Bell*, Clara Thomas has described Laurence's last meeting with Achebe in 1984, when Laurence "was already deliberating on the memoirs she would write and when he was struggling to finish his novel, *Anthills of the Savannah*" (265). During this meeting, Achebe undoubtedly spoke of his novel in progress, but in "Ivory Tower," published some years earlier, Laurence anticipated the problems Achebe had to overcome before the novel could take shape. It is unlikely that anyone will ever write with more understanding of the man she knew as a writer and a friend:

> Undoubtedly at some time it will become necessary for Achebe to write a novel out of the civil war, which will deal fictionally with the events of the Biafran holocaust. It will, I believe, be the most anguished work for him in his entire writing life. I also feel that if any novelist can write such a novel, with truth, strength, and integrity, that novelist is Achebe. He sees history in terms of people with names and conflicts and places of belonging. His sense of social injustice is like a white-hot sword wielded through his powerful irony. Yet he knows one of the most frightening facts of life, the thing every novelist must come to know — the enemy is also within, and the external enemy is also human and feels pain as real as anyone's. (22)

With these words Laurence emphasizes Achebe's own view of his responsibilities, as she pays tribute to a man whose respect for his art is such that he will only write from the highest of moral ground.

10

The Mysteries of Ogun:
Wole Soyinka

In *Long Drums and Cannons*, Margaret Laurence describes Soyinka's writing as "a juggling act." She admires his amazing dexterity, which allows him to "keep any number of plates — and valuable plates, at that — spinning in the air all at the same time" (11). She used the same image to explain that when she was writing a novel she felt like "a juggler trying to keep a dozen plates spinning up there in the air" ("Author's Commentary" 71). She could appreciate, from her own endeavours at conjuring, the extent of Soyinka's dexterity, and in *Long Drums and Cannons* she applauds his gifts in a long chapter entitled "Voices of Life, Dance of Death." Yet she is never completely sure of herself when discussing Soyinka. She has to speculate and presume as she interprets his work, but in this she has been joined by many others. Critics must still be prepared to employ imaginative guesswork when trying to explain Soyinka's intentions. Moreover, because Soyinka's drama has not yet had the audiences it deserves in the west, its effect in performance must often be imagined. In an interview with Lewis Nkosi, Soyinka has emphasized that his main aim has been "to provide excellent theatre," which means that he has put "liveliness and freedom" above "purpose or intentions," and this is sometimes forgotten when his work is discussed (173). The plays often have a multiplicity of themes, and analyzing them with only the printed page available can be an arduous process. If Laurence's chapter on Soyinka sometimes seems laboured, it is because of the complexity of his juggling act. Trying to identify and number the plates as they spin can mean that the overall effect of the performance is lost. To change the metaphor,

Laurence, and she is not alone in this, can make it difficult to see the forest for the trees, but it must be added that the trees that grow in Soyinka's forests are themselves worthy of close inspection.

When Laurence sent *Long Drums and Cannons* to her British publisher Macmillan, Soyinka was thirty-four, but he had already established his reputation as a major writer with ten plays and an inventive novel of remarkable interest. Laurence restricted her discussion to six of his plays, those which had been published and so were generally available. They were *A Dance of the Forests* and *The Lion and the Jewel*, both published in 1963, *The Strong Breed*, *The Swamp Dwellers*, *The Trials of Brother Jethro*, all published in 1964, and *The Road*, published in 1965. Soyinka's first novel, *The Interpreters*, which was also published in 1965, appeared in time for Laurence to include it in her survey.

While Achebe expresses in his writing the Igbo world-view, Soyinka opens up the very different Yoruba perspective. The Yoruba were traditionally organized into monarchical states and united as a people by an ancestral loyalty to the King of Ife. In a work published after *Long Drums and Cannons*, Eldred Durosimi Jones, a reliable guide to Soyinka's work, stresses the same points as Laurence does when outlining Soyinka's Yoruba inheritance. In *The Writing Life of Wole Soyinka*, Jones points out that ". . . Yoruba life is dominated by religion" (4). He explains how the deities closely interact with mortals in a culture dominated by religious ritual, in which masks and dance and song and sacrifice have their part. Laurence had also emphasized the dominance of the spiritual in Yoruba society, and in her critique she shows how this is reflected in Soyinka's drama where "Yoruba gods," as she succinctly phrases it, "inhabit his plays . . ." (12).

Beier in "Ibo and Yoruba," an article included in Laurence's bibliography, compares Igbo and Yoruba art, relating stylistic differences to "the general cultural pattern in the two societies" (49; see also Lindfors, "Characteristics"). With Green as a reliable guide and with Achebe's lucid descriptions before her, Laurence had been able to visualize the traditional Igbo way of life. She found it harder to relate what she had learnt of the Yoruba world to Soyinka's complex drama, which had only recently made its impact in London and Africa. To complicate matters further, Soyinka was not content to stick to traditional Yoruba mythology, but sought to enrich it, to use Michel Fabre's words, "through creative reinterpretation" (35). This was something Laurence immediately understood, and, though she sometimes found Soyinka obscure, she knew that he had made "something rich and strange and new" out of his traditional inheritance" (18).

Soyinka has himself explained the nature of that reinterpretation in an essay that was not available when Laurence was writing *Long Drums and Cannons*. Soyinka's fine apologia of tragedy, "The Fourth Stage," first appeared in *The Morality of Art*, a volume of essays put together in honour of Wilson Knight and published in 1969. Soyinka's arrest and imprisonment in 1967 had made it impossible for him to proof-read his essay before it went to press. So in 1976 he added it in revised form as an appendix to *Myth, Literature and the African World*, an edition of four lectures that he delivered for the Department of Social Anthropology at Cambridge University in 1973. Soyinka welcomed the chance to revise "The Fourth Stage," which develops a profound argument not always easy to follow. His second version is no less profound, but in it he clarifies some of his more complex ideas by eliminating what one of his students called the " 'elliptical' obstacles to its comprehension" (*Myth* ix).

Soyinka's explanation of Yoruba myth makes it easier to see repetitive patterns emerging in his work. To explain the role of the gods in his art, Soyinka turns for a parallel to Nietzsche's explanation of the birth of tragedy as the fusion of Dionysus's chaotic energy and Apollo's perfect form. In the Yoruba pantheon, Ogun and Obatala take the place of Dionysus and Apollo, but the parallel is not exact because, Soyinka writes, there are "inevitable, key departures" (140). Ogun represents for Soyinka the total process of creation, "Nietzsche's Dionysus-Apollo brotherhood," while Obatala, who is all "inner essence," stands for the serene beauty that is expressed in a finished work of art once the process of creation is over. "Obatala," for Soyinka, "is the placid essence of creation" while Ogun is "the creative urge and instinct, the essence of creativity" (141). Both Ogun and Obatala were created from shattered fragments of Orisa-nla, who was the primal Yoruba deity, but it was Ogun with whom Soyinka identified most closely. Ogun also calls to mind Prometheus as well as Dionysus and Apollo. Like Prometheus, Ogun undertook to bridge the gap that had grown between the gods and humans, but to do so he had to pass through the abyss or "fourth stage," the area of transition that separates the other three stages, the worlds of the dead, the living, and the unborn. Ogun had to endure violent disintegration before being reborn on earth, where he set the pattern in Yoruba tradition for the close association between the people and their gods. In "The Fourth Stage" Soyinka emphasizes the links between Ogun and the artist. The artist, Soyinka holds, must share Ogun's Orpheus-like dismemberment. Every act of creation is of necessity an act of self-destruction, but it is an act that can wrestle from chaos a finished and serene work of art. When bridging the abyss with an act of creation, the artist's struggle takes place in the half light on the frontier where death and life meet or, to view it in artistic terms, where unorganized and chaotic matter is wrought into ordered form. This concept is important to the interpretation of much of Soyinka's drama and fiction.

"The Fourth Stage" is especially important in that it reveals Soyinka's attitude, very much a personal and individual one, to the Yoruba gods, and in particular to Ogun, his preferred deity. If Laurence had written a few years later, with "The Fourth Stage" as a signpost, she would have found it easier to locate the focus of Soyinka's emphasis in the intertwining of themes that enrich his writing. Much of the recent critical work on Soyinka has made extensive and fruitful use of his exegesis, especially when concerned with the more complex of his plays, A Dance of the Forests and The Road.

These two plays caused problems for Laurence when she came to summarize their plots and explain their action in Long Drums and Cannons. Her method worked well with the other four plays, all of them comparatively short and compact, but A Dance of the Forests, which Laurence describes as "Soyinka's most intricate play" (29), and The Road, in which the ". . . theme is developed windingly and with a great many apparent detours . . ." (46), are both difficult to reduce to a plot outline, as she was not the only one to discover.

A note of despair creeps into Laurence's voice during her close reading of The Road, which she was fortunate to see performed in London in 1965 ("Ten Years'" 19–20). Having remarked that Soyinka scatters his work with fascinating but mystifying ideas that he does not immediately explain, Laurence complains that "[t]his kind of foreshadowing is sometimes overworked by Soyinka, because the memory of the reader or audience is severely taxed in retaining a multitude of details which will later prove meaningful" (52). Much of this significant foreshadowing concerns the mute Murano, who was knocked down by a lorry before the play opens. The accident occurred during the religious *Egungun* ceremonies while Murano was wearing the mask of Ogun. At the time he had entered the stage of "possession" and had become the mouthpiece of the god himself. Murano, rescued by the Professor, has not fully woken from his trance and, unable to speak, is still in part possessed by the god. His limp signifies that he has one foot in another world, the world of the dead. Murano's significance puzzles Laurence. While she recognizes that he is "the key to the whole thing" (59), the key in particular to the Professor's search for the "Word," the nature of the secret that he can reveal never becomes clear. Writing later than Laurence, Wilson Harris, who empathized with the ideas expressed in "The Fourth Stage," looks on *The Road* as a masterpiece, as a play that explores the boundary area between life and death, a "realm of partial images," where Ogun "comes to reside on the dark frontier of the imagination" (117). Laurence works carefully through the play and finally achieves something close to Harris's later understanding. She asks herself questions — "What does it really entail?" (54), and "Is Murano now dead or is he restored to himself?" (63) — few of which she can answer. "The only thing we can confidently expect from Soyinka," she acknowledges, "is that things will not turn out as anyone might on the surface expect them to do" (54).

The conclusion of the play is meant to suggest uncertainty, and Laurence's response is the right one. Many of her comments are perceptive, and some have influenced later interpretations. The Professor, an enigmatic figure — he could be played as a European or an African — has travelled the road searching for "the Word," and it is a road that leads inevitably to death. He dies with his questions unanswered, and Laurence suggests that he was all along engaged in an impossible quest. "Before he dies," Laurence argues, "Professor tells his people what little he has discovered, although his words are not going to be comprehended and are indeed only a broken series of words, for the final Word cannot be spoken or known — maybe does not even exist" (63). The ending of the play is open to this pessimistic reading. Jones, acknowledging *Long Drums and Cannons* in a footnote to *The Writing of Wole Soyinka*, accepts the possibility of this final tragic irony that Laurence has sensed. "There is," he adds, thinking of Laurence's critique, "an even more sardonic interpretation of the end of the play. What, if after all, there is no Word?" (71).

A *Dance of the Forests* has also kept the critics guessing. In this play Soyinka's central figure is an artist, the wood-carver Demoke. Laurence recognizes the appropriateness of Demoke's artistic bent because she knew that "Yoruba woodcarvers have always been of prime importance in Western Nigeria" (30). Demoke is closely involved in the climax of *A Dance of the Forests*, an ambiguous ending that has been interpreted in a variety of ways. Laurence to her credit undertook to solve the riddle. Anne Tibble in *African-English Literature: A Short Survey and Anthology of Prose and Poetry up to 1965* (1965) admitted that she could not understand the play. She considered it "a most puzzling play. Three or four careful readings can leave only glimmers of what it is about" (88).

Beier, who reviewed the play before it was performed, was the first to puzzle over the conclusion, which concerns an *abiku*, a figure to which Soyinka "attaches completely new meanings" (57). Laurence looked to Peter Morton-Williams's "Yoruba Responses to the Fear of Death" for an explanation of the traditional concept of the *abiku*, which is a child with death in its soul. If a woman lost a succession of infant children, it was believed that the same child was being "born again and again," fated each time to die, and such a child was called by the Yoruba an *abiku* (35). When an *abiku* was finally persuaded to stay among the living, it was as a person of unusual qualities. Soyinka, in his autobiographical work *Aké: The Years of Childhood*, describes his childhood friend Bukola who was an *abiku*, that is a "child which is born, dies, is born again and dies in a repetitive cycle" (16).

The Igbo call such children *ogbanje*, and Achebe and Cyprian Ekwensi bring them into their fiction. The most moving *ogbanje* in Nigerian literature is Okonkwo's daughter Ezinma. When discussing Ezinma, Laurence explains that ". . . the children who died were always the same children, born again and again, fated to die again and again, eternal bringers of anguish . . ." (101). Filia Enu, Ekwensi's heroine in *Iska*, is an *ogbanje*. Of her Laurence writes, ". . . Filia as a child was suspected to be an *Ogbanje*, 'one who comes to this world again and again,' or as the Yoruba say of the same type, whom they call *abiku*, 'the child born to die' " (167).

A *Dance of the Forests* ends with a power struggle between the gods Ogun and Eshuoro, in which the pawn is an *abiku*, separated from its mother. Finally Demoke, the artist, gains possession of the child, and he chooses to return it to its mother, thus presumably allowing all or part of the cycle of death and rebirth to continue. *A Dance of the Forests* was written and performed to mark Nigeria's independence, and the *abiku* has been seen as the symbol of the emerging nation, which is dying as a colony to be reborn in a new form. Laurence could not accept this reading though she felt that the occasion of the play's production could be a possible reason for some of its obscurities. The play criticizes corruption and warns against euphoria, and, writes Laurence, "[i]t was first performed — amazingly enough — as part of the Nigerian Independence celebrations in 1960. Either the authorities of that period were more liberal-minded than they subsequently became, or else they did not understand what *A Dance of the Forests* was all about" (29). What the *abiku* incident is all about continues to challenge the critics.

Beier in his review sees the final action as a death sentence for the *abiku* because Demoke "does not wish to live under the compulsion of old ideas perpetually reborn . . ." (58). Laurence finally suggests a more complex significance to Demoke's act. In returning "the child born-to-die to the Dead, to the ancestors, from whence it will be re-born and re-born," Demoke is driven, Laurence agrees with Beier, by the human urge to rid oneself of the past. She adds, however, that we can never discard our history since ". . . it is man's fate to carry along with him some of the anguish of the past, some of the unsolved mysteries at the core of his own heart." Caught by the suggestive power of Soyinka's writing, Laurence voices her fears of the unknown areas of the mind that he conjures up, "the never-ending cycle, the desire for oblivion born again into each soul, rarely recognised or admitted openly" (44). Soyinka's symbolism can and should be read on many levels, and one reading does not invalidate another. As Beier admits in his review, the "play is true symbolism, and like all real symbols can inspire more than one interpretation" (58). Jones is of the same opinion and thinks that "[e]ach succeeding reading produces insights which suggest a complete vision on the part of the author." He has high praise for Laurence's reading, which he finds "most sensitive" and one that "points a path through all these complexities" (*Writing* 33–34).[1]

Though she sometimes finds Soyinka's complexity difficult, Laurence was one of the first to recognize the outstanding quality of his work, and her discussion of his drama has proved of lasting value. Long before he won international fame with the Nobel Prize, she paid tribute to his genius. Thinking again of him as a conjuror, she praises his ability "to handle many themes simultaneously without ever endangering the reality of his characters," while also achieving "in his work an almost unbelievable amount of vitality" (11).

Laurence concludes her chapter on Soyinka with a commentary on *The Interpreters*, which when she wrote was a new and challenging work. As she remarks, this novel is at times "searingly funny" (73). Yet she realizes that it works on other levels. It is deeply concerned with a wide range of social themes while on another but integrated plane it deals with the relationship between the artist and the gods. It is an extremely difficult work to analyze since many of Soyinka's effects, especially the comic ones, are lost in the re-telling.

Soyinka's extravagant and irrepressible sense of comedy can only be appreciated in its setting, and Laurence, who savours his mockery, wisely praises his comic brilliance in general terms without trying to detail it. She can effectively suggest it, however, with her own ironic tone. For example she refers her readers to the scene when Chief Winsala comes to the office of the *Independent Viewpoint*, itself a slum building described in outrageous detail. Only Soyinka can do justice to what follows. Suffice it to say that Chief Winsala captures the female receptionist beneath his gown, made of *ankara* cloth with a design commemorating Nigerian independence, and attempts to have his way with her. Laurence suggests this moment of comedy with wit of her own. The "splendid" Chief Winsala, she writes, has "an extroverted personality and a cheerfully admitted lust which sends every young secretary and switchboard girl skittering for shelter" (66).

Laurence also discusses the social and psychological themes of the novel with perception. Her analysis of the chief characters, Egbo, Sagoe, Kola, Sekoni, and Bandele, the interpreters themselves, is thorough and helpful. Her admiration as a fellow novelist for Soyinka's remarkable achievement in sustaining the individual uniqueness of his five closely associated young intellectuals is warmly expressed. Yet there are parts of the novel that perplex her, and they mainly relate to the messianic figure Lazarus, who has returned from the dead, and his young convert Noah. They seem to her to have no place in the novel. In his article on *The Interpreters*, Jones shares Laurence's reservations; he feels that Lazarus and Noah lack the "inevitability" of the other characters and "seem to have been stuck in to fill the canvas" (45). Lazarus, an albino, cannot recall his former life, but he maintains that the villagers who released him when he woke from the dead told him he had been black when they put him in the coffin. Lazarus is yet another potential bridge, and by including him Soyinka recognizes the part played by the Christian faith in contemporary Nigeria. Though his novel, like his plays, is inhabited by Yoruba gods, there is also room for the prophet of another god whose covenant with his people was pledged to Noah with the rainbow. How reliable a prophet is a question Soyinka leaves open.

Once again "The Fourth Stage" would have helped Laurence, and she could have looked to Soyinka's explanation of the Yoruba pantheon to decipher the cryptic signals the novel contains. Kola the artist, Laurence writes, "is absorbed in painting a pantheon of the Yoruba gods," and much of the novel is concerned with his search for the right models — Egbo, for example, is sitting for the figure of Ogun (68). The relationship between the interpreters and the gods is not an easy one. Egbo turns away in disgust from Kola's portrayal of Ogun as the war lord, as Soyinka writes in *The Interpreters*, Ogun at his "drunkennest," "slaughtering his own men" (233). Before completing the painting, Kola incorporates another powerful figure into the painting. It is the arched resurrection figure of Lazarus, "the bridge of moon-beam piercing sky and earth" (237), portrayed as the rainbow god Esumare, "Kola's new dimension to the covenant" (232).

All the characters in *The Interpreters* are drawn into the need to cross the abyss stretching between themselves and the traditions of their past, to bridge, as Lazarus does, life and death, earth and heaven. The search for a trustworthy martyr or bridge is not a simple one in a novel that depicts the fragmentation and mingling of more than one faith. It is perhaps Sekoni, called Sheikh, with his mixed Islamic and Christian inheritance, who nevertheless best bridges the void. His first stammering words in the novel relate to bridges. " 'The b-b-bridge," Sekoni stutters, "is the d-d-dome of rreligion and b-b-bridges d-d-don't jjjust g-g-go from hhhere to ththere; a bridge also faces backwards' " (9). Sekoni, who creates the perfect carving of the wrestler after suffering a nervous breakdown and before dying in a violent road accident, is seen as a sacrificial offering to Ogun. Sekoni's act of creation involved great labour. Soyinka writes, ". . . the act of his creation which took him an entire month and over, was frenzy and desperation, as if time stood in his way" (99–100). Kola acknowledges that his finished painting lacks the power that Sekoni has achieved in his sculpture of a wrestling figure, for which Bandele is the model. Sekoni's figure, dressed in pilgrim's robes, is struggling with a serpent, a martyr god prepared to wrestle with the threatening forces on humanity's behalf.

Writing within a year of its publication, it is not surprising that Laurence did not grasp all the ideas contained in Soyinka's novel, which can still spring surprises with each new reading. It is a juggling act no less miraculous than any of his plays.

She does not as a writer identify as closely with Soyinka as she does with Achebe. Nevertheless, she sometimes has her own work in mind when discussing his. Halfway through her commentary on *A Dance of the Forests*, when she is describing how the honest Warrior was sold as a slave by King Mata Kharibu for a flask of rum, Laurence remarks that this "must be one of the very few places in contemporary Nigerian literature in which the question of the slave trade is mentioned. Either it is too far back in the past, or else there is some deep reluctance to look at it. Soyinka here deals with the guilt of the old African empires who sold their own people as slaves" (39). Soyinka's references to the slave trade in *A Dance of the Forests* are not out of place in a play that is remarkable for its historical breadth. Laurence must have recalled Nathaniel's allusions to the subject in *This Side Jordan*. In fact it is perhaps her own indignation that inspires Nathaniel's lament since his passionate concern about the slaves who lay in the dungeons of Elmina Castle is reminiscent of the outsider's reaction. It is not a subject, for example, that worries Achebe's Obi Okonkwo, who resembles Nathaniel in so many other ways.

The West Indian and American descendants of the slaves are, not surprisingly, most concerned about the slave trade. The Nigerian writers are more troubled about the years of colonization that gave shape to their own societies. Richard Wright in *Black Power* gives a personal and powerful commentary on the past. Another transatlantic but very different treatment of slavery can be found in C.S. Forester's *The Sky and the Forest*, which is a remarkable and under-rated novel. He portrays in moving terms the suffering of the slaves at the time of capture and deportation, and his response is one shared by Laurence. It is a subject about which they both feel strongly, but to which they cannot finally relate on a personal level. Laurence makes a revealing remark on the subject in an article, "In Pursuit of My Past on the Road from the Isles," published in 1966 (retitled "Road from the Isles" in *Heart of a Stranger*) and written when she was working on *Long Drums and Cannons*. After expressing her indignation about the treatment her Scottish ancestors received, she concludes that she is unable to feel the matter personally. She realizes that the only ancestral past that had any personal meaning for her was her Canadian heritage, which encompassed but "a very few generations" (157), and so did not include any Scottish history. "The story of the Highland Clearances," she writes, "moved me as much as the story of the slave trade in Africa, but no more" (155).

Her careful observation of Soyinka's work and her response to such aspects as his treatment of slavery give her critique its value. Her intuitive powers are strong and enable her to override the inevitable disadvantage of working so early in the field. Her assessment of Soyinka's writing can still stand today. Her peroration on his genius is as eloquent and as discerning as her final tribute to Achebe. Of Soyinka she concludes,

> Soyinka's writing is life-filled, overflowing with energy, capable of realising human personalities and catching the sound of one particular voice, at times intensely comic, coloured with rhythm and dance, with drums and masquerade. But underneath, there is a concern with the inner territory of the spirit, a painful appraisal of the usually hidden parts of the mind. This strong undercurrent in his writing places him, ultimately, among the chroniclers of the areas of darkness within us all. (76)

11

Forests, Cities, and Rivers:
Amos Tutuola, Cyprian Ekwensi,
and John Pepper Clark

The other essays in *Long Drums and Cannons* illustrate the point Irele makes, namely that it was difficult to evaluate Nigerian literature in English when it began to appear in a dazzling variety of new forms. Moore also discusses the problem in the introduction to his book, *Twelve African Writers* (1980), which was a revision and expansion of his earlier work, *Seven African Writers* (1962). With the benefit of hindsight he could see that early critics, of whom he was one, failed to evaluate the new writing with discrimination. The problem arose, he feels, because this writing was seen as "new" when it was in fact part of a continuing oral tradition. When Moore put together his second volume of writers, he believed that what was needed nearly twenty years later was a "largely new book, with different standards of selection, presentation and approach" (8). Amos Tutuola had been one of the original seven, but he was left out of Moore's later group of twelve. Moore maintains that the early promise of Tutuola's first book, which had, anyway, been welcomed for the wrong reasons, was not matched by his later writing.

Laurence makes far more use of secondary sources in her essay on Tutuola than anywhere else in her book, which indicates some uncertainty in her own line of approach.[1] In "Ways into Africa," a reviewer for the *Times Literary Supplement* notices that ". . . her essay on Tutuola is the least original." Laurence follows two earlier commentaries when she discusses his work: Moore's in *Seven African Writers* and Tibble's in *African-English Literature*. Laurence agrees with both earlier critics that Tutuola's first novel, *The Palm-Wine Drinkard*, was his best — "masterpiece" is the term used by Moore and Laurence — and that his succeeding novels never equalled it, though Tibble questions whether there was "a falling-off between his first book and his later books" (96). T.S. Eliot, who advised Faber to publish Tutuola's work, would have agreed with Tibble, and his remarks are quoted in a fascinating article by Bernth Lindfors, in which he tells the story of "Amos Tutuola's Search for a Publisher." Eliot would have accounted for Moore's reaction by explaining that, though there were " 'just as good things' " in Tutuola's second work as in *The Palm-Wine Drinkard*, ". . . the public appetite for this line of fiction may be satisfied with one book." Eliot himself found that his "attention did sometimes wander" while reading *My Life in the Bush of Ghosts* (103).

Laurence is not unaware of the controversial nature of the discussion that followed the publication of Tutuola's first novel. However, she does not investigate in any depth the questions raised by his work, and she draws back from offering any decisive or personal opinion. Laurence devotes nearly as much space, most of it given to plot summaries, to Tutuola as she does to Achebe.

Tutuola's story is now well known. According to Lindfors in "Amos Tutuola's Search for a Publisher," "[t]he story of Amos Tutuola's surprising rise to literary fame has been told so often that it has almost gained the stature of a legend or modern-day myth" (90). In the process, considerable injustice was done to Tutuola's reputation as a writer. He was born in Western Nigeria and wrote out of a traditional Yoruba background, though with an effect very different from that created by Soyinka. Unlike Soyinka, Tutuola received little formal education. He was, however, the first Nigerian to win international fame. When his book *The Palm-Wine Drinkard* was published in 1952, it was received enthusiastically, most notably by Dylan Thomas who described it as a "brief, thronged, grisly and bewitching story, or series of stories, written in young English by a West African . . ." (2). The reaction of western critics to the book, and especially to Tutuola's "young English," upset some Nigerians who resented the praise given Tutuola's quaint and ungrammatical language.

When Laurence turned her attention to Tutuola, the controversy had abated; both western hyperbole and African hypersensitivity had moderated. The problem with interpreting Tutuola has always been one of uncertainty; which of his effects were contrived and which spontaneous? His Faber editors were the first who had to find an answer when faced with his idiosyncratic English; what should they correct and what should they leave? Initially the policy was as Geoffrey Parrinder notes "to remove the grosser mistakes, clear up some ambiguities, and curtail repetition," without destroying the "original flavour of the style" (15). Because such a method required an arbitrary decision on the alterations needed, Faber later favoured a complete "hands-off" policy. This procedure was also criticized, most eloquently in a *Black Orpheus* review of *The Brave African Huntress*. The review was written by "Akanji," a pseudonym used by Ulli Beier (see table of contents in Lindfors, *Critical Perspectives*). Agreeing that Tutuola's style should not be tampered with, Beier nevertheless feels that obvious spelling mistakes should have been corrected because "Tutuola's language will lose none of its poetry, his style will not lose character if he is told that 'gourd' is not spelled 'guord' " (59). Laurence follows Beier's line of argument closely, devoting a paragraph to the question, which is obviously one she can understand personally and about which she is prepared to make a strong statement. After agreeing that it would have been wrong to alter Tutuola's imagery or phraseology, she adds that it would have been proper to correct the spelling: "Spelling is an entirely different matter," she argues, adding with feeling that "Tutuola is certainly not the only writer who makes spelling mistakes. Everybody makes them. The correction of such errors is common editorial practice, and the fact that it has not been done here seems to give weight to the feeling that many West Africans have had about Tutuola's work — that it was read in Europe and America only so that its language could be ridiculed" (142).

Other qualities of Tutuola's writing have also caused problems. As Tutuola's works followed each other in quick succession, initial enthusiasm for them waned, especially abroad. On the other hand, in Nigeria the initial outrage of some of Tutuola's compatriots had been replaced by a more sympathetic appreciation, best expressed by Achebe in the article "English and the African Writer." Achebe and Tutuola are often linked, not because they are alike, but because they demonstrate two different ways of adapting English to express African sensibilities. English needed to be Africanized if it was to convey an African outlook. Achebe was very deliberate in his methods of doing this; Tutuola seems to have done it instinctively.

Achebe describes Tutuola as "a natural" artist and himself as "a conscious" one. Of Tutuola he writes that "a good instinct has turned his apparent limitation in language into a weapon of great strength" (61). However, Achebe's use of "apparent" is indicative of the continuing enigmatic nature of Tutuola's work, and Laurence's use of "intentionally or unintentionally" when discussing the ending of *The Palm-Wine Drinkard* (132), confesses to a similar uncertainty about Tutuola's "naturalness."

Tutuola is an enigmatic and fascinating writer; beneath his apparent naturalness lies a well-defined moral purpose. When Achebe taught in America in the 1970s, he included Tutuola in his course, and, when he delivered the first Equiano Memorial lecture at the University of Ibadan in 1970, he chose to speak on "Work and Play in Tutuola's *The Palm-Wine Drinkard*." In his lecture, later published in *Hopes and Impediments*, Achebe argues that Tutuola's work is much more than the tall, devilish story that attracted Dylan Thomas. Behind the colourful and original narrative, which has strong links with "ancient oral, and moral, tradition," Tutuola, Achebe demonstrates, is concerned with the need to balance work and play, acknowledging the proper importance of both. Tutuola speaks, Achebe concludes, "strongly and directly to our times. For what could be more relevant than a celebration of work today for the benefit of a generation and a people whose heroes are no longer makers of things and ideas but spectacular and insatiable consumers?" (75–76).

Laurence could have delved more deeply into the questions Tutuola's work has raised, especially as she indicates her awareness of their existence. She chose, however, to concentrate on the episodic storylines of his first five books, which gain little from such treatment, though it does indicate that she had read his work carefully. As Achebe remarks in his lecture, ". . . many who talk about Tutuola one way or another are yet to read him" (69). Laurence refers frequently for clarification to the commentaries of Moore and Tibble. She does not accept all their readings, questioning, for example, Tibble's view of Tutuola's stories as " 'fine fairy tales' " (146), but for the most part she has little original comment to add. She appreciates those qualities that attracted Dylan Thomas: Tutuola's "strangely poetic writing" (126) and his "way of combining the macabre and the beautiful, the horrifying and the humorous, the familiar and the mysterious" (146). She fails, however, to discern any specific purpose to his writing and so does not, as Achebe does, argue convincingly on the importance of his work. She describes Tutuola with the same imagery that she had previously applied to Soyinka. She wrote with feeling about Soyinka's exploration of the areas of mysterious tension, but there is a false ring to her eloquence when she writes in the same way about Tutuola. She tends to use over-dramatic imagery when discussing his "intensely inward" imagination (147), as when, for example, she ends her summary of Tutuola's second novel with nebulous statements. The conclusion of *My Life in the Bush of Ghosts*, she feels, "does not seem to make sense in the external context, but it has specific meaning if it is viewed as another direct and indeed tragic statement from the inner world." Its author, she suggests, is "someone who has walked in the pit of hell, and who has been courageous enough to open his eyes while he was there" (136). Tutuola's fables, violent and bizarre though they may be, have a more direct and down to earth relevance than this would imply.

Cyprian Ekwensi no less than Tutuola is a fascinating figure whose writing has attracted considerable interest and acclaim. Laurence was one of the first to write extensively on Ekwensi, and she has much to say that is pertinent and perceptive. Ekwensi was born in Northern Nigeria of an Igbo family — like Filia Enu, the heroine of his novel *Iska* — and is a cosmopolitan in outlook. Ekwensi's first work, *When Love Whispers*, which Laurence does not discuss in detail, is accepted as the first example of Onitsha Market literature. Laurence describes this literature — mostly printed and sold in the market town of Onitsha — as "sentimental and highly moral," much like "many American and English women's magazines." She considers that in his best work Ekwensi manages to break away from this beginning: "Something of this sentimentality and superficiality can still be seen in his later books, although there is scarcely a trace of it in his best novels, *Jagua Nana* and *Iska*" (149).

Since the publication of *Long Drums and Cannons*, considerable research has been done on the nature of the Onitsha pamphlets, and Ekwensi at his best in fact stays true to their traditions, able at times to give them credibility and value. Emmanuel N. Obiechina has published extracts from the Onitsha pamphlets. He has also written extensively on the history and characteristics of the market literature and of the special place and time that caused it to flourish.

The town of Onitsha, essentially Igbo in character, was a trading centre that drew others to its famous market. Strategically placed on the Niger, Obiechina writes in *Onitsha Market Literature*, it was "the educational and commercial centre of the Eastern Region of Nigeria" and a meeting place for many people: Igbo from the hinterland, Hausa from the north, Ijaw fishermen, and Yoruba traders (4). It was busy and colourful and growing. Achebe, who wrote the foreword for Obiechina's *An African Popular Literature*, describes Onitsha as a place of "day schools and night schools, mission schools and private schools, grammar schools and commercial schools, of one-room academies and backyard colleges" (x). Achebe and Obiechina describe Onitsha as they remember it. "Onitsha," writes Achebe in *Morning Yet*, "had always attracted the exceptional, the colourful and the bizarre . . ." (91), and "Onitsha was a self-confident place where a man would not be deterred even by insufficient learning from aspiring to teach and improve his fellows" (92).

The pamphlets produced and sold in Onitsha in their thousands varied from romances to political commentaries to handbooks on how to get on in the world. Their heyday came in the years between the Second World War and Biafran Secession. They were rooted in contemporary life and had a serious side to them. Their authors, writes Achebe in his foreword, wished "to tackle seriously in the light of their own perception the social problems of a somewhat mixed-up but dynamic, even brash, modernizing community" (x). Writing *Onitsha Market Literature* after the Biafran War, Obiechina mourns the cost to Onitsha and its popular literature of the years of fighting:

> The pamphlet literature has suffered a number of serious setbacks. Onitsha Market which fathered the writing is one of the casualties of the recent civil war in Nigeria. It was totally gutted and its many thousand colourful and adventurous denizens scattered near and far. Onitsha itself, no less an important factor in the rise of the pamphlet literature than its market, lies battered and in ruins, drained of its vitality. (27–28)

Laurence recognizes the attractions of Ekwensi's writing, which appealed to young Nigerians who felt that ". . . here was someone who really understood them and accepted the fact that the world of today was not the world of their parents" (150). His novels, for the most part set in Lagos, portray the "city world of right-this-minute" (148), and the animation and noise of his streets, where the up-and-coming young city-dwellers live in rented rooms and frequent night-clubs, would have reminded Laurence of Accra. Something of the city's restlessness transfers itself into Ekwensi's narrative, especially, as Laurence notices, in *People of the City*, where the plot is "jittery" (150). Ernest Emenyonu quotes with approval Laurence's description of this novel, which, he notes, "Margaret Laurence has so correctly described by her remark that 'the story leaps about spasmodically like a nervous cricket' " (Emenyonu 45; Laurence 150). Laurence rightly acknowledges Ekwensi's sympathetic and spirited portrayal of women, and she responds to his greatest character, Jagua Nana, in imaginative and fitting terms. This is Laurence at her best as a critic:

> [Jagua] has a temper like red pepper, but she is capable of great affection. She can screech and claw like a she-eagle one moment, and the next moment be as generous with her money and herself as though her whole future were assured. She is tough, enduring, and completely without self-pity. She accepts the world as she finds it, seeing its meanness with an undeceived eye and enjoying its pleasures whenever she can. As a fictional character she will remain alive for a long time. (157)

Laurence also notices Ekwensi's concern about the distrust between the different peoples of Nigeria and the threat it poses for his contemporary characters. In Ekwensi's novels the different peoples of Nigeria mix as they used to in Onitsha's market place. In *Iska*, Filia Enu, an Igbo, marries the northerner Dan Kaybi, and the novel, as Laurence notes, has a serious theme because it deals with the Igbo-Hausa riots that led ultimately to the Biafran War. *Iska* is a prophetic novel, no less than Achebe's *A Man of the People*, and Laurence notes that Ekwensi was "deeply involved" in the events he describes (162).

His novels are for the most part sentimental and superficial like the popular pamphlet literature, but they serve the purpose for which they were designed. Ekwensi said in an interview that his "audience consists of the ordinary working man. I don't pretend to aim at any intellectuals. If I am in a taxi and the taxi driver recognizes me and talks about what I have written, it makes me feel that I am reaching the masses" (44). In her essay "Ivory Tower" Laurence recalls "reading an interview with Cyprian Ekwensi, who said that among the people who bought and read his books the Lagos taxi drivers ranked high" (18).

Laurence could have profitably omitted the mundane plot outlines and concentrated on those qualities of Ekwensi's fiction that she had identified as noteworthy. Ekwensi's novels, written for and about contemporary society, are animated, colourful, and popular, like Onitsha in its heyday.

Throughout her study Margaret Laurence, while giving priority to her primary texts, makes good use of the limited secondary reading that was available to her. Having absorbed the observations of writers like Green and Beier, she can begin to identify the Igbo characteristics of Achebe's and Ekwensi's writing and the Yoruba nature of Soyinka's and Tutuola's work. In the essay on John Pepper Clark, she examines the different traditions of the Ijaw people. Her debt to secondary sources in this case is substantial, though the appropriateness of the material she uses has been questioned.

The fisher people who live in the mangrove swamps of the Niger Delta have a distinct and fascinating culture that reflects their close relationship with their watery environment. Laurence earlier noticed that Soyinka had been drawn to the Ijaw landscape in *The Swamp Dwellers*, the play in which he left "his usual Yoruba background" for the world of those "who live in the tidal mangrove swamps of the Eastern Niger Delta" (24).

Robert M. Wren, in a study of Clark written after the publication of *Long Drums and Cannons*, evokes the landscape of the Delta. The annual floods continually change the shape of the swamp islands, but they also wash down rich deposits to fertilize the soil in those areas where the in-coming salt-water tides cannot reach. The river is the source of wealth for the village fishers, and the waters of its creeks and swamps were seen as the dwelling places of powerful spirits. As Wren puts it, ". . . the central economic factors in all Ijo [Wren uses this spelling] communities are the water and the canoe that floats upon it" (2–3). Laurence is herself attracted by Clark's use of the watery environment in his work. When discussing *The Raft*, she commends "the picture it gives of the life of the creeks and swamps, set down lovingly and with the kind of close-up detail that shows a lifelong knowledge and an inner understanding of a place" (90).

But once again Laurence needed some guidance from an anthropologist as she considered another set of complex traditions. The authority Laurence uses is Robin Horton, who wrote a series of articles, published in the early 1960s, on the Kalabari people, whom he describes as "part of the great bloc of Ijo-speaking peoples who fill the Delta; but they form a distinct sub-group both in dialect and in culture" ("The Kalabari World-View" 197). The Kalabari people live on the eastern edges of the Delta, whereas, Wren notes, Clark's home, Kiagbodo, lies in "the extreme north of the Western Delta" (4). Horton's articles, therefore, have been considered inappropriate background material for a discussion of Clark's plays. This opinion was voiced in "Ways into Africa" by the reviewer of *Long Drums and Cannons* who pointed out that ". . . J.P. Clark — though indeed an Ijaw — was born in what was then Western Nigeria, and a very long way away from the Kalabari, who speak an Ijaw dialect in Eastern Nigeria, and who are the people described by Robin Horton" (8). However, the different groups of the Ijaw people shared common traditions, and an understanding of the Kalabari customs is relevant to Clark's drama, as Laurence's discussion demonstrates. Clark himself was familiar with Horton's work, which he uses, on the whole with approval, when discussing his own drama in *The Example of Shakespeare*.

Horton, describing the Kalabari religion in "The Kalabari World-View: An Outline and Interpretation," names the three forces that influence the daily life of the people: the ancestors, the village heroes, and the water spirits (Horton calls them "the water people"). "Perhaps," he writes, "it would not be going too far beyond Kalabari conceptions if we visualized ancestors, heroes, and water people as forming the corners of a triangle of forces" (203). Laurence expands this and explains that "[t]he structure of the traditional Ijaw world, spiritually speaking, rests upon the ancestors and upon the village heroes who have mainly come in from the outside and have been innovators and bringers of change, and upon the water people — the gods and demi-gods who dwell in the swamps and creeks and who exercise a considerable influence over the lives of men" (78).

Laurence introduces her discussion of Clark's plays with two explanatory sections, "Ekine Drama" and "Ijaw View of the Personality." In these sections Laurence used notes she had made from Horton's articles, often echoing his phraseology. In his articles Horton covers many aspects of Kalabari art and religion, discussing the Ijaw conception of *teme*, something akin to the Igbo *chi*, and describing in detail the masquerade plays that the Kalabari *Ekine* societies perform in the dry seasons.

In "Destiny and the Unconscious in West Africa," Horton describes the Kalabari view of the human personality as two-fold, and he draws a parallel with Freudian concepts. One half of the soul is the "*biomgbo*, which corresponds most closely to what we should call the 'conscious mind.' This is the agency associated with all the feelings, desires, and thoughts of which the individual is aware." The other, and more important half, "is the *teme*, an immaterial agency which is in existence before the individual is born and which survives his death." Drawing their imagery from their environment the ". . . Kalabari liken the *teme* to the steersman of the personality" (113). In her discussion of *teme*, Laurence clearly follows Horton's argument, picking up his reference to Freudian theory. Laurence accepts Horton's interpretation that "[t]he personality, in the Ijaw view, is layered, just as it is in the Freudian view. The *biomgbo* or personal soul, containing the individual's desires and feelings, corresponds to the conscious mind. The *teme* or steersman of the soul is comparable to the unconscious . . ." (80).

When discussing the Kalabari masquerades in "The Kalabari *Ekine* Society: A Borderland of Religion and Art," which share many of the characteristics of the English medieval mystery plays, Horton explains that "[e]ach society stages a cycle of thirty to fifty masquerade plays — a cycle which in former times was probably completed in the drier part of every year. The commonest way of beginning the cycle is for *Ekine* members to go down in canoes to a spot far out in the creeks known as 'Beach of the Water Spirits'" (95). That Laurence uses Horton as her source can be clearly seen from her description, which echoes his: "Each year a cycle of thirty to fifty plays is put on. The cycle begins with the Ekine members' visit to the Beach of the Water Spirits, far out in the creeks of the Niger Delta" (79).

Horton has been told that the water spirits often attend the masqueraders closely, eventually possessing them. "Possession," relates Horton, "is in fact encouraged, and is regarded as the seal of a successful performance" (95). Laurence expands this when she remarks that "The plays are performed by masked dancers, who are often possessed by the spirit of the mask. This state of trance enables a dancer to perform beyond his normal skill" (79). Horton lists the characters that are typical of the masquerades. He names *Ikaki*, a "cunning, amoral hypocrite," and he describes at some length "the native doctor *Ngbula*," who makes his appearance "grunting around with grim concentration in search of bad medicines and evil spirits: suspicious like all of his profession that people are talking ill of him. . . ." Notable among the female parts is *Igoni*, "a garrulous, self-pitying old widow who alternately bemoans her own and everyone else's troubles" (97). Laurence comments on the same characters, "types such as Ikaki, the amoral hypocrite, Ngbula the herbal doctor who imagines that people are talking maliciously about him, and Ijona, a self-pitying widow" (79). She appears to have misread her notes as she refers to the widow Igoni as "Ijona."

It is easy and fascinating to follow Laurence as she makes notes for use in her own text. For example she changes Horton's adjective "native" to "herbal" when talking about doctor Ngbula. This is typical of her realization after her years in Africa of the sensitivity of certain words — another word she came to distrust was "bush," which she used freely when working on *A Tree for Poverty*, but avoids when writing *The Prophet's Camel Bell*. Laurence ignores the most scurrilous characters mentioned by Horton, "sexy, good-for-nothing aristocrat *Igbo*, of whom they sing: 'His father sent him to market to buy yams; but instead he bought woman's vagina' " (97).

Laurence thinks it more important to relate Clark's drama to "the culture and mythology of his own people" (77) than to trace the undoubted influence on his work of Greek or Shakespearean drama. With Horton's help she succeeds in her aim. Her summary of Clark's first play, *Song of a Goat*, which she considers his best, is thorough and sympathetic. Laurence gives a fine reading of the main character, the poor fisherman Zifa, showing how he is compelled by his *teme* to fulfil his tragic destiny. This reading parallels her interpretation of Okonkwo and his relationship with his *chi*. Laurence presents Okonkwo and Zifa in the same tragic terms as noble and generous figures. They are very different people as Clark himself has pointed out in *The Example of Shakespeare* (23), but both are driven to suicide, and Laurence's explanation of their actions is not only fine critical writing but also a sign of her own compassionate understanding of human vulnerability.

In her discussion of *Ozidi*, Laurence could not take advantage of the five essays Clark wrote in the 1960s and which were published in 1970 in a volume called *The Example of Shakespeare*. These essays, especially "Aspects of Nigerian Drama," in which Clark makes clear his passionate interest in Ijaw masquerades, are particularly helpful to a discussion of *Ozidi*. While Laurence prefers *Song of a Goat*, she knows that Clark attached more importance to his dramatization for the stage of the epic Ijaw saga about the hero Ozidi. Clark saw as his mission the preservation of the traditions of the masquerades, which could last for days and which, "because they demand so much energy and time, are more or less dying out today" (84). As part of the process of preservation, which includes adapting it for new audiences, Clark has made a tape recording of the Ijaw saga about Ozidi, an English translation, and a film. In his description of the filming of *Ozidi*, Clark has an interesting comment on the state of trance, which Horton had described as typical of masquerades. In "Aspects of Nigerian Drama," Clark describes possession as "the attainment by actors in the heat of performance of 'actual freedom of spirit from the material world' . . . ." He adds that "[t]his phenomenon features regularly in sacred plays, especially the masquerade kind. It was a constant cause of hold-ups in my filming of the Ozidi saga at Oru[a.]" (87). He also wrote his own dramatic version in English, *Ozidi*, an attempt to stage the saga for the enclosed theatre with some of the effects that were traditionally part of the village performances. While Laurence has understandable reservations about the suitability of Clark's play for actual performance, she recognizes the importance of his achievement, that of breathing new life into the old traditions. Her examination of Clark's rendering of this Ijaw epic reveals "the complexity of his traditional sources and the ways in which he has drawn — in all his plays — upon forms and concepts of Ekine masquerade drama, extending these and using them as a means of expressing conflicts which are both contemporary and universal" (95).

Laurence writes with limited success on Clark, mainly because she excludes a full discussion of his poetry. She draws some comparisons between his plays and Soyinka's, clearly considering the latter as the more skilled dramatist. She believes that Clark suffers "from an insufficient knowledge of theatre" (95). His plays have, indeed, been difficult to stage; Wren describes some of the disastrous performances of *Song of a Goat*, which involve a sacrifice of a goat on stage (44). Laurence rightly sees Clark as "primarily a poet" (78), but could not demonstrate this because *Long Drums and Cannons* is concerned only with fiction and drama. She does, however, comment on his fine use of language in his first play. There ". . . the language is spare and yet rich, full of poetic images drawn from the land and the creeks" (86). She concludes with the remark that, while Clark does not have Soyinka's "gift for creating character," he does have "a poetic fluency which, when it is going well, goes very well indeed" (96).

12

Other Voices

In her final essay, Laurence turns to six other Nigerian voices. She explains that they are writers who did not at the time merit full-length discussion because they had not produced a body of work of a consistently high standard, though some of them had written a first work of promise. Here, it is only too easy to question her choice of authors because among them are some who have not lived up to expectations and some who have exceeded them. This final chapter, however, shares the few faults and many virtues of the book as a whole. Within it is found the same fascinating ethnic mix: T.M. Aluko is a Yoruba, Elechi Amadi, Nkem Nwankwo, Flora Nwapa, and Onuora Nzekwu are Igbo, and Gabriel Okara an Ijaw. With ready sympathy Laurence discusses work of differing quality, always reluctant to criticize and quick to recognize the good points of any work.

Some of the novels she discusses are more interesting as social histories than as literary works. This is above all true of T.M. Aluko, whose novels, Laurence admits, "contain many flaws" (169). She can see value in Aluko's work and concentrates on *One Man, One Matchet*, which is easily Aluko's best novel and which hinges on the European attempt to treat diseased cocoa trees. She astutely points out that it "should be required reading for every European or American technician and teacher involved in aid schemes in Africa, as well as for every African government official dealing with development projects . . ." (171). Ngugi Wa Thiong'o has written of Aluko's work, in particular *One Man, One Matchet*, as satire directed against the contemporary Nigerian neo-colonialist élite, who have used independence to further their own ends. Ngugi recognizes that Aluko does not have Achebe's imaginative capacity, that his characters are stereotypes, but he commends Aluko's social responsibility. "Everything in this novel," Ngugi maintains, "although it is set in an earlier period, carries overtones of the violence, corruption and anarchy of contemporary Nigerian politics" (58). It is this aspect of his work that allows Ngugi to discuss Aluko in the same article as Soyinka, though in every other respect these two Yoruba writers cannot be compared. Laurence also recognizes Aluko's clear and honest viewpoint and remarks that his "social satire is deft" (170).

Laurence could have left a discussion of Onuora Nzekwu out of the book. In just over two pages she finds little to say of his three novels beyond a brief summary of plot outline. Like Ekwensi, Nzekwu was born of an Igbo family in a railway town in Northern Nigeria. Patrick Ikenga, the hero of Nzekwu's novel *Blade Among the Boys*, shares these biographical details with his creator, and the evocation of the life of railway workers in Northern Nigeria is realistically done. Nzekwu, however, too often echoes the worst of the Onitsha Market pamphlets, without ever rising above them, as Ekwensi was able to do. Laurence has some words of praise for the portrayal of the heroine in *Highlife for Lizards*, but Agom, an "[i]ntelligent and passionate" woman, who "marries a man who is basically weaker than herself . . ." (192–93), has none of the originality and spirit of Jagua.

Only one Nigerian woman, Flora Nwapa, had written a novel before the outbreak of the Biafran War, and Laurence was naturally interested in it. It is an evocative novel and one that Achebe recommended for publication. Nwapa's account of Igbo village life lacks the vision and purpose that gives Achebe's novels their power, but, as Laurence points out, she has an ear for women's voices and succeeds because she lets them tell her story. "*Efuru*," Laurence observes, "takes place almost totally within the minds and the society of women," and Nwapa's compassionate description of life in the village is done "from the viewpoint of a participant rather than an observer" (190).

Another Igbo writer, Elechi Amadi, published his first novel, *The Concubine*, in 1966. His second novel, *The Great Ponds*, 1970, came too late for inclusion in Laurence's book. However, with only one novel before her, Laurence recognized the strength of Amadi's work, and her short discussion of *The Concubine* reaches beyond simple description to perceptive critical appreciation, in part due to her understanding of Igbo traditions. She is one of the first to write on

Amadi as *The Concubine* appeared too late to be included in Tibble's 1965 survey. Laurence points out the important differences between Achebe's and Amadi's novels. *The Concubine*, no less than Achebe's historical novels, conveys a sense of "unfaltering authenticity" in its depiction of the Igbo world-view, but Amadi portrays a world where the European has no part. Unlike Achebe's Umuofia, where the fabric of society is cracking, Laurence notes that Amadi's Omokachi is a village where "[t]he tribal system is still stable and capable of coping with its own disasters in its own way. Amadi tells the story wholly from the inside, never attempting to give a contemporary interpretation to events, but adhering meticulously to the concepts and life-view held by the people within the novel" (177). Laurence remarks on the slow pace of the narrative, which, without ever being dull, matches the tempo of village life. Her reading of the end of the novel is both masterly and moving; when she describes Ekwueme's death, she writes of a man possessed with much the same courage and vulnerability that she grants her own characters:

> Ekwueme may be doomed by his love for Ihuoma, but he is not defeated by the gods. He does not become less than he is. Despite his previous timidity and his present fear, he declares that he will marry Ihuoma even if she is the beloved of the Sea King. He does not want to do battle with the gods, but when he is forced into this role he does not draw back. He goes on, only too aware of his vulnerable humanity, but stronger within himself than he has ever managed to be before. The victory, with Ekwueme's death, does not entirely belong to the gods. (184)

Alastair Niven, writing "The Achievement of Elechi Amadi" after the appearance of *The Great Ponds*, praises both novels, pointing out, as Laurence had done, how Amadi, in contrast to Achebe, shows a pattern of life persisting, not breaking down. Niven quotes directly from *Long Drums and Cannons*, praising the way Laurence interprets Amadi's portrayal of "man's relation to the gods" (96).

Two novels published in 1964 complete Laurence's discussion of Nigerian writing: *Danda* by Nkem Nwankwo and *The Voice* by Gabriel Okara. The former is a light work saved from mediocrity by its principal character, whom Laurence describes as "vibrant and memorable" (187). Okara, who is considered a better poet than a novelist, has attracted considerable interest because of his experimental use of English in his novel. Irele has discussed the problem faced by African writers who must choose between writing in their own language or that of the European colonizer. It is not a question of whether the writer can master the second language, but whether that language can adequately express cultural sensibilities. There is always, Irele maintains, a "disparity between his African material and his medium of expression" (50). Laurence approved of the position taken by Achebe, who claims English as his own. "I have been given," Achebe writes in "English and the African Writer," "this language and I intend to use it" (62). He has used the language in his own way, absorbing Igbo vocabulary and imagery into his narrative. He never attempted, however, to alter the structure of English syntax. It is generally felt that Achebe succeeded in, as Irele notes, "re-appropriating the European language to place it at the service of an African vision" (51). Laurence would certainly not question Achebe's success in this respect.

When discussing Tutuola's work, Achebe acknowledges in "English and the African Writer" that imperfectly learnt English can also be effective when it is used by a "natural" (61). Okara opened up a third possibility, that of deliberately using perfectly learnt English imperfectly. Okara's re-appropriation of English is in syntactic as well as semantic terms, but as an experiment it is not convincing, possibly because it is overdone. Clark, who like Achebe regarded English as one of his inherited languages, felt that Okara's example proved that ". . . for the African writer in a European language, the use of external and formalistic devices like special syntax and sentence-structures from the vernacular, although tempting, carries with it risks that can lead even the genius to disaster" (*Example* 37). At much the same time, but independently, Laurence was coming to the same conclusion as Clark, though as always her criticism is understated. She felt that the experimental use in *The Voice* of Ijaw linguistic constructions was not always successful and the resulting English could "appear strained" (196). Laurence does not see the attempt as wholly unsuccessful and finds that some of the descriptive passages read as "highly effective prose-poetry" (197). It is not within her terms of reference to comment on Okara's poetry, but she justly holds that the poetic quality of the writing makes *The Voice* "one of the most memorable novels to have come out of Nigeria" (193). This assessment has weight, coming as it does at the end of a book in which she has brought to her readers' attention a great many fascinating fictional works that have come out of Nigeria.

As Laurence notes in *Dance on the Earth*, her purpose in writing *Long Drums and Cannons* had been to make Nigerian literature "better known and more accessible" (185). This she did in warm and enthusiastic terms, her own experience as a writer making her perceptive and sympathetic. It was, indeed, a wise decision on the part of Macmillan to ask a Canadian writer of her stature to comment on an emerging literature in another part of the Commonwealth. The manner of her response produces the kind of criticism Healy asks for, a criticism that does not place African works in a museum, but evaluates each one as an independent and living creation, while at the same time relating it to all the literary traditions from which it has grown. Laurence locates each new text within its regional context, but she never denies it a place within a wider field of reference, within a world where boundaries are recognized, but only because they can be crossed.

The Spirit in the Ascent

When bringing together the diverse writings that resulted from Margaret Laurence's "seven years" in Africa — years, indeed, of plenty — it is helpful to use the obvious metaphor of a journey. Morley has rightly noted in "Canada, Africa, Canada" that "[t]he journey is one of Margaret Laurence's favorite metaphors and one that is particularly relevant to her own experience" (81). Travel as theme or metaphor acts as a framework for much of her African writing. *The Prophet's Camel Bell* is above all an account of a journey. In *A Tree for Poverty*, she interprets the oral literature of the Somali nomads as an integral part of their life of endless wandering through the desert. In her African fiction, the journey is one to independence in the promised land, involving the escape from slavery in Egypt and the final crossing of Jordan.

Hers was a journey through space and time. However, while she recognizes the importance of recalling the past, both the period before the colonial power encroached upon the traditional way of life as well as the years of colonization, what most concerns her is the environment of her contemporary characters and their quest for freedom. Their way forward is not easy, but it is essentially one of ascent, as she looks with them towards independence. She recognizes that progress, in all senses of the word, cannot be achieved without sacrifice: the death of Kofi and the tears of Ruth. In her study of the Nigerian writers, Laurence emphasizes the same themes in their work, thus relating it to her own. She commends the reassessment they give of their starting point — the historical past — but she points out in *Long Drums and Cannons* that "[t]he most persistent theme in Nigerian writing of today is today itself" (200).

The road Laurence took through Africa brought its rewards, for Laurence as well as for her readers. Much of the continent remained unknown to her, but the two areas she visited were markedly different from each other and gave her a sense of Africa's diversity. The desert Muslims of the Somaliland Protectorate, who had fought off the encroachments of the imperialists, lived in a world very unlike the Ashanti forest region, where the Akan people had seen their proud kings defeated by the white colonials. The time spent with the Somali nomads and then the peoples of West Africa gave her a compassionate understanding of the problems that divide one race from another. This knowledge sharpened her perception, not only of others, but also of herself. Her writing, fiction and nonfiction, while it centres on the solitary quest of the individual, also exploits the richness, complexity, and fascination of a diversity of cultures that were, for her, unfamiliar. It was the strangeness of these places that forced Laurence to prove herself as a writer, and the effects of her journey in Africa are evident not only in her African writing but also in the Manawaka works that brought her writing career to its climax.

Woodcock in an excellent essay entitled "Many Solitudes," which focuses on *The Prophet's Camel Bell*, has pointed out some of the direct connections between Laurence's travels and all her fiction. He remarks on "the importance to novelists like Margaret Laurence of an organic link between creative sensibility and the living environment" (150). In his essay he quotes in full the passage describing Laurence's encounter with the Somali woman who, her water finished, was travelling with her child through the Haud when the *Jilal* was at its height. Woodcock describes the account of this meeting as having an "epiphanic quality" (140). The two women came together for a brief moment, but for Laurence the result was of lasting consequence. The details of the scene remained with her and found an outlet later in her fiction. The sight of a mother "squatting in the sand," watching her child die, a symbol of inequity all too familiar today, inevitably shamed Laurence into protest (*Prophet's* 65–66). Philip Thrane, in "Mask of Beaten Gold," living by the sea in West Africa, is haunted by the scene Laurence witnessed in the Haud. While watching his "quick and laughing" wife, Philip thinks of others of her colour whose life has been less easy. He momentarily imagines her as "a skeletal woman in a shred of septic cloth that would soon double as shroud, a woman with vacant eyes, squatting in the red dust somewhere, by some roadside, not understanding the politics of famine, knowing only that her child and her own flesh were dying" (11–12).

In "Mask of Beaten Gold" the Somali woman is recalled as a symbol of those who suffer helplessly in an unjust world. She is heard again in Laurence's fiction, but on a different continent where she speaks with a Canadian accent. In that desert encounter, Laurence stepped back in time and came face to face with Hagar, Sarah's proud Egyptian handmaid. The Haud was the landscape through which Abraham wandered, and the Somalis, as the Children of Israel had done, "lived in the palm of God's hand" (*Prophet's* 53). Laurence identified the Somali woman and her child with Hagar and her son Ishmael. In this way the Old Testament story acquired new force, and Abraham's Hagar, despairing but unbeaten, stands like an indistinct shadow behind Laurence's first Canadian protagonist, who belongs without question to the Manitoban prairies, but who nevertheless in *The Stone Angel* describes herself as an "Egyptian" (40), "Pharaoh's daughter" (43).

Yet Hagar Shipley's life is not a retelling of the Bible story, though the cross-references are important and obvious. In an introduction to *The Stone Angel*, New explores its biblical references closely, demonstrating that they include allusions to Abraham's other family, descended from Sarah. Hagar Shipley's sons, Marvin and John, must both wrestle with an angel as Jacob did. New argues that ". . . Laurence's story of Hagar is based not so much on the *Genesis* story" (which is told from Sarah's viewpoint), as on St. Paul's reference to it in Galatians 4: 22–27, where the apostle lays emphasis on both of Abraham's families (viii). New's explanation is fascinating, but it leads to contradictions. In the end it is preferable not to look for a tight relationship between Bible and novel, but to see the association as a loose one. In "Margaret Laurence on *The Stone Angel*," an interview with Fabre, Laurence said ". . . I did not want the parallel to be too exact" (15). Laurence also told Sullivan in her interview that in her novel ". . . at various points there is an oblique reference to the story of the Biblical Hagar," but she adds that she "intended it only as a sort of echo" (68). The echo is most pronounced in Hagar's need for water. Water was as precious in the dusty Prairies as in the desert wilderness. When Hagar Shipley is dying, she takes into her own hands a glass full of water, saying "I'll drink from this glass, or spill it, just as I choose" (308). Water is a sign of God's mercy for Bram Shipley's Hagar in hospital as it was for Abraham's Hagar in the desert.

After her time in Somaliland, water became an important source of imagery for Laurence. "Water," as she explains to Fabre, "comes into, perhaps, a lot of my writing. . . . It is probably because it is one of the basic elemental symbols of life" (19). Yet, when she came to read Rattray's work, she would have been struck by the importance of water in Akan death rites, and the memory of those rites may well have added for her at any rate another dimension to Hagar's death. Rattray discovered that the Ashantis considered it important, when "the soul leaves the body, to pour a little water down the throat of the person who is dying" (*Religion* 148). Any doubts Laurence had about the importance of this rite would have ended when she found Nketia emphasizing that ". . . it is considered essential that before a person draws his final breath, he should be given a little drink of water to help him on in the journey that lies before him. The giving of the water is considered a sacred duty and an important preparation for the journey to the next world" (7). Doris gives the dying Hagar Shipley the glass of water, which she takes into her own hands. Water as the symbol of life and death allows Laurence to end the novel with a death scene that stops short of closing off Hagar's hold on life. In her last novel, *The Diviners*, Laurence returns to her literary beginnings in Africa for the potent image implicit in her title: the search for water in the arid desert world of today.

Laurence's use of biblical imagery in *The Stone Angel* is successful because it is natural, not forced.[1] Her use of biblical allegory is not limited to the story of Hagar. It can be found elsewhere in her West African and Canadian fiction. Names provide the best indication to its presence, though the connection should always be loosely not rigidly understood. Ruth in "The Rain Child" and Rachel in *A Jest of God* represent only in part their biblical namesakes. Ruth, standing "in tears amid the alien corn" (Keats, "Nightingale" line 67) and Rachel, who was barren and envied her sister, are remembered for only a part of their stories. The closest use of a biblical story is found in "Godman's Master," where the cross-references are extensive. The biblical imagery is an integral and natural part of Laurence's work, her familiarity with the Old and New Testaments was so complete that she drew on them almost unconsciously and certainly did not expect her allusions to be taken too literally. On one occasion confusion was the result of her natural inclination to use such reference. In the first published version of "The Drummer of All the World," there is a dramatic but, as Laurence decided later, expendable passage in which Matthew recalls the initiation of a fetish priest.

The passage concludes with Matthew likening himself to Isaac as a sacrificial victim. "Africa," Matthew acknowledges, "took unto itself my father's God. But at a price. I was your Isaac, of Abraham my father. This sacrifice, too, was never completed" (496). Laurence correctly realized that her biblical reference here was both inappropriate and muddled, and it was omitted in the version revised for *The Tomorrow-Tamer*.

Laurence's understanding of the Bible, strengthened in the hotel room in Antwerp, was sharpened into contemporary focus in the Haud, leaving her with unforgettable images. She even saw herself as a figure from Exodus, a stranger in the land of Egypt. Many of the mission-educated African writers knew the Bible as well as she did and used it with the same unconscious fluency. Laurence's comment on Achebe's use of the story of Abraham and Isaac in *Things Fall Apart* could be adapted to apply to her own such use of a Bible story in, for example, *A Jest of God*. In his first novel, Laurence notes in *Long Drums and Cannons*, "Achebe draws an unforced and unexplained but deeply ironic parallel . . . between Okonkwo and the Biblical patriarch Abraham, and the son Isaac who was once offered up as sacrifice . . ." (104).

In "Ten Years' Sentences," Laurence has referred to her relationship with Africa as "a seven years' love affair with a continent" (18), adding that during those years she was "young and full of faith" (19). Her commitment in those days was total. She sympathized with the political aspirations of the people among whom she lived, participated in the endeavours of those who were chronicling the present, and assisted in the task of restoring dignity to the past. It was not, as she admitted, "a lifetime commitment" (18), but while it lasted it was an intense one. Laurence was never an optimistic writer; however, in her West African fiction she is at times hopeful, occasionally even joyful. Certainly, in the 1950s in the Gold Coast, Laurence saw the realization of the "dream-goal of the promised land" as possible (19).

In the succeeding decade, Laurence watched as the spirit of hope died, and the promised land provided little milk or honey. The love affair had ended: "I guess I will always care about Africa. But the feeling I had, in everything I wrote about it, isn't the feeling I have now" (Ten Years' " 19). This is not an uncommon human experience. It parallels, for example, Wordsworth's disappointment as the French Revolution betrayed its ideals, and, though Laurence would not have expressed her feelings in his terms, there were times in Africa when one could exercise hope and joy: "Bliss was it in that dawn to be alive" ("The Prelude: Book Eleventh" line 108). The disappointment that followed was difficult to bear, and developments in Somalia and Ghana seemed incomprehensible to one who had come to know and admire both nations.

She viewed post-colonial developments in Africa from a distance, and her comments on neo-colonialism are few. Her aversion to the colonial mentality remained, and she found answers to many of her troubled questions in Mannoni's psychological study of colonization. She adopted his theory with eagerness, but its effect on her writing is not always a fortunate one. "The Voices of Adamo," the least convincing, at any rate for this reader, of all her stories, was written to illustrate Mannoni's ideology.

The coming of disillusion changed her attitude to her writing. She has described her African fiction as being about the nature of freedom, whereas her Canadian fiction concentrates on the possibility of merely surviving. As she looked back to the African years in "Ten Years' Sentences," she could see that "The world had changed; I had grown older," she admits, and her belief in the promised land was less certain, "even the promised land of one's own inner freedom. Perhaps an obsession with freedom is the persistent (thank God) dance of the young" (20). Along with this disillusion went the disquiet she felt about her attempt to convey the thoughts of African people: "I had decided I could never get deeply enough inside the minds of African people — or, at least, I'd gone as far as I personally could as a non-African" ("Gadgetry" 82). However, her disillusion and disquiet should not be allowed to detract from what she did achieve, which can be best assessed by an African. Githae-Mugo, who in *Visions of Africa* moves from Laurence's work to that of Achebe and Ngugi with no sense of difference, maintains that Laurence's "rather harsh and unfair self-assessment should be treated as part of Mrs. Laurence's tendency to be too ruthless a critic of herself and her own work. . . . [She] has — perhaps above any other Western writer on Africa — richly contributed to the field of African literature" (13). Laurence's identification with her African characters is remarkably close. Indeed, in her Canadian fiction she is sometimes unsure of her material to a degree that is rare in *This Side Jordan* and *The Tomorrow-Tamer*. In "Margaret Laurence's *The Diviners*: The Problems of Close Reading," Keith has shown that Laurence has an "uncertain command of realistic detail outside Manawaka," especially when she takes Morag and Brooke Skelton to Toronto, and it could be reasonably argued that Nathaniel is a far more convincing character than Brooke (112). In *The Diviners* Laurence returns to the theme of colonization, seeing Brooke as the Prospero figure, suggesting the roles of Caliban and Miranda for Jules and Morag. Morag's relationship with Brooke, and indirectly with Jules, is not consistently convincing, and this is in part because Laurence is preoccupied with feminist and political causes. These concerns were important to Laurence, but Brooke and Jules, who have to carry the burden of the author's crusade, pale beside Christie Logan, who stands out not because he carries a message, which he does since he is one of the diviners, but because he has been realized first as an individual.

Laurence's concern with the political aspirations of the people of Africa does not destroy the realism of her African writing, because she is able to incorporate it naturally into the background and imagery of her narrative and keep it subservient to the creation of the individual. When her symbolism and realism harmonize, Laurence writes at her best. She mastered the art in her African fiction and perfected it in *The Stone Angel*. "Godman's Master," Laurence says in her interview with Sullivan, is a story about freedom "in political and individual terms," and it succeeds because Laurence is sure of her ground both on the symbolic and realistic level (65).

Realism is the hallmark of Laurence's best writing, and Africa provided excellent material with which to achieve fine graphic effects. Because her personal response to the local setting was enthusiastic and wide-ranging, she writes about Africa with colour and variety. She was well aware that this response marked her out as a visitor or, at worst, a tourist. After she had written *Long Drums and Cannons*, she compared her interpretation of West Africa with that given by the Nigerian writers, and it was natural that she should see theirs as more authentic than hers. In a private annotation to the introduction of *Long Drums and Cannons*, she describes all her African writing as "tourism": "It might be a fairly subtle tourism. It might even be an understanding tourism to some extent. But it was tourism all the same. It could not go deeply enough" ("Long Drums and Cannons," ts.). Once again, she is unfair to herself.

Laurence, with her understanding of place and time and with her knowledge of local detail, writes more like an inhabitant than a tourist. The similarities between her work and Achebe's, for example, have been discussed. It should be remembered that her African writing is contemporary with, if not ahead of, that of the Africans who first found an English voice in the 1950s and 1960s, and she cannot be said to have been influenced by them. In "Ten Years' Sentences" she notes that when she lived in England in the 1960s she began to read "contemporary African writing in English" and realized that she had not been working alone, that "already many young African writers were exploring their own backgrounds, their own societies and people" (19).

Some of the similarities between her African fiction and that of the Nigerian authors she studied show how her responses to the African setting were often the same as theirs. For example, the lorries that transported people and goods about the country were a familiar sight. They were important to the economy of the Gold Coast and Nigeria, and the strength of Soyinka's great play is that the road was an obvious but nevertheless inspired choice for theme and metaphor. He chose a subject that had immediate and everyday relevance, and, as Laurence writes in *Long Drums and Cannons*, "[n]o more contemporary characters could be imagined than the drivers, thugs and layabouts who move through *The Road*" (46). More importantly, it was a theme that had already acquired a mythology of its own, one that was readily exploited in fiction, as Laurence among others realized.

West Africans attach great importance to the lorry traffic that provides the main means of transport for the average citizen. That importance is reflected in the names and slogans painted on the vehicles themselves. It is part of the myth that the drivers are reckless, the passengers innocent, and the touts, whose business is to drum up customers, unscrupulous. Ekwensi, whom Laurence considered above all the "chronicler of right-now" (168), often has his characters using the mammy-lorries. In *Jagua Nana*, when Jagua returns to her village by mammy-lorry, she argues her way to the "first class" seat at the front of the vehicle. In Port Harcourt, however, even Jagua is out-manoeuvred by the touts. There the mammy-lorry slogans take on ironic meaning for her. She pays her fare to the owner of GOD's CASE NO APPEAL because she has been led to believe that it will depart ahead of TRUST NO MAN. Ekwensi writes:

> She soon discovered her folly. The men and women seated on the benches in GOD's CASE had been hired to deceive. They were

not travellers but had been put there to fill the benches and to convey an impression of readiness to unwary travellers. TRUST NO MAN. She should have heeded the sign. One of the men seated in GOD's CASE got up to make room for her and she never saw him again. (68)

Laurence's characters use the mammy-lorries, and she shows herself aware of their importance as a means of communication. The people of Kofi's village in "The Tomorrow-Tamer" rely on the lorry *God Helps Those*, which replenishes Danquah's store fortnightly (79). Her perception of social nicety is demonstrated in "Godman's Master," where she explains that Moses is driving a car he can ill-afford because ". . . he had not wanted to ride a mammy-lorry, like any labourer or bushboy, when he went to see his parents after four years away at university in England" (135). In "The Pure Diamond Man," Tetteh, like Jagua, travelled in the mammy-lorry as a first-class passenger when he went to his village. Tetteh rode up front while the "other passengers, several dozen of them, sat or crouched or perilously clung at the back of the lorry, amid the sacks of sugar and crates of yellow soap." It was a particularly colourful mammy-lorry, "green and lustrous as a mango leaf, and it had KING KONG painted on the front and GOD SAVE SOULS on the back" (189).

The imaginative slogans of African mammy-lorries intrigued Laurence, and she chose four, which express the buoyant mood of pre-independent Gold Coast, as an epigraph for *This Side Jordan*: "The Day Will Come / Authority Is Never Loved / Flee, Oh Ye Powers Of Darkness / Rise Up, Ghana" (vii). Laurence was one of the first to appreciate the creativity shown by the sign-writers and the symbolic potential of their signs.

In Achebe's novel, *Anthills of the Savannah*, set in the 1980s, Chris Oriko, who has been accustomed to driving his own car, is forced to escape north by bus. Though the buses are now "factory-built and fitted out with upholstered seats," they still have their messages. Chris takes careful note of the inscriptions on the bus he boards. "The one at the back of the bus . . . said simply: *Ife onye metalu —* What a man commits. At the sides the inscriptions switched to English: *All Saints Bus*; and in front, also in English, they announced finally (or perhaps initially!) *Angel of Mercy*." Chris, about to set out on a fateful journey, observes that the sign-writers who paint the slogans on the buses seek "in their work to capture the past as well as invent a future" (201–02). With regard to the present and the future of Africa, Laurence is not inferior as a sign-writer to the best African writers. Depicting the past, one with which she had no personal connection, was, of course, a more difficult task. Wisely she did not attempt it in fictional terms on a large scale and restricted herself to the dreams and memories of her characters. In her fictional and nonfictional work, she made thorough and meticulous use of the records of the past that were available and related them carefully to the contemporary scene.

Laurence's contribution to the field of African studies is considerable. In a conversation with Robert Kroetsch she refers to *A Tree for Poverty* as a landmark since it contained "the first Somali poetry that had ever been translated from that part of Africa into English" (54). In 1966 Laurence returned to Hargeisa for Independence Day celebrations, a journey she describes in "The Wild Blue Yonder," an article written in 1973 and included in *Heart of a Stranger*. She went as the invited guest of the Somali government in recognition of her "small book of Somali poetry and prose translations" (137). There, as she told Kroetsch, she encountered the Somali "with whom [she] had worked on this poetry," undoubtedly Galaal, who, she recalls, spoke warmly of *A Tree for Poverty*. " 'You know,' " Galaal said to her, " 'a strange thing happened. That was the first little book and then others came out and so on. And my people had had this vast body of oral poetry, but until the book came out we never really knew that we had a literature.' " Kroetsch can see the importance to the Somalis of a book that "helped them discover — invent — themselves" (55). *A Tree for Poverty* also helped outsiders discover the richness of Somali oral literature. Laurence's work has been widely acknowledged and, as has been shown, was not without influence in the formation of a current view, notably Finnegan's, on the composition and nature of oral poetry.

Laurence's contribution to the understanding of African story-telling is also important. Her Somali stories have their place among the many collections made by visitors to Africa. It is inevitable that these stories bear the individual mark of those who record them, however careful the attempt to act as a neutral reporter may be. One of the most comprehensive of modern collections of African stories is that made by W.H. Whiteley for the first volume of *A Selection of African Prose*. Whiteley includes fifteen Somali tales, all of which were translated for him by Andrzejewski. One of these stories is also found in *A Tree for Poverty*, though with a different title. Laurence's story, "Tale of Two Thieves," appears told by Andrzejewski in Whiteley's collection as "The Two Tricksters." There are many details common to both versions, but the two accounts admirably illustrate the way a story can be individually handled by its story-teller. Laurence, influenced probably by Hersi's acting, dramatizes hers with lively dialogue; Andrzejewski adopts a dryer and more laconic style. Whiteley remarks that Somali prose style is restrained, but he adds that ". . . the bareness of the Somali narrative is richly compensated for, under natural conditions, by artistic effects which cannot be written down; a good narrator changes the quality of his voice when he impersonates different characters in the dialogue, while his facial expressions and his movements help the audience to reach an illusion of reality" (1: 134–35). Laurence's fine ear, which could catch the subtleties of Hersi's performance, meant she was able to capture many of the story-teller's effects.

Story-telling as an oral art has its own typical stylistic devices. Some of these devices can be easily adapted to the printed page to suggest the nature of the oral voice. Most collections of African stories provide evidence of typical oral story-telling techniques. Finnegan lists the characteristics of the Limba stories she collected and then published in 1967. She mentions the use of repetition, direct speech, stock phrases, and the active participation of the audience. Like other westerners she sees the stories as night-time tales because "Limba stories are most frequently told in the evenings, after the sun has set" (64). Many of these characteristics are also obvious from Laurence's collection of the Somali stories told "[i]n the evenings, around the camp-fires . . ." (*Tree* 1).

Laurence imparts life to her collection of stories through her appreciation of their merit, as does a very different traveller in Africa, who was also enchanted by the stories he heard. Henry M. Stanley, as he travelled through Africa, encouraged the "nightly custom of gathering around the camp fire, and entertaining one another with stories" (1). In 1893 he published these stories that he considered "not wholly devoid of a certain merit as examples of Central African lore, and oral literature" (3). His tone reflects the patronizing attitude of his age, but his enthusiasm for African oral literature is genuine, and his collection matches Laurence's in vitality and entertainment.

Those who are able to suggest the vital qualities of the stories, as Stanley and Laurence were, perform as great a service for African oral literature as the linguists and anthropologists who work with dedication to provide more accurate and perhaps authentic transcriptions. The purpose of Galaal's devoted study of his country's oral traditions was two-fold, as he notes in an interview with Lee Nichols: young educated Somalis should be reminded of their culture, and this culture should be properly understood abroad (88). He acknowledged the contribution made to his cause by *A Tree for Poverty*.

Each of the five books that Laurence wrote about Africa has a different value, and that value is assessed according to the standpoint of each reader. *A Tree for Poverty* is highly regarded by those who are interested in oral literature and who have specialized in African studies. *Long Drums and Cannons* was welcomed by the Nigerian writers whom it concerned, although as a work of literary criticism it has not received much attention outside Africa. In Canada, *The Prophet's Camel Bell* has been recognized as an unusual book, but its relation to its African context is not always understood. The success of Laurence's Canadian fiction has meant that her African fiction has been to some extent neglected. *The Tomorrow-Tamer* has inspired some scholarly criticism of a high standard, but *This Side Jordan*, a first novel of unusual quality, has been generally regarded as the work of an inexperienced beginner and given less critical attention than it deserves.

In recent years the study of African literatures has opened up areas of theoretical discussion that are complex as well as controversial. When Laurence wrote *Long Drums and Cannons* many of these issues had surfaced, but she chose not to discuss them in detail, concentrating instead on the texts. The question of negritude, with its implications of a distinct African psychology, is only briefly raised in her preface. There she points out that the Nigerian writers "seem to have been able to by-pass the negritude phase" (9). She did not consider the vehicular versus vernacular language debate as one that needed discussion. The negritude question and the language debate have resulted in the drawing of divisive lines between Africans themselves, and this goes against the spirit of Laurence's work. Throughout *Long Drums and Cannons*, she seeks to emphasize the positive qualities of Nigerian writing. She considers it a body of work "which is of interest and value not only in Africa but everywhere in the world" (203). She sees "both contemporary and universal" qualities (95) in Clark's work, as in the work of all her chosen authors.

Tutuola's themes, she writes, "can in no sense be said to exclude any one of us" (146). In her introduction she argues that "the best of these Nigerian plays and novels reveal something of ourselves to us, whoever and wherever we are" (10). Though Laurence recognizes the difficulty of communicating across cultural barriers, she believes literature can make it possible. She affirms this of the African literature she studied, but her own fiction could be equally said to do the same.

As a literary critic she does have faults. Though her judgement is sound and her research thorough, the critical stance taken by Laurence sometimes requires defence. She does not in the final analysis remain uncommitted. Her sympathy for those who write is stronger than her responsibility to those who read, a fact recognized by William French. In "A Salute to a Writer of Rare Integrity," he recounts a personal memory: "When Laurence first came to Toronto in 1969," he recalls, "I enlisted her to do book reviews for The Globe and Mail. After she did several reviews of Canadian fiction, I began to sense a problem. Her sympathies were always with the author, and she couldn't bring herself to say an unkind word about a novel, even when it was obviously necessary. She came to me and said friends who read her reviews told her she had no critical standards." Among the books she reviewed after she had left the Gold Coast were some with an African theme. In 1962 Ralph Allen's novel *Ask the Name of the Lion* was published, and Laurence reviewed it for *Canadian Literature*.

Allen was a good journalist. Like Laurence he began his working life as a reporter in Winnipeg. In 1938 he moved to Toronto and later to Europe where he worked as war correspondent for *The Globe and Mail*. Between 1950 and 1960 he was editor of *Maclean's*. When he relinquished that position, he continued to contribute articles to the magazine, travelling as its reporter in Africa. In June and July of 1961 he visited South Africa and the Congo, and he wrote of his experiences in a series of articles for *Maclean's*. Introduced with lurid headlines, Allen's reports are sensational, which is not surprising because he toured the Congo at a time of great lawlessness. He suggested that the only way to come to terms with the horrific events that he had witnessed was through fiction. "It may be no accident," he writes in "Why Both Sides Will Lose the Black-White Struggle for Africa," "that the most prophetic words ever written about Africa have been in the form of fiction. That lustrous, gleaming, tortured, terrible and magnificent continent is far larger than life. It can never be described by any mere recital of fact" (19). The novel Allen wrote is closely related to fact, and it is possible to identify many of his characters as people he met in the Congo and described in his reports. For example, Sierra Ramon in the novel is clearly the Spaniard Gustavo Duran working for the United Nations, whom Allen describes in "Is Africa the Graveyard of the UN," the *Maclean's* report of 17 June. Allen, however, is unable to transform the fact into imaginative fiction, and *Ask the Name of the Lion* is not a good novel.

Laurence found the novel disturbing, but not for literary reasons. She realized it was written by someone with whom she had to disagree, someone who could in all seriousness put this question: *"If the white man is expelled or if his flight becomes a total one, must Africa revert to the Heart of Darkness and its ancient legacy of superstition, ignorance, disease, poverty and hatred?"* ("Why Both Sides Will Lose" 19).[2] She devotes her review, "Illusions of Simplicity," not to the reasons why Allen's novel is bad fiction, but to refuting the implication that Africa's past had been one of darkness. She must, however, face the reality of the contemporary situation in the Congo and find an explanation for it. She examines the attitude of the Canadian protagonist of Allen's novel, Dr. Grant, whom she sees as "a western liberal whose lifelong attitudes of tolerance and goodwill no longer seem to have much relevance in the midst of the horrors and irrationalities of the Congo situation" (57). Young and idealistic, Grant left Canada to work in the newly independent Republic of the Congo, sacrificing a lucrative career in the process. The brutal behaviour of the Congolese soldiers destroys his idealism, which turns to sour disillusion because the Africans are not grateful for what has been done on their behalf. Laurence recognizes that Grant is a better man without his liberal idealism, without that "first fine careless rapture of the essentially patronizing do-gooder," and she adds that he was not wrong to condemn the Congolese for their acts of violence and brutality. Whatever the colour of the perpetrator, cruelty and oppression must be condemned. Laurence denounces "the false liberalism of those who conscientiously condemn Dr. Verwoerd for silencing his opposition but are quite prepared to excuse Dr. Nkrumah for doing the same thing" (58). Grant should not, however, have been so quick to accuse the Africans of ingratitude. He should have examined his own hunger for their gratefulness.

Turning from Grant to the author, she suggests he should have examined the psychological reasons for the "drunken, stupid, irresponsible, murderous" behaviour of the Congolese (60).

Laurence's review was written in the same period as her story "The Voices of Adamo," and it does not come as a surprise to find her using Mannoni when she tries to explain the violence that has erupted in post-independent Congo. She would explain it as she explained the crime committed by Adamo; the parallel is for her only too plain. Mannoni had proved, certainly to Laurence's satisfaction, that when young African soldiers were torn from their traditional way of life and recruited into a European army, they were quick to accept military discipline as a substitute for the authority that had rested in the tribe. The African, Mannoni believed, needed to be a dependent and for that reason finds independence difficult to cope with. The Congolese soldiers, Laurence therefore argues, without their Belgian masters, found that their world had "quite literally fallen apart" (61). Their only reaction could be a violent one. The violence of post-colonial Africa is not so easily explained, but, as Fanon recognized in *The Wretched of the Earth*, violence was perhaps inevitable: ". . . decolonization is always a violent phenomenon" (35). Laurence, however, grasped at Mannoni's theory as a way of comprehending the situation. This is, of course, an unusual book review, reaching as it does beyond literary criticism into political commentary. Allen saw only violence and corruption when he visited Africa. He had little conception of the true nature of Africa's past and could not appreciate the extent of the tragedy he was witnessing.

Laurence also reviewed two later novels, one set in Nigeria and one in Ghana, both depicting the troubled years that followed independence. Her reviews of David Knight's *Farquharson's Physique: And What It Did to His Mind* and of Dave Godfrey's *The New Ancestors* are limited to plot summaries and generous praise, and they are disappointing after her interesting treatment of Allen's book. Indeed, "African Experiences," her review of Knight's book, seems totally devoid of critical judgement, and there is a suggestion of flippancy in her tone that undercuts her praise of this "splendid" novel (77). Some of this flippancy is amusing. Laurence describes Farquharson's wife, for example, as taking "to Africa like a sparrow to new wet concrete" (78). To be fair to Laurence, other reviews of Knight's novel now seem equally uncritical. Anthony Boxill praised it in terms that one would hesitate to apply even to Laurence's fiction.

"By blending Conrad and Bellow with Achebe and Soyinka," Boxill speculates, "he [Knight] has advanced the already rich tradition of fiction about Africa. This is a remarkable achievement" ("Farquharson's Quest" 119). In "Caverns to the Mind's Dark Continent," Laurence treats Godfrey's work more seriously, and, though her review is again structured around a plot summary, she interprets Godfrey's complex novel with perception and sympathy. In this case her plot outline is helpful because Godfrey's novel is not easy to read.

In these reviews, as in *Long Drums and Cannons*, when Laurence can feel a personal involvement, her voice is strong. When she comments on themes and problems that have concerned her either as a writer or as a visitor in Africa, she writes with intensity. She felt, for example, the full tragedy of the Biafran War, which seemed to negate all the national spirit she had celebrated in the work of the Nigerian writers. She had chosen her title for *Long Drums and Cannons* because in Okigbo's poem the drums and cannons were sounded to summon his ancestors to the sacred groves. As her book went to press she was shocked to hear of his death, to realize that he had himself been summoned to join his ancestors, and her title then seemed "cruelly ironic" (10).[3]

Her time in Africa, as many have noted, taught Laurence to look closely at others, and this in its turn helped her with the more difficult task of looking closely at herself. She closes *Long Drums and Cannons* affirming that ". . . there are people who find in literature one way of discovering more fully the reality of others and of exploring the mystery of themselves" (203). Canadians have had a problem defining their identity, and in *The Bush Garden: Essays on the Canadian Imagination* Northrop Frye perceived that it was essentially a territorial predicament: "It seems to me that Canadian sensibility has been profoundly disturbed, not so much by our famous problem of identity, important as that is, as by a series of paradoxes in what confronts that identity. It is less perplexed by the question 'Who am I?' than by some such riddle as 'Where is here?'" (220).

In the Manawaka novels Laurence provides her own answer to the riddle. She identifies in literary terms "A Place To Stand On," what she calls in *Heart of a Stranger* her "own place of belonging" (14). Laurence may well have left Canada with a sense of alienation, but she returned from Africa with a very clear idea of where she belonged. It was by journeying beyond the borders of her hometown that Laurence was finally able to define its qualities for those who lived within and without its boundaries, thus making it accessible to the outsider and to herself.

But the achievement of this self-identification in Canadian terms should not overshadow her success in understanding "the other." Laurence, the first lady of Manawaka, was also a citizen of the world. She crossed foreign boundaries in a spirit of humility, eager to learn and ready to respond sympathetically. She travelled in East and West Africa with notebook and pencil in hand, asking many questions and listening to the answers so that she came to understand and share the aspirations and fears of the people she met. Her literary record of the years spent in Africa is invaluable, and the tribute she has paid as a writer to her fellows is moving, be it to the greatest of the Somali *gabei* artists, the warrior Sayyid, or to Okigbo, the young Nigerian poet who died at the moment when his spirit had been in the ascent.

APPENDIX

In "Ten Years' Sentences" Laurence refers to her "seven years' love affair with a continent" (11). Laurence spent nearer six than seven years in Africa, but the figure of seven years is metaphorically appropriate, and, indeed, she fell in love with Africa before she arrived there. However, it is important to establish the date of her arrival in Somaliland, which is often given as 1950.

Certain facts are clear. She left Canada in 1949. She left Somaliland in 1952 (in the Spring after the *Gu* rains) and arrived in the Gold Coast the same year. She left the Gold Coast in 1957 just before independence (March 1957).

In *The Prophet's Camel Bell*, she describes leaving England in December ("sleet-sodden English December" [2]), waiting "seven days" in Rotterdam (2), and then spending a month on the Norwegian boat that took her to Aden ("The *Tigre* was our home for a month . . ." [5]). Laurence describes spending Christmas on the boat (6). She, therefore, arrived in Somaliland at the beginning of a New Year.

This could be January 1950 or more likely January 1951. From other evidence it seems Laurence was in England during 1950. In "Books That Mattered to Me," Laurence refers to her time in England:

> It is a letter I wrote from England, in 1950, to Adele's parents in Winnipeg. My husband and I were preparing to go to Somaliland, in East Africa, where Jack was to be in charge of a scheme to build *ballehs*, large earth dug-outs, to catch the once-yearly rainfall across the Haud Desert. (243)

From this evidence it must be assumed that, though Laurence left England in 1950, she did not arrive in Somaliland until January 1951.

NOTES

Into Africa

[1] This is the spelling Laurence uses in her essay on the Sayyid, "The Poem and the Spear," which appears in *Heart of a Stranger*. In *The Prophet's Camel Bell* she uses the spelling Mohamed Abdullah Hassan.

1. *Water and Shade*

[1] When the post of Engineer was first advertised, the hope was expressed that the *ballehs* would each hold 10,000,000 gallons of water (*Prophet's* 2). As the work progressed a more realistic target was adopted.

2. *Something More Than Nothing*

[1] Musa Galaal was born in the pastoral interior about 1914 and died in 1980. Andrzejewski wrote a moving tribute to his friend and colleague "Muuse Xaaji Ismaaciil Galaal" for *Horn of Africa*.

[2] This was Burton's description of the Eesa tribe (127). I.M. Lewis considered it so apt he used it as the epigraph for his book about the northern Somali Bedouin, *A Pastoral Democracy*.

[3] I am grateful to Adele Wiseman and Jocelyn and David Laurence for permission to quote from this letter.

[4] The Somali original has 71, lines which Andrzejewski and Lewis follow exactly. Laurence prefers to divide the long Somali line in two and also to expand where necessary, so there are 162 lines in her translation.

[5] This story is also told by Major H. Rayne, Margery Perham's brother-in-law, in his chapter on "The Yibir" in *Sun, Sand and Somals* with the difference that Mohamed Hanif's dispute is with Sheikh Ishaak. Rayne describes in detail the Yibir ritual involved when a Somali baby boy is born.

[6] Mentioning *A Tree For Poverty*, Andrzejewski and Lewis give the line in Somali, adding a literal translation (42).

3. *"Bits and Pieces"*

[1] Samatar gives December 1920 and influenza as the cause of the Sayyid's death (136); Andrzejewski, in "Somali Literature," writes that the Sayyid "died

of an illness in 1921 at Iimey" (393).

2 This incident is mentioned by Jardine in *The Mad Mullah* (44). A full account is given by Samatar (117–18).

3 Hamilton never uses "mad" when he refers to the Mullah, and he is one of the few people to give a description of the Sayyid, one that contrasts with the legendary stories of his obesity. However, the description does apply to the year 1895: "Tall, lithe, energetic, Mahomed Abdullah's wiriness seemed to be emphasized by the thin goatee beard he wore" (49).

4 Abdillahi and Andrzejewski refer their readers to Laurence's translation: "One of ['Ilmi's] longer poems, not given in our text, is available in an excellent English translation with annotations in *A Tree for Poverty* by Margaret Laurence" (204).

4. *In Search of a Cast of Characters*

1 North American voices are largely absent from Laurence's African fiction. The notable exception is Amory Lemon, the proselytizer from the Angel of Philadelphia mission ("The Merchant of Heaven"). In *This Side Jordan* an American, Eric Banning, who is studying the drum language, is mentioned. Doree's diction ("The Perfume Sea") indicates that she comes from North America. She variously gives Montreal, Chicago, and "once, daringly, Mexico City" as her previous place of residence, thus adding to the mystery of her unexpected presence in Africa.

2 Rattray's collection has many stories of Ananse, the man/spider, frequently referred to in Laurence's stories.

7. *An African Consciousness*

1 Leney writes, ". . . Laurence has employed the trite symbol of the woman as African continent" (69).

2 Laurence read Elliott P. Skinner's article, "Strangers in West African Societies," in later years when writing *Long Drums and Cannons*. Skinner explains how colonial governments caused the movement of many Africans to foreign areas; in particular "Yoruba, Togolese, Ewe, Dahomeyans, Mossi and Songhay migrated to the former Gold Coast" (309).

10. *The Mysteries of Ogun: Wole Soyinka*

1 In 1976 Nick Wilkinson, with extensive reference to Laurence, discussed the question in "Demoke's Choice in Soyinka's *A Dance of the Forests*." He

writes, "There are as many interpretations of Wole Soyinka's *A Dance of the Forests* as there are commentators" (22).

11. *Forests, Cities, and Rivers: Amos Tutuola, Cyprian Ekwensi, and John Pepper Clark*

[1] Laurence covers five of Tutuola's novels: *The Palm-Wine Drinkard* (1952), *My Life in the Bush of Ghosts* (1954), *Simbi and the Satyr of the Dark Jungle* (1955), *The Brave African Huntress* (1958), and *Feather Woman of the Jungle* (1962).

The Spirit in the Ascent

[1] The name itself is also right. Hagar was not an unnatural name to give a Canadian girl of Scots descent — Hagar, as Laurence writes in *The Stone Angel*, "had been named, hopefully, for a well-to-do spinster great-aunt in Scotland" (14).

[2] There is no evidence that Laurence had read Allen's reports, but this attitude can be sensed within the novel.

[3] See Clara Thomas, "Ascent and Agony": ". . . the book's title touches everything in it with tragic irony" (93).

WORKS CONSULTED

NOTE: Part I contains a chronological list of major works by Margaret Laurence. Part II includes critical works relating to Laurence's African writing — books and works that provide further relevant African background information. Laurence's book reviews and magazine articles have only been included if they have reference to Africa. A comprehensive bibliography of Laurence's writings and secondary sources to 1979, compiled by Susan Warwick, can be found in *The Annotated Bibliography of Canada's Major Authors*, ed. Robert Lecker and Jack David, vol. 1 (Downsview, ON: ECW, 1979).

I

Laurence, Margaret. "African Experience." Rev. of *Farquharson's Physique: And What It Did to His Mind*, by David Knight. *Journal of Canadian Fiction* 1.1 (1972): 77–78.

____ . "Author's Commentary [On "The Tomorrow-Tamer"]." *Sixteen by Twelve: Short Stories by Canadian Writers*. Ed. John Metcalf. Toronto: Ryerson, 1970. 71–73.

____ . *A Bird in the House*. Toronto: McClelland, 1970.

____ . "Books That Mattered to Me." Friends of the Bata Library, Trent U. Peterborough, 1981. Printed in Verduyn 239–49.

____ . "Calliope." *Vox* [United College, Winnipeg] 18.3 (1945): 10–12.

____ . "Canadian Literature." Interview. With Alan Twigg. *For Openers: Conversations with 24 Canadian Writers*. By Alan Twigg. Madeira Park, BC: Harbour, 1981. 261–71.

____ . "Caverns to the Mind's Dark Continent." Rev. of *The New Ancestors*, by Dave Godfrey. *The Globe Magazine* [*The Globe and Mail*] 5 Dec. 1970: 18.

____ . "A Conversation about Literature: An Interview with Margaret Laurence and Irving Layton." With Clara Thomas. *Journal of Canadian Fiction* 1.1 (1972): 65–69.

____ . "A Conversation with Margaret Laurence." With Robert Kroetsch. *Creation*. By Robert Kroetsch, James Bacque, and Pierre Gravel. Toronto: new, 1970. 53–63. Rpt. in Woodcock, *Place* 46–55.

____ . *Dance on the Earth: A Memoir*. Toronto: McClelland, 1989.

____ . *The Diviners*. Toronto: McClelland, 1974.

____ . "The Drummer of All the World." *Queen's Quarterly* 62 (1955–56): 487–504. Rpt. in Laurence, *Tomorrow* 1–19.

____ . "The Epic Love of Elmi Bonderi." *Holiday* Nov. 1965: 35, 37, 39–40. Rpt. as "The Epic Love of Elmii Bonderii" in Laurence, *Heart* 77–85.

____ . "A Fetish for Love." Laurence, *Tomorrow* 161–81.

____ . *The Fire-Dwellers.* Toronto: McClelland, 1969.

____ . "Gadgetry or Growing: Form and Voice in the Novel." U of Toronto. Toronto, 1969. Printed in *Journal of Canadian Fiction* [The Work of Margaret Laurence] 27 (1980): 54–62. Rpt. in Woodcock, *Place* 80–89.

____ . "Godman's Master." *Prism* 1.3 (1960): 46–64. Rpt. in Laurence, *Tomorrow* 134–60.

____ . "A Gourdful of Glory." *Tamarack Review* 17 (1960): 5–20. Rpt. in Laurence, *Tomorrow* 225–44.

____ . *Heart of a Stranger.* Toronto: McClelland, 1976.

____ . "Illusions of Simplicity." Rev. of *Ask the Name of the Lion*, by Ralph Allen. *Canadian Literature* 14 (1962): 57–58, 60–62.

____ . "In Pursuit of My Past on the Road from the Isles." *Maclean's* 2 May 1966: 26a–26h. Rpt. as "Road from the Isles" in Laurence, *Heart* 145–57.

____ . Interview. With Clara Thomas. *Canadian Writers on Video.* Videotape. Toronto: ECW, 1985.

____ . Interview. With Earle Toppings. *Canadian Writers on Tape.* Audiotape. By Earle Toppings. Toronto: OISE, 1971.

____ . Interview. With Graeme Gibson. Gibson 185–208.

____ . Interview. With Rosemary Sullivan. Woodcock, *Place* 61–79.

____ . "Ivory Tower or Grassroots?: The Novelist as Socio-Political Being." *A Political Art: Essays and Images in Honour of George Woodcock.* Ed. William H. New. Vancouver: U of British Columbia P, 1978. 15–25.

____ . *Jason's Quest.* Toronto: McClelland, 1970.

____ . *A Jest of God.* London: Macmillan, 1966.

____ . "Letter to Bob Sorfleet." *Journal of Canadian Fiction* [The Work of Margaret Laurence] 27 (1980): 52–53.

____ . *Long Drums and Cannons.* London: Macmillan, 1968.

____ . "Long Drums and Cannons." Box 1.f3, ts. and notes. The William Ready Division of Archives and Research Collections, McMaster U.

____ . "Man of Honour." Rev. of *Gabriel Dumont: The Métis Chief and His Lost World*, by George Woodcock. *Canadian Forum*, Dec.–Jan. 1975–76: 28–29. Rpt. (revised) as "Man of Our People" in Laurence, *Heart* 204–12.

____ . "Margaret Laurence: The Black Celt Speaks of Freedom." With Donald Cameron. *Conversations with Canadian Novelists — 1.* By Donald Cameron. Toronto: Macmillan, 1973. 96–115.

_____ . "Margaret Laurence on *The Stone Angel*." Interview. With Michel Fabre. *Etudes canadiennes/Canadian Studies* [*The Stone Angel*: A Collection of Critical Essays] 11 (1981): 11–22. [The interview took place on 5 Aug. 1980.]

_____ . "Mask of Beaten Gold." *Tamarack Review* 29 (1963): 3–21.

_____ . "The Merchant of Heaven." *Prism* 1.1 (1959): 52–74. Rpt. in Laurence, *Tomorrow* 50–77.

_____ . "My Final Hour." Trent Philosophy Society, Trent U. Peterborough, 29 March 1983. Printed in Verduyn 250–62.

_____ . Papers. Accession 2, box 4.f83. York U. North York, ON.

_____ . "The Perfume Sea." *Winter's Tales* 6. Ed. A.D. Maclean. London: Macmillan, 1960. 83–120. Rpt. in Laurence, *Tomorrow* 20–49.

_____ . *The Prophet's Camel Bell*. Toronto: McClelland, 1963. Rpt. as *New Wind in a Dry Land*. New York: Knopf, 1964.

_____ . "The Pure Diamond Man." *Tamarack Review* 26 (1963): 3–21. Rpt. in Laurence, *Tomorrow* 182–204.

_____ . "A Queen in Thebes." *Tamarack Review* 32 (1964): 25–37. Rpt. in *Journal of Canadian Fiction* [The Work of Margaret Laurence] 27 (1980): 41–51.

_____ . "The Rain Child." *Winter's Tales 8*. London: Macmillan, 1962. 105–42. Rpt. in Laurence, *Tomorrow* 105–33.

_____ . "Sources." *Mosaic* 3.3 (1970): 80–84. Rpt. as "A Place To Stand On" in Laurence, *Heart* 13–18.

_____ . "The Spell of the Distant Drum." *Saturday Evening Post* 5 May 1962: 24–25, 76, 78, 80–82. Rpt. as "The Voices of Adamo" in Laurence, *Tomorrow* 205–24.

_____ . "A Statement of Faith." Convocation Address, Emmanuel College, Victoria U/U of Toronto. Toronto, 6 May 1982. Printed in Woodcock, *Place* 56–60.

_____ . *The Stone Angel*. Toronto: McClelland, 1964.

_____ . "Tal des Walde." *Vox* [United College, Winnipeg] 19.3 (1947): 3–5, 39–40, 54.

_____ . "Ten Years' Sentences." *Canadian Literature* 41 (1969): 10–16. Rpt. in New, *Margaret Laurence* 17–23.

_____ . *This Side Jordan*. Toronto: McClelland, 1960.

_____ . "Time and the Narrative Voice." *The Narrative Voice: Short Stories and Reflections by Canadian Authors*. Ed. John Metcalf. Toronto: McGraw, 1972. 126–30. Rpt. in New, *Margaret Laurence* 156–60.

_____ . "The Tomorrow-Tamer." *Prism* 3.1 (1961): 37–54. Rpt. in Laurence, *Tomorrow* 78–104.

_____ . *The Tomorrow-Tamer*. Toronto: McClelland, 1963.

____, ed., introd., and trans. *A Tree for Poverty: Somali Poetry and Prose.* Nairobi: Eagle, 1954. Hamilton: McMaster U Library P, 1970.

____. "Uncertain Flowering." *Story 4.* Ed. Whit Burnett and Hallie Burnett. New York: Wyn, 1953. 9–34.

____. "The Very Best Intentions." *Holiday* Nov. 1964: 107–08, 111, 125. Rpt. in Laurence, *Heart* 33–43.

I I

Abdi Sheikh-Abdi. "Sayyid Mohamed Abdille Hassan and the Current Conflict in the Horn." *Horn of Africa* 1.2 (1978): 61–65.

Abdillahi, Mohamed Farah, and B.W. Andrzejewski. "The Life of 'Ilmi Bowndheri, a Somali Oral Poet Who Is Said To Have Died of Love." *Journal of the Folklore Institute* 4 (1967): 191–206.

Abrahams, Cecil. "Margaret Laurence and Chinua Achebe: Commonwealth Storytellers." *ACLALS Bulletin.* 5th ser. 3 (1980): 74–85.

Achebe, Chinua. *Anthills of the Savannah.* London: Heinemann, 1987.

____. *Arrow of God.* London: Heinemann, 1964.

____. "English and the African Writer." *Transition* 4.18 (1965): 27–30. Rpt. as "The African Writer and the English Language" in Achebe, *Morning Yet* 55–62.

____. Foreword. Obiechina, *African Popular Literature* ix–x.

____. Foreword. Whiteley, *A Selection of African Prose* 1: vii–x.

____. *Hopes and Impediments: Selected Essays 1965–1987.* London: Heinemann, 1988.

____. *A Man of the People.* African Writers Ser. 31. London: Heinemann, 1966.

____. *Morning Yet on Creation Day: Essays.* Studies in African Literature. London: Heinemann, 1975.

____. *No Longer at Ease.* African Writers Ser. 3. London: Heinemann, 1960.

____. "The Novelist as Teacher," Achebe, *Morning Yet* 42–45.

____. *Things Fall Apart.* London: Heinemann, 1958.

Africa [International African Institute] 1 (1928)– .

"African Crosscurrents." Rev. of *The Tomorrow-Tamer*, by Margaret Laurence. *Times Literary Supplement* 25 Oct. 1963: 869.

Akanji [pseud.]. See Beier, Ulli.

Allen, Ralph. *Ask the Name of the Lion.* New York: Doubleday, 1962.

____. "Is Africa the Graveyard of the UN?" *Maclean's* 17 June 1961: 11, 52–53.

____. "The Most Appalling Jungle War of All — The Handcuffed Fight against

Disease." *Maclean's* 17 June 1961: 12, 54–56.

_____. "Report from Africa. The Question: How Much More Tyranny for Whites?" *Maclean's* 3 June 1961: 66–67.

_____. "A Reporter at Large among the Congolese Meets the Evolués — and Recent Cannibals." *Maclean's* 17 June 1961: 13, 57–59.

_____. "Why Both Sides Will Lose the White-Black Struggle for Africa." *Maclean's* 1 July 1961: 18–19, 38, 40.

Aluko, T.M. *Kinsman and Foreman*. London: Heinemann, 1966.

_____. *One Man, One Matchet*. London: Heinemann, 1964.

_____. *One Man, One Wife*. 1959. London: Heinemann, 1967.

Amadi, Elechi. *The Concubine*. London: Heinemann, 1966.

_____. *The Great Ponds*. London: Heinemann, 1969.

Andrzejewski, B.W. "The Art of the Miniature in Somali Poetry." *African Language Review* 6 (1967): 5–16.

_____. "The Development of a National Orthography in Somalia and the Modernization of the Somali Language." *Horn of Africa* 1.3 (1978): 39–45.

_____. "The Literary Culture of the Somali People." *Somalia in Word and Image*. Ed. Katheryne S. Loughran, John William Johnson, and Said Sheikh Samatar. Bloomington, IN: Indiana UP, 1986.

_____, ed. *Literatures in African Languages*. Cambridge: Cambridge UP, 1985.

_____. "Muuse Xaaji Ismaaciil Galaal (1914–1980): A Founding-Father of Written Somali." *Horn of Africa* 4.2 (1981): 21–25.

_____. "Oral Literature." Andrzejewski, *Literatures in African Languages*.

_____. "Somali Literature." Andrzejewski, *Literatures in African Languages*.

_____. "The Two Tricksters." Whiteley 1: 139–40.

Andrzejewski, B.W., and Musa H.I. Galaal. "A Somali Poetic Combat." 3 Pts. *Journal of African Languages* 2 (1963): 15–28, 93–100, 190–205.

Andrzejewski, B.W., and I.M. Lewis. *Somali Poetry: An Introduction*. Oxford: Clarendon, 1964.

Armah, Ayi Kwei. *The Beautyful Ones Are Not Yet Born*. Boston: Houghton, 1968.

Babalola, Adeboye. "Ijala: The Traditional Poetry of Yoruba Hunters." *Black Orpheus: A Journal of African and Afro-American Literature* 1 (1957): 5–7.

Babalow, Anthony. Rev. of *This Side Jordan*, by Margaret Laurence. *British Columbia Library Quarterly* 25.1 (1961): 31, 34.

Beardsley, Doug. Rev. of *Heart of a Stranger*, by Margaret Laurence. *Canadian Fiction Magazine* 24–25 (1977): 163–65.

Beer, David F. "Somali Literature in European Languages." *Horn of Africa* 2.4 (1979): 27–35.

Beier, Ulli. *Art in Nigeria*. London: Cambridge UP, 1960.

____. "Ibo and Yoruba Art." *Black Orpheus: A Journal of African and Afro-American Literature* 8 (1960): 46–50.

____. "Obatala: Five Myths of the Yoruba Creator God." *Black Orpheus: A Journal of African and Afro-American Literature* 7 (1960): 34–35.

____ [pseud. Akanji]. Rev. of *The Brave African Huntress*, by Amos Tutuola. *Black Orpheus: A Journal of African and Afro-American Literature* 4 (1958): 51–53. Rpt. in Lindfors, *Critical Perspectives* 58–60.

____. Rev. of *A Dance of the Forests*, by Wole Soyinka. *Black Orpheus: A Journal of African and Afro-American Literature* 8 (1960): 57–58.

Bell, C.R.V. *The Somali Language.* London: Longman, 1953.

Bellow, Saul. *Henderson the Rain King.* New York: Viking, 1959.

Benson, Peter. *Black Orpheus, Transition, and Modern Cultural Awakening in Africa.* Berkeley: U of California P, 1986.

Black Orpheus: A Journal of African and Afro-American Literature [Ibadan] 1 (1957)–22 (1967).

Black Orpheus: A Journal of the Arts from Africa [Ibadan] 2.1 (1968)–2.3 (1968).

Boxill, Anthony. "Farquharson's Quest: A Canadian in Africa." Rev. of *Farquharson's Physique: And What It Did to His Mind*, by David Knight. *Fiddlehead* 97 (1973): 116–19.

____. Rev. of *Long Drums and Cannons*, by Margaret Laurence. *Fiddlehead* 80 (1969): 105–06.

Brodie, Fawn M. *The Devil Drives: A Life of Sir Richard Burton.* 1967. London: Eland, 1986.

Brydon, Diana. "Re-Writing *The Tempest*." Proc. of the 6th Triennial Conference of ACLALS. 10–17 Aug. 1983. *World Literature Written in English* 23.1 (1984): 75–88.

Burton, Richard F. *First Footsteps in East Africa.* 1856. London: Dent, 1910.

Cahill, Kevin M. *Somalia: A Perspective.* Albany: State U of New York P, 1980.

Cameron, Donald. "The Mysterious Literary Fondness for Darkest Africa." *Maclean's* Aug. 1971: 64.

Canadian Women's Studies [Margaret Laurence: A Celebration] 8.3 (1987).

Carroll, David. "Letters in Canada: 1970. Literary Studies." Rev. of *Long Drums and Cannons*, by Margaret Laurence. *University of Toronto Quarterly* 40 (1970–71): 359–60.

Cary, Joyce. *The African Witch.* 1936. Carfax ed. London: Joseph, 1951.

____. *Aissa Saved.* 1932. Carfax ed. London: Joseph, 1949.

____. *An American Visitor.* 1933. Carfax ed. London: Joseph, 1952.

____. *The Case for African Freedom and Other Writings on Africa.* 1941. London: Secker, 1944.

_____ . *Mister Johnson*. 1939. Carfax ed. London: Joseph, 1952.

Cerulli, Enrico. *Somalia: scritti vari editi ed inediti*. 3 vols. Roma: Istituto Poligrafico, 1957–64.

Chadwick, Hector Munro, and Nora Kershaw Chadwick. *The Growth of Literature*. 3 vols. Cambridge: Cambridge UP, 1932–40.

Charles, Gerda. Rev. of *Border Country*, by Raymond Williams; *This Side Jordan*, by Margaret Laurence; *Evvie*, by Vera Caspary; *Frontier of the Unknown*, by Henri Queffelec; and *Frame for Julian*, by Yvonne Mitchell. *New Statesman* 19 Nov. 1960: 800, 802.

Clark, John Pepper. "Aspects of Nigerian Drama." Clark, *Example* 76–96.

_____ . *The Example of Shakespeare*. London: Longman, 1970.

_____ . *The Masquerade*. Clark, *Three Plays* 49–88.

_____ . *Ozidi*. London: Oxford UP, 1966.

_____ . *The Raft*. Clark, *Three Plays* 89–134.

_____ . *Song of a Goat*. Clark, *Three Plays* 1–48.

_____ . *Three Plays*. London: Oxford UP, 1964.

Collins, Harold R. *Amos Tutuola*. Twayne's World Authors Series. 62. New York: Twayne, 1969.

Commonwealth SP1 (1989). [A special issue on Wole Soyinka *A Dance of the Forests*.]

Curle, A.T. "The Ruined Towns of Somaliland." *Antiquity: A Quarterly Review of Archaeology* 11 (1937): 315–27.

Dale, James. "Valuable Addition to the Mac Library." Rev. of *Long Drums and Cannons*, by Margaret Laurence. *Hamilton Spectator* 8 Mar. 1969: 26.

Danquah, J.B. *The Akan Doctrine of God*. 1944. London: Cass, 1968.

Dixon, Michael. "Letters in Canada: 1976. Humanities." Rev. of *Heart of a Stranger*, by Margaret Laurence. *University of Toronto Quarterly* 46 (1977): 477–79.

Dobbs, Kildare. "Outside Africa." Rev. of *This Side Jordan*, by Margaret Laurence. *Canadian Literature* 8 (1961): 62–63.

Downey, Deane E.D. "The Canadian Identity and African Nationalism." *Canadian Literature* 75 (1977): 15–26.

Drake-Brockman, Ralph E. *British Somaliland*. London: Hurst, 1912.

Ekwensi, Cyprian. *Beautiful Feathers*. London: Hutchinson, 1963.

_____ . *Burning Grass: A Story of the Fulani of Northern Nigeria*. African Writers Ser. 2. London: Heinemann, 1962.

_____ . Interview. Conducted in Enugu. Nichols.

_____ . *Iska*. London: Hutchinson, 1966.

_____ . *Jagua Nana*. London: Hutchinson, 1961.

_____ . *Lokotown and Other Stories*. London: Heinemann, 1966.

____ . *People of the City*. London: Dakers, 1954. Rev. ed. London: Heinemann, 1963.

____ . *When Love Whispers*. Onitsha: Tabansi, [1947].

Emenyonu, Ernest. *Cyprian Ekwensi*. Modern African Writers. London: Evans, 1974.

Etudes canadiennes/Canadian Studies [*The Stone Angel* by Margaret Laurence: A Collection of Critical Essays] 11 (1981).

Fabre, Michel. "Soyinka's Use of Yoruba Mythology in *A Dance of the Forests*." *Commonwealth* SP1 (1989): 35.

Fanon, Frantz. *Black Skin, White Masks*. [1952 French ed.] Trans. Charles Lam Markmann. London: MacGibbon, 1968.

____ . *The Wretched of the Earth*. [1961 French ed.] Trans. Constance Farrington. Evergreen Black Cat ed. New York: Grove, 1968.

Farah, Nuruddin. *Close Sesame*. London: Allison, 1983.

____ . "Coming Out of Oral Tradition To Write about Dictatorship." Interview. With Mary Langille. *The Varsity* [U of Toronto] 26 Nov. 1987: S7.

____ . *From a Crooked Rib*. African Writers Ser. 80. London: Heinemann, 1970.

____ . *Maps*. London: Picador, 1986.

____ . *A Naked Needle*. African Writers Ser. 184. London: Heinemann, 1976.

____ . *Sardines*. London: Allison, 1981.

____ . *Sweet and Sour Milk*. London: Allison, 1979.

Finnegan, Ruth. *Limba Stories and Story-Telling*. Oxford: Clarendon, 1967.

____ . *Oral Literature in Africa*. Oxford: Clarendon, 1970.

____ . *Oral Poetry: Its Nature, Significance and Social Context*. Cambridge: Cambridge UP, 1977.

____ , ed. *The Penguin Book of Oral Poetry*. Harmondsworth, Eng.: Penguin, 1982.

Flecker, James Elroy. "Gates of Damascus." *The Collected Poems of James Elroy Flecker*. Ed. and introd. J.C. Squire. London: Secker, 1916. 151–57.

Forester, C.S. *The Sky and the Forest*. Boston: Little, 1948.

Freedman, Adele. "The Once and Future Past of Margaret Laurence." Rev. of *Heart of a Stranger*, by Margaret Laurence. *Saturday Night* Nov. 1976: 49–50.

French, William. "Colorful Tales of Modern Africa." Rev. of *The Tomorrow-Tamer*, by Margaret Laurence. *The Globe and Mail Magazine* [*The Globe and Mail*] 1 Feb. 1964: 14.

____ . "A Salute to a Writer of Rare Integrity." *The Globe and Mail* 6 Jan. 1987: C5.

Frye, Northrop. *The Bush Garden: Essays on the Canadian Imagination*. Toronto: Anansi, 1971.

Fuja, Abayomi. *Fourteen Hundred Cowries: Traditional Stories of the Yoruba.* London: Oxford UP, 1962.

Fulford, Robert. "On the Colonial Heritage: The Whites Aren't All Black-hearted." Rev. of *The Prophet's Camel Bell*, by Margaret Laurence. *Maclean's* 19 Oct. 1963: 81–82.

Galaal, Musa. Interview. With Lee Nichols. Nichols 186–92.

Gibbs, James, ed. *Critical Perspectives on Wole Soyinka.* Critical Perspectives 5. Washington: Three Continents, 1980.

Gibson, Graeme. *Eleven Canadian Novelists.* Toronto: Anansi, 1973.

Girling, H.K. Rev. of *The Prophet's Camel Bell*, by Margaret Laurence. *Queen's Quarterly* 71 (1964–65): 456–57.

Githae-Mugo, Micere [see also Micere (Githane [sic]) Mugo]. *Visions of Africa: The Fiction of Chinua Achebe, Margaret Laurence, Elspeth Huxley and Ngugi Wa Thiong'o.* Nairobi: Kenya Literature Bureau, 1978.

Gleason, Judith. "Out of the Irony of Words." *Transition* 4.18 (1965): 34–38.

Godfrey, Dave. "Figments of the Northern Mind." Rev. of *Agaguk*, by Yves Thériault; *Hungry Hills*, by George Ryga; *Julian, the Magician*, by Gwendolyn MacEwen; *Fasting Friar*, by Edward McCourt; and *The Tomorrow-Tamer*, by Margaret Laurence. *Tamarack Review* 31 (1964): 87–93.

——. Interview. With Graeme Gibson. Gibson 155–79.

——. *The New Ancestors.* Toronto: new, 1970.

——. "Piquefort's Column." Rev. of *Long Drums and Cannons*, by Margaret Laurence. *Canadian Forum* Feb. 1969: 249.

Goldsborough, Diana. "Inside Somaliland." Rev. of *The Prophet's Camel Bell*, by Margaret Laurence. *Tamarack Review* 31 (1964): 98.

Gotlieb, Phyllis. "On Margaret Laurence." Rev. of *The Fire Dwellers* and *Long Drums and Cannons*, by Margaret Laurence; and *Margaret Laurence*, by Clara Thomas. *Tamarack Review* 52 (1969): 76–80. Rpt. in New, *Margaret Laurence* 41–44.

Great Britain. British Protectorate of Somaliland. "Memorandum by the Acting Financial Secretary on the Draft Estimates 1st Apr. 1949–31st Mar. 1950." Hargeisia.

Great Britain. Colonial Office. *The Colonial Office List.* London: HMSO, 1951, 1952.

——. *Report on the Somaliland Protectorate for the Years 1950 and 1951.* London: HMSO, 1952.

Green, Margaret Mackesen. *Ibo Village Affairs, Chiefly with Reference to the Village of Umueke Agbaja.* 1947. 2nd ed. London: Cass, 1964.

Greene, Graham. *A Burnt-Out Case.* 1960. London: Heinemann, 1961.

——. *Collected Essays.* New York: Viking, 1969.

____. *The Heart of the Matter*. 1948. Harmondsworth, Eng.: Penguin, 1962.

____. *In Search of a Character: Two African Journals*. London: Bodley Head, 1961.

____. *Journey without Maps*. 1936. London: Heinemann, 1978.

Gunnars, Kristjana, ed. *Crossing the River: Essays in Honour of Margaret Laurence*. Winnipeg: Turnstone, 1988.

Gurr, Andrew. *Writers in Exile: The Identity of Home in Modern Literature*. Brighton: Harvester, 1981.

Hamilton, Angus. *Somaliland*. 1911. Westport: Negro UP, 1970.

Harris, Wilson. "The Complexity of Freedom." *Explorations*. Mundelstrup: Dangaroo, 1981. 113–24.

____. "The Fabric of the Imagination." *Third World Quarterly* 12.1 (1990): 175–86.

____. "The Frontier on Which *Heart of Darkness* Stands." *Explorations*. Mundelstrup: Dangaroo, 1981. 134–41.

Harrison, James. "The Rhythms of Ritual in Margaret Laurence's *The Tomorrow-Tamer*." *World Literature Written in English* 27 (1987): 245–52.

Hatch, John. *Nigeria: A History*. London: Secker, 1971.

Healy, Jack. "The Louvre, the Musée de l'Homme and the Criticism of African Literature." *ACLALS Bulletin* 5th ser. 3 (1980): 13–25.

Henderson, Richard N. *The King in Every Man: Evolutionary Trends in Onitsha Ibo Society and Culture*. New Haven: Yale UP, 1972.

Hesse, Herman. *The Glass Bead Game (Magester Ludi)*. Trans. Richard Winston and Clara Winston. Harmondsworth, Eng.: Penguin, 1972.

Hicks, Granville. "Neighbor to the North Makes News." *Saturday Review* 13 June 1964: 25–26. Rpt. in New, *Margaret Laurence* 114–16.

Hind-Smith, Joan. *Three Voices: The Lives of Margaret Laurence, Gabrielle Roy, Frederick Philip Grove*. Toronto: Clarke, 1975.

Hood, Hugh. *You Cant Get There from Here*. Ottawa: Oberon, 1972.

Horton, Robin. "Destiny and the Unconscious in West Africa." *Africa* 31 (1961): 110–16.

____. "The Kalabari *Ekine* Society: A Borderland of Religion and Art." *Africa* 33 (1963): 94–113.

____. "The Kalabari World-View: An Outline and Interpretation." *Africa* 32 (1962): 197–219.

Howells, Coral Ann. "Free-Dom, Telling, Dignidad." Rev. of "A Gourdful of Glory," by Margaret Laurence; *The Handmaid's Tale*, by Margaret Atwood; and *The Measure of Miranda*, by Sarah Murphy. *Commonwealth Essays and Studies* 12.1 (1989): 39–46.

Hunt, John A. *A General Survey of the Somaliland Protectorate 1944–1950*.

Hargeisa: Printed in London for the Somaliland Government, 1951.

"Imperial and Foreign News Items." *Times* [London] 19 Mar. 1921: 9.

Irele, Abi[o.]la. *The African Experience in Literature and Ideology*. Studies in African Literature. London: Heinemann, 1981.

Jardine, Douglas J. "The Mad Mullah of British Somaliland." *Blackwood's Magazine* 208 (1920): 108–21.

———. *The Mad Mullah of Somaliland*. London: Jenkins, 1923.

Johnson, John W. *Heellooy Heelleellooy: The Development of the Genre Heello in Modern Somali Poetry*. Bloomington: Indiana UP, 1974.

———. "Somali Prosodic Systems." *Horn of Africa* 2.3 (1979): 46–54.

Jones, Eldred Durosimi. *Othello's Countrymen: The African in English Renaissance Drama*. London: Oxford UP, 1965.

———. *Wole Soyinka*. New York: Twayne, 1973.

———. "Wole Soyinka's *The Interpreters*: Reading Notes." *African Literature Today* 2 (1969): 42–50.

———. *The Writing of Wole Soyinka*. London: Heinemann, 1973.

Journal of Canadian Fiction [The Work of Margaret Laurence] 27 (1980).

Journal of Canadian Studies [Margaret Laurence] 13.3 (1978).

Keith, W.J. *Canadian Literature in English*. Longman Literature in English Ser. London: Longman, 1985.

———. "Margaret Laurence's *The Diviners*: The Problems of Close Reading." *Journal of Canadian Studies* 23.3 (1988): 102–16.

———. " 'Uncertain Flowering': An Overlooked Short Story by Margaret Laurence." *Canadian Literature* 112 (1987): 202–05.

Killam, G. Douglas. *Africa in English Fiction: 1874–1939*. Ibadan: Ibadan UP, 1968.

———, ed. *African Writers on African Writing*. Studies in African Literature. Evanston: Northwestern UP, 1973.

———. Introduction. *This Side Jordan*. By Margaret Laurence. New Canadian Library 126. Toronto: McClelland, 1976. ix–xviii.

———. "Notes on Symbolism in *The Stone Angel*." *Etudes canadiennes/Canadian Studies* [*The Stone Angel* by Margaret Laurence: A Collection of Critical Essays] 11 (1981): 89–103.

———. *The Novels of Chinua Achebe*. London: Heinemann, 1969.

———. "On African Writing." Rev. of *Whispers from a Continent: The Literature of Contemporary Black Africa*, by Wilfred Cartey; and *Long Drums and Cannons*, by Margaret Laurence. *Journal of Commonwealth Literature* 9 (1970): 109–13.

King, Bruce Alvin, ed. *Introduction to Nigerian Literature*. London: Evans, 1971.

Kirk, J.W.C. *A Grammar of the Somali Language*. Cambridge: Cambridge UP, 1905.

____ . *Notes on the Somali Language*. London: Frowde, 1903.

Kirkwood, Hilda. "The Compassionate Eye." Rev. of *The Tomorrow-Tamer*, by Margaret Laurence. *Canadian Forum* July 1964: 94.

____ . "Place of Meeting." Rev. of *The Prophet's Camel Bell*, by Margaret Laurence. *Canadian Forum* Jan. 1964: 259.

Knight, David. *Farquharson's Physique: And What It Did to His Mind*. Toronto: Hodder, 1971.

Kom, Dorothée. "From Ghana to Manawaka: Continuity in Margaret Laurence's Fiction." *Etudes canadiennes/Canadian Studies* 14 (1983): 89–100.

Kreisel, Henry. "The African Stories of Margaret Laurence." Rev. of *This Side Jordan*, by Margaret Laurence. *Canadian Forum* Apr. 1961: 8–10. Rpt. in New, *Margaret Laurence* 105–10.

____ . "A Familiar Landscape." Rev. of *The Tomorrow-Tamer and Other Stories* and *A Bird in the House*, by Margaret Laurence. *Tamarack Review* 55 (1970): 91–92, 94. Rpt. in New, *Margaret Laurence* 143–45.

"A Language in Common I–XI." *Times Literary Supplement* 10 Aug. 1962: 567, 570–71, 572, 578, 584–85, 588–89, 590, 594, 596–97, 600–01, 602. [A series of articles on the use of English in the Commonwealth.]

Leney, Jane. "Prospero and Caliban in Laurence's African Fiction." *Journal of Canadian Fiction* [The Work of Margaret Laurence] 27 (1980): 63–80.

Le Fanu, Richard. Rev. of *This Side Jordan*, by Margaret Laurence. *Transition* 2.4 (1962): 28.

Lewis, I.M. *The Modern History of Somaliland*. New York: Praeger, 1965.

____ . *A Pastoral Democracy: A Study of Pastoralism and Politics among the Northern Somali of the Horn of Africa*. London: Oxford UP, 1961.

____ . Rev. of *A Tree for Poverty: Somali Poetry and Prose*, by Margaret Laurence. *Africa* 25 (1955): 305–06.

Lindfors, Bernth. "Amos Tutuola's Search for a Publisher." *Journal of Commonwealth Literature* 17.1 (1982): 90–106.

____ . "Characteristics of Yoruba and Igbo Prose Styles in English." Rutherford 47–61.

____ , ed. *Critical Perspectives on Amos Tutuola*. Critical Perspectives 1. Washington: Three Continents, 1975.

Livesay, Dorothy. *Collected Poems: The Two Seasons*. Toronto: McGraw, 1972.

____ . *The Colour of God's Face*. Vancouver: Unitarian Church of Canada, 1964.

Lloyd, P.C. "Sacred Kingship and Government among the Yoruba." *Africa* 30 (1960): 221–37.

Lord, Albert B. *The Singer of Tales*. Cambridge: Harvard UP, 1960.

Maclean, Una. "Soyinka's International Drama." *Black Orpheus: A Journal of African and Afro-American Literature* 15 (1964): 46–51.

Mannoni, O. *Prospero and Caliban: The Psychology of Colonization*. [1950 French ed.] Trans. Pamela Powesland. London: Methuen, 1956.

Mason, Philip. Foreword. Mannoni 9–15.

Mathews, A.G. Quoted in Great Britain, Colonial Office, *Report on the Somaliland Protectorate*.

Matthews, John Pengwerne. *Tradition in Exile: A Comparative Study of Social Influences on the Development of Australian and Canadian Poetry in the Nineteenth Century*. University of Toronto Department of English Studies and Texts 10. Toronto: U of Toronto P, 1962.

Meyerowitz, Eva L.R. *The Sacred State of the Akan*. London: Faber, 1951.

Miller, Charles. "Weathering the Wind of Change." Rev. of *New Wind in a Dry Land*, by Margaret Laurence. *Saturday Review* 13 June 1964: 33–34, 66.

Monk, Patricia. "Shadow Continent: The Image of Africa in Three Canadian Writers." *Ariel* 8.4 (1977): 3–25.

Moore, Gerald. "Amos Tutuola: A Nigerian Visionary." *Black Orpheus: A Journal of African and Afro-American Literature* 1 (1957): 27–35. Rpt. in Lindfors, *Critical Perspectives* 34–42.

_____ . *Seven African Writers*. London: Oxford UP, 1962.

_____ . *Twelve African Writers*. London: Hutchinson U Library for Africa, 1980.

_____ . "The Writer and the Cargo Cult." Rutherford 73–84.

Morley, Patricia. "Canada, Africa, Canada: Laurence's Unbroken Journey." *Journal of Canadian Fiction* [The Work of Margaret Laurence] 27 (1980): 81–91.

_____ . "The Long Trek Home: Margaret Laurence's Stories." *Journal of Canadian Studies* 11.4 (1976): 19–26. Rpt. in Verduyn 38–51.

_____ . *Margaret Laurence*. Twayne's World Authors Series 591. Boston: Twayne, 1981.

_____ . "Margaret Laurence's Early Writing: 'a world in which Others have to be respected.' " *Journal of Canadian Studies* [Margaret Laurence] 13.3 (1978): 13–18. Rpt. in Verduyn 10–20.

Morton-Williams, Peter. "The Yoruba Ogboni Cult in Oyo." *Africa* 30 (1960): 362–74.

_____ . "Yoruba Responses to the Fear of Death." *Africa* 30 (1960): 34–40.

Mphahlele, Ezekiel. *The African Image*. London: Faber, 1962.

"Muddling into Maturity." Rev. of *This Side Jordan*, by Margaret Laurence. *Times Literary Supplement* 4 Nov. 1960: 705. Rpt. in New, *Margaret Laurence* 101–02.

Mugo (Githane [sic]), Micere [see also Micere Githae-Mugo]. "Somali Litera-ture in Translation." Rev. of *A Tree for Poverty: Somali Poetry and Prose*, by Margaret Laurence. *Journal of Canadian Fiction* 1.2 (1972): 86–87.

Munton, Ann. Rev. of *Heart of a Stranger*, by Margaret Laurence. *Dalhousie Review* 57 (1977–78): 397–400.

Myatt, Frederick. *The Golden Stool*. London: Kimber, 1966.

New, William H. *Among Worlds: An Introduction to Modern Commonwealth and South African Fiction*. Erin, ON: Porcepic, 1975.

____. "Canadian Literature and Commonwealth Responses." *Canadian Lit-erature* 66 (1975): 14–30.

____. Introduction. *The Stone Angel*. By Margaret Laurence. New Canadian Library 59. Toronto: McClelland, 1968. iii–x.

____, ed. *Margaret Laurence*. Critical Views on Canadian Writers. Toronto: McGraw, 1977.

____. "The Other and I: Laurence's African Stories." Woodcock, *Place* 113–34.

____. "A Shaping of Connections." *A Shaping of Connections: Common-wealth Literature Studies — Then and Now: Essays in Honour of A.N. Jeffares*. Eds. Hena Maes-Jelinek, Kirsten Holst Petersen, and Anna Ruther-ford. Sydney: Dangaroo, 1989.

____. "Text and Subtext: Laurence's 'The Merchant of Heaven.'" *Journal of Canadian Studies* 13.3 (1978): 19–22. Rpt. in Verduyn 52–57.

Ngugi Wa Thiong'o [James Ngugi]. *Homecoming: Essays on African and Caribbean Literature, Culture and Politics*. Studies in African Literature. London: Heinemann, 1972.

Nichols, Lee, ed. *Conversations with African Writers: Interviews with Twenty-Six African Authors*. Washington: Voice of America, 1981.

Niven, Alastair. "The Achievement of Elechi Amadi." Rutherford 92–100.

____. Rev. of *Long Drums and Cannons*, by Margaret Laurence. *The Legon Observer* 6 June 1969: 15–17.

Nketia, J.H. *Funeral Dirges of the Akan People*. 1955. New York: Negro UP, 1969.

Nwankwo, Nkem. *Danda*. London: Deutsch, 1964.

Nwapa, Flora. *Efuru*. African Writers Ser. 26. London: Heinemann, 1966.

Nwoga, Donatus I. "The *Chi* Offended." Letter. *Transition* 4.15 (1964): 5.

Nzekwu, Onuora. *Blade among the Boys*. London: Hutchinson, 1962.

____. *Highlife for Lizards*. London: Hutchinson, 1965.

____. *Wand of Noble Wood*. London: Hutchinson, 1961.

Obiechina, Emmanuel N. *An African Popular Literature: A Study of Onitsha Market Literature*. Cambridge: Cambridge UP, 1973.

_____ , ed. *Onitsha Market Literature*. New York: Africana, 1972.

Okara, Gabriel. *The Voice*. London: Deutsch, 1964.

Ong, Walter. *Orality and Literacy: The Technologizing of the Word*. London: Methuen, 1982.

Opland, J. " 'Scop' and 'Imbongi': Anglo-Saxon and Bantu Oral Poets." *English Studies in Africa* 14.2 (1971): 161–78.

Parkinson, John. "An 'Unsolved Riddle' of Africa: Mysterious Ruins in Somaliland." *Illustrated London News* 26 Jan. 1935: 126–27.

Parrinder, Geoffrey. Foreword. *My Life in the Bush of Ghosts*. By Amos Tutuola. London: Faber, 1978. 9–15.

Parry, Milman. *SerboCroatian Heroic Songs*. Ed. Albert Bates Lord. 3 vols. Belgrade: Serbian Academy of Sciences; Cambridge: Harvard UP, 1953–74.

Perham, Margery. *The Colonial Reckoning*. London: Collins, 1962.

_____ . *Major Dane's Garden*. 1922. London: Collins, 1970.

Pickrel, Paul. "Triple Debut." Rev. of *The Tomorrow-Tamer*, *New Wind in a Dry Land*, and *The Stone Angel*, by Margaret Laurence. *Harper's Magazine* July 1964: 100–02. Rpt. in New, *Margaret Laurence* 120–22.

Prescott, Orville. "Life with the Nomads of Somaliland." Rev. of *New Wind in a Dry Land*, by Margaret Laurence. *New York Times* 17 June 1964: 41.

Press, John, ed. *Commonwealth Literature: Unity and Diversity in a Common Culture*. London: Heinemann, 1965.

Rao, Raja. *The Serpent and the Rope*. London: Murray, 1960.

Rattray, R.S., ed. and trans. *Akan-Ashanti Folk-Tales*. Illus. members of the Ashanti, Fanti, and Ewe Tribes. Oxford: Clarendon, 1930.

_____ . *Ashanti*. Oxford: Clarendon, 1923.

_____ . *Ashanti Law and Constitution*. Oxford: Clarendon, 1929.

_____ . *The Leopard Priestess*. London: Butterworth's, 1934.

_____ . *Religion and Art in Ashanti*. London: Oxford UP, 1927.

Ravenscroft, Arthur. "Africa in the Canadian Imagination of Margaret Laurence." *Re-Visions of Canadian Literature*. Proc. of Seminar in Canadian Literature, U of Leeds, Leeds, Apr. 1984. Ed. Shirley Chew. Leeds: Institute of Bibliography and Textual Criticism, U of Leeds, 1984. 29–40.

Rayne, H. *Sun, Sand and Somals*. London: Witherby, 1921.

Reece, Alys. *To My Wife — 50 Camels*. London: Harvill, 1963.

Reece, Gerald. "The Horn of Africa." *International Affairs* 30 (1954): 440–49.

Renault, Mary. "On Understanding Africa." Rev. of *This Side Jordan*, by Margaret Laurence. *Saturday Review* 10 Dec. 1960: 23–24. Rpt. in New, *Margaret Laurence* 103–04.

Robertson, George. "An Artist's Progress." Rev. of *The Tomorrow-Tamer* and *The Stone Angel*, by Margaret Laurence. *Canadian Literature* 21 (1964):

53–55. Rpt. in New, *Margaret Laurence* 123–25.

Ross, Ian [Zeres]. *"Blackwood" Tales from the Outpost: IX Tales from Africa.* Edinburgh: Blackwood, 1936.

Rutherford, Anna, ed. *Common Wealth.* Proc. of Conference of Commonwealth Literature. 26–30 April 1971. Aarhus: Aarhus U, 1971.

Samatar, Said S. *Oral Poetry and Somali Nationalism.* Cambridge: Cambridge UP, 1982.

Sandison, Alan. *The Wheel of Empire: A Study of the Imperial Idea in Some Late Nineteenth and Early Twentieth-Century Fiction.* London: Macmillan, 1967.

Shelton, Austin J. "The Offended *Chi* in Achebe's Novels." *Transition* 3.13 (1964): 36–37.

Skinner, Elliott P. "Strangers in West African Societies." *Africa* 33 (1963): 307–20.

Soyinka, Wole. *Aké: The Years of Childhood.* 1981. New York: Random, 1983.

____ . *A Dance of the Forests.* Soyinka, *Five Plays* vii–89.

____ . *Five Plays: A Dance of the Forests, The Lion and the Jewel, The Swamp Dwellers, The Trials of Brother Jero, and The Strong Breed.* London: Oxford UP, 1964.

____ . "The Fourth Stage." *The Morality of Art: Essays Presented to G. Wilson Knight by His Colleagues and Friends.* Ed. D.W. Jefferson. London: Routledge, 1969. 119–34. Rpt. in Soyinka, *Myth* 140–60.

____ . *The Interpreters.* London: Deutsch, 1965.

____ . Interview. With Lewis Nkosi. *African Writers Talking: A Collection of Radio Interviews.* Ed. Cosmo Pieterse and Dennis Duerden. New York: Africana, 1972. 171–77.

____ . *The Lion and the Jewel.* Soyinka, *Five Plays* 91–156.

____ . *Myth, Literature and the African World.* Cambridge: Cambridge UP, 1976.

____ . *The Road.* London: Oxford UP, 1965.

____ . *The Strong Breed.* Soyinka, *Five Plays* 235–76.

____ . *The Swamp Dwellers.* Soyinka, *Five Plays* 157–98.

____ . *The Trials of Brother Jero.* Soyinka, *Five Plays* 199–233.

Stanley, Henry M. *Tales from Africa.* 1893. Gloucester: Sutton, 1985.

Swayne, H.G.C. *Seventeen Trips through Somaliland and a Visit to Abyssinia.* London: Ward, 1903.

Swayze, Walter E. "Less a Stranger." Rev. of *Heart of a Stranger,* by Margaret Laurence. *Canadian Forum* Feb. 1977: 54–55.

Tahir, Ibrahim. "Anthropological Curiosity?" Rev. of *The Tomorrow-Tamer,* by Margaret Laurence. *West Africa* 9 Nov. 1963: 1273.

Tapping, Craig. "Margaret Laurence and Africa." Gunnars 65–80.

Thomas, Audrey. *Mrs. Blood.* 1970. Vancouver: Talon, 1975.

_____ . *Munchmeyer and Prospero on the Island.* Indianapolis: Bobbs, 1971.

Thomas, Clara. Afterword. *The Prophet's Camel Bell.* By Margaret Laurence. New Canadian Library. Toronto: McClelland, 1988. 265–68.

_____ . "Ascent and Agony." Rev. of *Long Drums and Cannons,* by Margaret Laurence. *Canadian Literature* 42 (1969): 91–93.

_____ . Introduction. *The Tomorrow-Tamer and Other Stories,* by Margaret Laurence. New Canadian Library 70. Toronto: McClelland, 1970. xi–xvii.

_____ . *The Manawaka World of Margaret Laurence.* Toronto: McClelland, 1975.

_____ . *Margaret Laurence.* New Canadian Library: Canadian Writers 3. Toronto: McClelland, 1969.

_____ . " 'Morning Yet on Creation Day': A Study of *This Side Jordan.*" Woodcock, *Place* 93–105.

_____ . "The Novels of Margaret Laurence." *Studies in the Novel* 4.2 (1972): 154–64. Rpt. in New, *Margaret Laurence* 55–65.

_____ . "The Short Stories of Margaret Laurence." *World Literature Written in English* 11.1 (1972): 25–33.

Thomas, Dylan. "Blithe Spirits." Rev. of *The Palm-Wine Drinkard and His Dead Palm-Wine Tapster in the Deads' Town,* by Amos Tutuola. *Observer* 6 July 1952: 7. Rpt. in Lindfors, *Critical Perspectives* 7–8.

Thompson, Denys. *Distant Voices: Poetry of the Preliterate.* London: Heinemann, 1978.

Tibble, Anne, ed. *African-English Literature: A Short Survey and Anthology of Prose and Poetry up to 1965.* London: Owen, 1965.

Tracy, Honor. "A Writer of Major Talent." Rev. of *The Stone Angel* and *The Tomorrow-Tamer,* by Margaret Laurence. *New Republic: A Journal of Opinion* 20 June 1964: 19–20. Rpt. in New, *Margaret Laurence* 117–19.

Transition [Kampala and Accra] 1 (1961)–(1968).

Tutuola, Amos. *The Brave African Huntress.* London: Faber, 1958.

_____ . *Feather Woman of the Jungle.* London: Faber, 1962.

_____ . *My Life in the Bush of Ghosts.* London: Faber, 1954.

_____ . *The Palm-Wine Drinkard and His Dead Palm-Wine Tapster in the Deads' Town.* London: Faber, 1952.

_____ . *Simbi and the Satyr of the Dark Jungle.* London: Faber, 1955.

Verduyn, Christl, ed. *Margaret Laurence: An Appreciation.* Peterborough: Broadview, 1988.

Vernon, Lorraine. "Poor Find Richness in Words." Rev. of *A Tree for Poverty: Somali Poetry and Prose,* by Margaret Laurence. *Vancouver Sun* 28 July 1972: A31.

Walsh, Langton Prendergast. *Under the Flag and Somali Coast Stories*. London: Melrose, [1932].

Ward, Barbara. *Faith and Freedom*. London: Hamilton, 1954.

Ward, W.E.F. *A History of the Gold Coast*. 1948. Rpt. as *A History of Ghana*. London: Allen, 1958.

Watt, F.W. "Letters in Canada: 1960. Fiction." Rev. of *This Side Jordan*, by Margaret Laurence. *University of Toronto Quarterly* 30 (1960–61): 406–07.

____. "Letters in Canada: 1964. Fiction." Rev. of *The Tomorrow-Tamer*, by Margaret Laurence. *University of Toronto Quarterly* 34 (1964–65): 375–76.

Waugh, Evelyn. *Black Mischief*. London: Chapman, 1932.

____. *When the Going Was Good*. London: Duckworth, 1946.

"Ways into Africa." Rev. of *Long Drums and Cannons*, by Margaret Laurence; and *A History of Neo-African Literature*, by Janheinz Jahn. *Times Literary Supplement* 2 Jan. 1969: 8.

Wescott, Joan. "The Sculpture and Myths of Eshu-Elegba, the Yoruba Trickster." *Africa* 32 (1962): 336–54.

Whiteley, W.H., ed. *A Selection of African Prose*. 2 vols. Oxford: Clarendon, 1964.

Wilkinson, Nick. "Demoke's Choice in Soyinka's *A Dance of the Forests*." *Journal of Commonwealth Literature* 10.3 (1976): 22–27. Rpt. in Gibbs 69–73.

Wiseman, Adele. "Somali Literature." Rev. of *A Tree for Poverty: Somali Poetry and Prose*, by Margaret Laurence. *Queen's Quarterly* 62 (1955–56): 610–11.

Woodcock, George. "Jungle and Prairie." Rev. of *The Tomorrow-Tamer and Other Stories* and *A Bird in the House*, by Margaret Laurence. *Canadian Literature* 45 (1970): 82–84. Rpt. in New, *Margaret Laurence* 146–48.

____. "Many Solitudes: The Travel Writings of Margaret Laurence." *Journal of Canadian Studies* 13.3 (1978): 3–12. Rpt. in Woodcock, *Place* 135–51.

____, ed. *A Place To Stand On: Essays by and about Margaret Laurence*. Western Canadian Literary Documents Ser. 4. Edmonton: NeWest, 1983.

Wren, Robert M. *J.P. Clark*. Twayne's World Authors Series 734. Boston: Twayne, 1984.

Wright, Richard. *Black Power: A Record of Reactions in a Land of Pathos*. London: Dobson, 1954.

Xiques, Donez. "New Light on Margaret Laurence's First African Short Story." *Canadian Notes and Queries* 42 (1990): 14–21.

Zabus, Chantal. "A Calibanic Tempest in Anglophone and Francophone New World Writing." *Canadian Literature* 104 (1985): 35–50.

243

INDEX

Printed in Canada
Imprimerie Gagné Ltée